UNDERSTANDING CONTEMPORARY EDUCATION

Understanding Contemporary Education offers an essential exploration of key concepts and issues in education that will allow education studies students, as well as trainee and practising teachers, to engage in reflection, not only on work at the classroom level, but on education more broadly. Using detailed examples, the book problematizes many popular and taken-for-granted views, allowing the reader to challenge and seriously consider the nature of the education enterprise.

In each chapter, a concept is carefully considered, with major features, controversies, and strengths and weaknesses highlighted. Key follow-up questions challenge the reader to reflect on specific issues, and encourage involvement, not just in their own teaching, but in the planning and determination of the total programme of their school and, where possible, that of the nation.

The book is divided into seven main parts:

- The Social Context of Education
- Education Policy
- Curriculum
- Teaching and Learning
- Leadership in Education
- Teacher Preparation
- International Developments in Education.

Drawing upon a wide variety of theoretical positions, *Understanding Contemporary Education* provides an accessible introduction to key themes and concepts in education, challenging readers to fully consider the purpose of education and to reflect intelligently on issues that affect all schools. It is a must-read book for those on education studies courses, as well as trainee and practising teachers.

Tom O'Donoghue is Professor of Education in the Graduate School of Education, The University of Western Australia, Australia.

UNDERSTANDING CONTEMPORARY EDUCATION

Key themes and issues

Tom O'Donoghue

Routledge
Taylor & Francis Group

LONDON AND NEW YORK

First published 2017
by Routledge
2 Park Square, Milton Park, Abingdon, Oxon OX14 4RN

and by Routledge
711 Third Avenue, New York, NY 10017

Routledge is an imprint of the Taylor & Francis Group, an informa business

British Library Cataloguing in Publication Data
A catalogue record for this book is available from the British Library

Library of Congress Cataloguing in Publication Data
Names: O'Donoghue, T. A. (Tom A.), 1953– author.
Title: Understanding contemporary education : key themes and issues / Tom O'Donoghue.
Description: New York, NY : Routledge, [2016]
Identifiers: LCCN 2016002698| ISBN 9781138678255 (hardback) |
ISBN 9781138678262 (pbk.) | ISBN 9781315559070 (ebook)
Subjects: LCSH: Education.
Classification: LCC LB17 .O36 2016 | DDC 370.1–dc23
LC record available at http://lccn.loc.gov/2016002698

ISBN: 978-1-138-67825-5 (hbk)
ISBN: 978-1-138-67826-2 (pbk)
ISBN: 978-1-315-55907-0 (ebk)

Typeset in NewsGothic
by Wearset Ltd, Boldon, Tyne and Wear

CONTENTS

Introducing this book

This book has been written primarily for students of education studies, student teachers, college and university lecturers, practising teachers and education leaders. It should also be of interest to parents, policy makers and politicians. It is based on the fundamental principle that the study of education studies can provide one with key concepts that can facilitate reflection on education more broadly than just at the classroom level. This is also the third of three principles which, it is held, should guide the development of programmes on how classroom practitioners at the pre-service and on-going teacher-development levels should be prepared for, and guided in, their work. These principles are as follows:

- Teachers should have a very good command of the subject matter of their teaching areas.
- Teachers should know how to teach.
- Teachers, along with students of education studies and policy makers, should engage in reflection not only on work at the classroom level, but also on education more broadly.

The position is that, while the third of these principles should underpin introductory programmes in education studies, all three should underpin programmes of pre-service and on-going teacher preparation in order for teaching to be considered a profession and for teachers to be considered professionals.

An exposition on the three principles is provided in Chapter 1, with the principal emphasis being on the third one since it constitutes the foundation of the view of education studies that underpins the remainder of the book. With regard to pre-service teachers and those partaking in programmes of on-going professional development, the generation of this third principle also arose out of a view that for teachers to be professionals they need to be involved, through genuine participation, not just in the teaching of their teaching-area specialisms, but also in the planning and determination of the total programme of the school and, wherever and to whatever extent possible, that of the nation. This is important so that education policy generated by central-level bureaucrats and politicians should be informed by those who have to implement it in the classroom. Such a position, in turn, requires that teachers must be able to reflect intelligently on issues that involve the relationship of the school to the social order and to education policy, curricula, teaching and learning, education leadership and teacher preparation.

The book can be used as the basis of a core unit or programme of work for students of education studies at various levels and also for a core unit or programme for pre-service and practising teachers, as well as to inform a variety of other stakeholders. It opens with a selection of key themes that can facilitate reflection on education at the broad societal level. This is followed by five other sets of themes, each organized in terms of the following central areas of concern to educationists: education policy, curriculum, teaching and learning, leadership in education and teacher preparation. The book concludes with a section that considers a set of themes that relate to contemporary international developments in education.

The themes covered in each section are as follows:

The social context of education

- the functions of education;
- education versus training;
- stages of education development;
- education and national development;
- globalization and internationalization of education.

Education policy

- key foci of policy analysis;
- education policy orientations;
- models for analysing education policy;
- policy borrowing;
- policy changes in higher education.

Curriculum

- orientations to curriculum;
- approaches to curriculum planning;
- outcomes-based education;
- alternatives to the objectives model for curriculum planning;
- the curriculum ideas of Kieran Egan.

Teaching and learning

- learning and the conditions that enhance learning;
- questioning some taken-for-granted assumptions about teaching and learning;
- approaches to teaching;
- learning through making and doing;
- direct instruction.

Leadership in education

- approaches to leadership;
- leadership for learning;

- leadership in assessment for learning;
- leadership for change;
- some challenging positions for leaders in education.

Teacher preparation

- the evolution of teacher preparation;
- a model to inform planning for teacher preparation;
- globalization, internationalization and teacher preparation;
- teacher induction;
- alternative models of teacher preparation.

International developments in education

- standardized testing;
- national curriculum;
- education in countries in transition;
- shadow education;
- the challenge of ICT in the classroom.

While the book draws upon a wide variety of theoretical positions on education, a number of other positions are not explicitly considered, including those of post-structuralists and post-modernists. Nevertheless, plenty of opportunities can be created by lecturers and tutors to address these and other perspectives when cogitating the variety of themes that are detailed in the various chapters. In the same way, lecturers and tutors should use every opportunity which presents itself when discussing the content of each chapter to also consider eight of the most important areas that should constantly concern all educationists and how they can have an impact on students in multiplicative rather than additive ways. These eight areas are as follows:

- class;
- equality;
- ethics;
- gender;
- race;
- sexuality;
- social class;
- social justice.

The challenge presented for lecturers and tutors is to generate questions in these areas to accompany the more topic-specific questions posed at the end of each chapter.

There are also no chapters dealing specifically with the history and philosophy of education. Nevertheless, historical and philosophical aspects of the concepts examined in each chapter are considered where appropriate. The same situation prevails in relation to comparative education, especially in the last section of the book. The specific influence on adopting this approach is the contention that one of the best ways to come to an understanding of one's own and one's nation's situation is by cogitating the conditions that prevail in very different situations.

The book can be considered to be 'a primer'. The term comes from 'primus', the Latin word for 'first'. This is an appropriate term to use as the work covers the basic elements of the themes addressed. In other words, it seeks to get readers ready for more in-depth study, rather than provide a comprehensive exposition on any one area.

Finally, no claim is made that the themes and issues considered in the book are the only ones available. On the contrary, they constitute only a small selection. Also, no claim is made that they constitute the 'best' available to assist one when trying to understand education developments and when reflecting on them. It is recognized that others might, quite legitimately, wish to draw upon a different selection of concepts, or highlight some to which they would attach more priority. If they are stimulated to do so on reading this book then it will have achieved its purpose.

1   The scope of the book

Introduction

This book, as has already been pointed out, is based on the fundamental principle that education studies can provide one with key themes that can facilitate reflection on education more broadly than just at the classroom level. It has also been pointed out that this is the third of three principles which, it is held, should guide the development of programmes on how classroom practitioners at the pre-service and on-going teacher-development levels should be prepared for, and guided in, their work. The principles are as follows: teachers should have a very good command of the subject matter of their teaching areas; they should know how to teach; and they should engage in reflection not just in relation to their work at the classroom level, but also in relation to education more broadly. The view is that these principles need to underpin programmes of pre-service and on-going teacher preparation in order for teaching to be considered a profession and for teachers to be considered professionals. It is also held that students of education studies, student teachers, practising teachers, and others, including parents, politicians, education leaders and policy makers, could benefit from understanding this view, from embracing it, from supporting teacher educators in their efforts to produce teachers educated in accordance with it and from supporting teachers who are the product of it.

The book is primarily concerned with the third principle outlined above, namely, that teachers of education studies, student teachers and practising teachers should engage in reflection not just in relation to work at the classroom level, but also in relation to education more broadly. On this, it provides a set of concepts to assist one in the task. Before outlining these themes in subsequent chapters, it is necessary at this point to elaborate on each of the three principles so that the relation of the third one to the first two can be fully appreciated.

Teachers should have a very good command of the subject matter of their teaching area

Back in 1968, Stanley (1968) could state with confidence that there can be no argument with the proposition that teachers should have a good general education and that they should be thoroughly grounded in the subject or subjects they are expected to teach. At the time, there was little contestation of this position. Indeed, there were growing calls for an increase in academic studies for future teachers (Bloom, 1987; Hirsch, 1987). The countries that were loudest in their advocacy in this regard were those that were most concerned about, and critical of, the education standards in their schools, and of the perceived lack of basic knowledge and skills on the part of their teachers. In the USA, for example, the National Commission on Excellence in Education (1983, p. 5) had this to say about standards in the nation's schools:

> If an unfriendly foreign power had attempted to impose on America the mediocre educational performance that exists today, we might well have viewed it as an act of war. As it stands, we have allowed this to happen to ourselves.

The Holmes Group (1986, p. 4) took the same line when it stated that 'America cannot afford any more teachers who fail a twelfth grade competency test', as did the Carnegie Task Force (Carnegie Corporation, 1986), which was concerned that some people who were unable to spell, write, speak grammatically correctly or solve arithmetical word problems were graduating from college and becoming teachers.

The concerns expressed in the USA in the 1980s and early 1990s continue to be voiced in other parts of the world today. This is not surprising since, in many, though certainly not all, countries the academic calibre of recruits to teaching has presented challenges (Cochran-Smith and Zeichner, 2009). The problem is that many are drawn from the lower half or even the lower quarter of the range of achievement of all students in higher education. This is unfortunate because both common sense and empirical evidence reveal that teachers' knowledge of their subject matter has a major influence on student achievement (Cochran-Smith, 2005). Thus, what is alarming at present is not that authorities in many countries continue to advocate for high academic standards for those entering teacher preparation courses, but that there are some who argue that we can settle for the status quo as long as applicants display a love of children, a desire to teach and an aptitude for teaching. This, rather disturbingly, is like saying that those with lower levels of academic achievement on graduation from high school could become good doctors if they could indicate that they would be likely to have a good bedside manner, or could become good lawyers if they could indicate they would be likely to have a commitment to social justice.

Anyone in a position of power and authority arguing against the need for high academic achievement for those entering programmes of teacher preparation is indicating either an ignorance of, or an ulterior motive regarding, the results of decades of research conducted by those embracing the 'effective schools' movement' (Calman, 2010). As early as 1991, Lockheed and Verspoor (1991) were able to conclude convincingly from the large body of studies produced as part of this movement that teachers and parents agree that academic achievement, basic skills acquisition and appropriately structured learning activities are important in the development of effective schools. Because such schools establish clearly defined goals for academic achievement and set high expectations for work (Ainscow, 2006), it follows that teachers themselves need to be of a high academic calibre. It is also arguable that both primary and secondary school teacher preparation should take place in institutions which are an integral part of the university system so that not only can student teachers be brought to an undergraduate degree level of achievement in their teaching areas, they can also be exposed to, rub shoulders with and benefit from engaging with undergraduate peers intent on other career paths.

There is also a significant body of literature arising out of research focused on the 'subject-matter knowledge' (SMK) of the subject disciplines or learning areas one teaches (Darling-Hammond and

Bransford, 2005; OECD, 2008). While it has long been recognized that SMK is an essential aspect of teaching, it was not the focus of sustained research until the mid-1980s. Since then, there has been a growing number of studies on the SMK of teachers in such subject disciplines as mathematics, English literature, history, biology and social science. Overall, the conclusion has been that one needs a depth of SMK to help shape and orientate teachers' planning, selection of teaching materials, classroom teaching and the assessment of student learning (Kind, 2009).

Within the associated academic literature, the notion of SMK has not been limited to discussion on the length of time spent on learning one's teaching subject area or the grades obtained in it, although both can serve as observable indicators of a teacher's SMK. Grossman *et al.* (1989) paved the way in systematizing thinking on this when they produced a model of SMK with four dimensions:

- Content knowledge: this is what is generally understood as subject matter by the layperson. It can roughly be interpreted as the contents of textbooks and it comprises factual information, organizing principles and central concepts. Also, content knowledge is shaped by both substantive and syntactic knowledge.
- Substantive knowledge: this is the knowledge of 'paradigms or frameworks within a discipline that guide the focus of inquiry, dictating in many ways the questions researchers ask and the directions they pursue' (Grossman *et al.*, 1989, p. 29).
- Syntactic knowledge: this consists of the 'canons of evidence that are used by members of the disciplinary community to guide inquiry in the field. They are the means by which new knowledge is introduced and accepted into the community' (Grossman *et al.*, 1989, p. 29).
- Beliefs: while not part of the structure of a discipline, beliefs are seen to be so closely intertwined with the three dimensions of SMK that Grossman *et al.* (1989) consider it to be a fourth dimension. Beliefs are seen to be different from knowledge in that they are more difficult to investigate and they are subjective, drawing more on the affective aspect of human nature.

Back in the 1990s, Borko and Putnam (1996) carried out a thorough review of studies on knowledge and beliefs about subject-matter as part of their analysis of research on the learning of teachers and found a strong positive correlation between teachers' depth and breadth of SMK and the way they carried out their teaching in class.

Ball and McDiarmid (1995) also found that students' learning opportunities were affected by their teachers' understanding of SMK; there was a qualitative difference in teaching performance between teachers with greater SMK and those who had superficial understanding of their subject. Teachers with greater SMK organized and planned their teaching differently from those with less knowledge. They also tended to stress the conceptual, problem solving and inquiry aspects of their subject. On the other hand, teachers with superficial knowledge of their subjects were found to adhere closely to textbooks, emphasizing facts, rules and procedures. These teachers missed opportunities to focus on key ideas, or draw links between them. The importance of such findings was reiterated by Ball *et al.* (2008) in more recent years.

The evidence from the comparative education literature on the need for teachers to have a solid grasp of the subject matter they teach is also compelling. Finland is a good example of a country that produces extremely high-achieving students academically. Simola (2005) has pointed out that this outcome is related to the relatively high image of schooling in the country. This image can be seen in the popularity of the teaching profession among Finnish students year after year (Kansanen, 2003). Simola (2005) has also pointed out that, in 2004, it was found amongst those in the final grades in upper secondary school in Finland that teaching was clearly the number one career choice and had overtaken such traditional favourites as physician, lawyer, psychologist, engineer and journalist. This ensured that those embarking on a university course to become teachers were already at a high level of academic achievement. More recently, Sahlberg (2011) has recorded that, due to the popularity of teaching and becoming a teacher, only Finland's best students in terms of possessing high scores in their matriculation examinations are able to gain a place in teacher preparation programmes.

Teachers should know how to teach

The second main principle underlying the thinking upon which this book is based is that teachers should know how to teach. In other words, not only do teachers need to be competent in the subject matter that they teach, they also need a range of pedagogical skills to implement the curriculum (Roehrig, 2015). At the broadest level, these skills include classroom management and organization, appreciation of each student's characteristics and preconceptions, and formal and informal evaluation of students, along with personal reflection and critical self-analysis. On the more specific matter of knowledge transmission, there is a clear connection between knowledge of one's subject and how one needs to think about it from a pedagogical point of view. Lockheed and Verspoor (1991, p. 98) summarized Shulman's (1986, 1987) position on this as follows:

> Teachers must understand the subject matter for themselves and be able to elucidate that knowledge in new ways, recognize and partition it, and clothe it in activities, emotions, metaphors, exercises, examples, and demonstrations so that it can be grasped by the students.

Coupled with this is the argument that it is important not to try to impose pre-ordained teaching approaches uncritically without considering the cultural context of the school, the pupils and the wider socio-economic environment (Clarke and O'Donoghue, 2013, 2015).

The latter point takes on major significance when one considers the extent to which, over the past two decades, with greater centralization in many countries of various aspects of education than has hitherto been the case, not only are there calls for the invention and discovery of sure-fired prescriptive approaches to teaching and learning (Darling-Hammond, 2006), great credence has also been given to the exponents of these calls by education policy makers, administrators and leaders at the school level (Luke *et al.*, 2013). Associated with this is the expectation that teachers should be 'trained' appropriately in order to ensure the successful implementation of the prescribed approaches.

To adopt the latter position is to ignore the wisdom of the past, including that of William James, one of the most famous psychologists of the modern era. Back in the 1890s, when considering the function of the study of psychology for educationists, he stated that one makes a great mistake to think that the discipline can provide definite programmes, schemes and methods of instruction for specific classroom contexts. Rather, he went on:

Psychology is a science, and teaching is an art. An intermediary inventive mind must make the application, by using its originality. The science of logic never made a man reason rightly, the science of ethics never made a man behave rightly. The most such sciences can do is to help us catch ourselves up, check ourselves, if we start to reason or behave wrongly; and to criticise ourselves more articulately if we make mistakes. A science only lays down lines within which the rules of the art must fall, laws which the follower of the art must not transgress; but what particular thing he shall positively do within those lines is left exclusively to his own genius ... and so while everywhere the teaching must agree with the psychology, it may not necessarily be the only kind of teaching that would so agree; for many diverse methods of teaching may equally well agree with the psychological laws.

(James, 1958, p. 15)

For many decades this position was overlooked as educationists sought, rather misguidedly, to identify 'best practice' in relation to a variety of areas, find 'the one best way' to proceed and seek to 'train' leaders at the individual school level to make sure their teaching staff acted in accord with prescribed pedagogical approaches.

Over 30 years ago, Eisner (1983) was one of the key players to question this view. Like James, he highlighted the importance of considering context. His argument was that because of the changing uniqueness of the practical situations that make up the education domain, only a portion of professional practice can be usefully treated in the manner of a prescriptive science. The gap between general prescriptive frameworks and successful practice is, he held, dependent more on the reflective intuition, the craft and the art of the professional practitioner than on any particular prescriptive theory, method or model. The implication for teachers is that they should be cognisant of this view and be guided by it in making decisions on teaching and learning.

Certain psychologists, as O'Donoghue and Clarke (2010) have pointed out, have lent support to this position, with some powerful voices criticizing many of the findings presented around the world in education psychology textbooks on the grounds that they are based on research with such atypical populations as American psychology undergraduates. Sears (1986), for example, questioned the unwarranted influence of studies founded on a narrow data base generated in the laboratory with college sophomores as participants. More recently, Henrich *et al.* (2010) reiterated this position, criticizing the quest in psychological research for generalizations about human nature and the neglect of the actual diversity of humankind.

Bridges (2007) took up the same point when questioning some of the assumptions of the 'evidence-based practice' movement. In particular he called into question the view that the generalizations derived from large population studies can lead to recommendations at the national level for implementation at the local level. He summarized his position as follows:

you cannot logically derive lessons for a single specific instance from such generalizations. They always have to be linked to consideration of local conditions which might well point to a different recommendation ... a teacher or school may test out different teaching strategies in their own environment and find out 'what works' for them. The fact that this enquiry was small scale and local does not invalidate it as a reliable basis for local practice even if it might be regarded as an unreliable basis for national policy without some further work.

(Bridges, 2007, p. 2)

Thus, Bridges concluded, one cannot treat local and national decisions as if they have exactly the same requirements. To put it another way, rather than presenting them with blueprints of one-best-way-of-teaching, teachers need to be introduced both to a multitude of evidence-based teaching and learning theories and to associated practices as 'tools' for thinking intelligently about their work.

Hopkins (1993) had already argued along similar lines when stating that, even when evidence-based, education theories (which include theories about teaching and learning) and associated practices do not consist of revealed knowledge. Rather, they are frameworks for making sense of the world. In promoting this argument, he leant heavily on the position of Stenhouse (1975), who held that 'it is teachers who in the end, will change the world of the school by understanding it'. Stenhouse (1975, p. 69) elaborated on this as follows:

> Good teachers are necessarily autonomous in professional judgment. They do not need to be told what to do. They are not professionally the dependents of researchers or superintendents, of innovators or supervisors. This does not mean that they do not welcome access to ideas created by other people at other places or in other times. Nor do they reject advice, consultancy or support. But they do know that ideas and people are not of much real use until they are digested to the point where they are subject to the teacher's own judgment. In short, it is the tasks of all educationists outside the classroom to serve the teachers; for only teachers are in the position to create good teaching.

This is a very different view to one which holds that instructions issued from central education bureaucracies should be put into practice with total fidelity at the appropriate level lower down the organization. The latter approach, in the view of Hopkins (1993) and reiterated by Horn and Evans (2013), tends to equate schools to factories which operate on a rational input–output basis, with pupils as raw materials, teachers as mechanics, the curriculum as the productive process and the school leaders as factory managers. What is required instead, Hopkins (1993) argued, is that teachers acquire a wide range of curriculum and pedagogical approaches so that they can test them out in their classrooms to see if they work for them with their pupils in their particular circumstances.

Education studies relates to being able to reflect on education at the broad societal level

Historically, teacher preparation was for a long time undertaken in accord with the first two principles already considered in this chapter, in that it included preparation in one's teaching subject area(s) and teaching practice. Slowly, student teachers were also exposed in their courses to some history of education and psychology of education. Both subjects were offered to place teaching on a more professional footing, the former being aimed at locating it within a great tradition and the latter at providing a scientific basis for pedagogical approaches. Little by little, various other theoretical strands were added to courses (Gardiner *et al.*, 2011; Rohstock and Trohler, 2014). These included the study of the progressive education movement, child development and the antecedents of what we now term philosophy of education and sociology of education, while all of the time a practical focus was also maintained. In this way, a third strand developed in courses of teacher preparation, namely, one aimed at producing teachers able to reflect on education at the broad societal level. While this strand became known by a variety of terms, 'education studies' emerged as the most common and neutral of them.

Education studies became a recognized component of teacher preparation programmes and was generally well received by staff, students and education authorities. Nevertheless, the associated syllabi in many countries by the late 1960s and early 1970s consisted of such a disconnected set of academic areas that educationists were forced to address themselves seriously to defining the nature of this area of studies in fairly precise terms. In Britain, the philosopher of education Hirst (1974) made a major contribution to the debate in his distinction between 'forms of knowledge', 'fields of knowledge' and 'practical theories'. Put simply, he contended that, over history, human beings mutually constructed specific modes of thought, or ways of knowing, namely, philosophy, mathematics, physical sciences, social sciences, morals, religion, literature and fine arts. These modes of thought, ways of knowing or forms of knowledge, are complex ways of understanding experience which are publicly specifiable and require justification. Each deals with different concepts, possesses a different logical structure, contains distinctive expressions which are testable against experience, utilizes different techniques and skills for exploring experiences and defines its own criteria for distinguishing true from false and good from bad. Also, each form of knowledge has developed within it specialist subjects, or disciplines.

'Fields of knowledge' are akin to what we call interdisciplinary studies. In Hirst's terms, they consist of selections from different forms of knowledge (and also from subject disciplines within them) organized around a central unifying concept. Examples of fields of knowledge in this sense are geography, women's studies and peace studies. 'Practical theories', on the other hand, are defined as being composed of relevant knowledge from the various forms of knowledge (and also from subject disciplines within them) organized around certain central practical problems in order to help one to understand these problems as fully as possible and to assist one in coming up with possible solutions for dealing with them. Medicine fits into this category since it consists of knowledge organized around a series of medical problems. Engineering, law, architecture and education can be conceptualized in a similar manner.

Around the same time as Hirst was clarifying his thinking, Broudy *et al.* (1967) at the University of Illinois Urbana-Champaign in the USA were designing a model for professional preparation in education which was consistent with Hirst's views. This included inducting students into education studies. Their starting point in this regard was a justification for the autonomous existence of professional areas of study, or what Hirst called 'practical theories'. On this, Broudy and colleagues (1967) adopted the following position:

- For an area of study to justify an autonomous existence it must have a set of special problems that direct and focus its enquiries.
- For an area of study to be professionalized it must use and organize facts and principles taken from diverse disciplines (e.g. chemistry, physics and psychology) around the demands of its own problems.
- If an area of study is to be professional, it has to utilize practice in order to illuminate theory and to use theory as a guide to practice.

Overall, the position they put forward is that a profession is related to engagement in a practical enterprise; it is goal oriented. This was summarized by arguing that law, medicine, agriculture, engineering and education, as areas of study, should have distinctive social functions, rendering service to clients. To this end, a professional field of study generates rules or practice as well as principles or generalizations that guide practice.

From this position, a schema for education studies as a professional area of study was developed. A modified version of this can be represented as follows:

Table A

	Education problem areas				
	Policy	Curriculum	Teaching and learning	Leadership	Teacher preparation
Philosophical perspectives					
Historical perspectives					
Psycho-social perspectives					
Socio-cultural perspectives					

In identifying major education 'problem' areas along the lines indicated above, Broudy and colleagues were equating the study of education with the study of medicine, which defines itself by drawing upon such disciplines as anatomy, physiology and psychology, and organizing relevant bodies of knowledge from them around a series of medical problems to give us such areas of study and research as psychiatry, paediatrics, gynaecology and so on. Engineering can be similarly viewed. It defines itself by drawing upon such disciplines as physics, chemistry and mathematics, and organizing relevant bodies of knowledge from them around a series of engineering problems to give us such areas of study and research as chemical engineering, structural engineering, nautical engineering, electrical engineering and nuclear engineering.

If we relate Hirst's view on education studies to the schema based on the work of Broudy and colleagues outlined above, we can speak about engaging in academic study and research in areas identifiable from left to right. For example, if one is interested in working in philosophy of education, one becomes concerned with drawing from existing knowledge within philosophy to help one understand better, and come up with suggestions for improvement in, the areas of education policy, curriculum, teaching and learning, leadership in education and teacher preparation. Broudy and colleagues recommended an equally helpful approach which, if one refers to the schema outlined above, is tantamount to arguing that education studies can be organized by proceeding from top to bottom in their schema. This means that one can start with a contemporary issue within one of these major education problem areas and investigate it from the position of its philosophical, historical, psych-social and socio-cultural aspects, or from a position that adopts a combination of them. It is when viewed from this perspective that it makes sense to talk of the study of 'education policy studies', 'curriculum studies', 'teaching and learning studies', 'leadership studies in education' and 'the study of how best to prepare teachers' (as distinct from studying specifically to be a teacher).

Broudy and colleagues' identification of the five major education problem areas is also extremely helpful when considered in relation to the manner in which they are organized from left to right in the schema outlined above. There is nothing haphazard about this arrangement. The implication is that in any education system, from the national level right down to the classroom level, we should initially be clear about our education policy. It is only in light of this that we should make pronouncements about curriculum. Furthermore, it is only when we are clear about the curriculum that we should pronounce on matters of teaching and learning. Once we are clear on all of these areas we can pronounce on leadership in education. Finally, we can then go on to pronounce on teacher preparation, both pre-service and on-going.

This might all seem very obvious. Here, however, it is suggested that this is not how it is in many quarters. Take, for example, the fact that a great deal of education research conducted over the last 10–15 years has been on teaching and learning. That emphasis is excellent. Nevertheless, much of it has taken place divorced from considerations like those being promoted in this chapter so far. To put it another way, research on teaching and learning has taken place as if teaching and learning are neutral activities, that all one needs to do is investigate the efficacy of as wide a variety of approaches as possible and then pick and choose from them on the basis of the evidence of 'what works' and 'what is best practice'. Yet, cognisance of the importance of making clear one's aims and policy, and from there making clear what curriculum should follow, should surely suggest that teaching, and drawing on the results of research on teaching and learning, is not a neutral activity. Indeed, the history of education is replete with accounts of particular pedagogical approaches being rejected by various interest groups on philosophical, religious, ethical and moral grounds.

To bring this section to a conclusion, it is helpful to recall that education studies developed in different, yet related, ways. Some institutions continued to adopt the disjointed approach mentioned already. Others adopted a Hirst-type approach, promoting especially what they termed the foundation disciplines of history of education, philosophy of education, psychology of education and sociology of education. Others yet again adopted an approach like that advocated by Broudy and colleagues in promoting the study of education policy, curriculum studies, the study of teaching and learning, the study of leadership in education and the study of the preparation of teachers. It was also not uncommon to have institutions offering courses in education studies based on a combination of the Hirst approach and that of Broudy and colleagues.

By the 1980s, however, all approaches were criticized as the preparation of teachers throughout much of the developed English-speaking world came under intensive scrutiny. Initial attacks relied heavily on stereotypes, with reference being made increasingly to what was termed 'the remoteness of schools from the real world', and to 'the vacuousness and subversiveness of education theory' (Lawn and Furlong, 2011). Particularly controversial were criticisms that education studies, which provided students with understandings on such matters as the role of education in society, consisted of pseudo-disciplines irrelevant to the practical world of the classroom and the preaching of a spurious gospel of equality. This created a fear mentality that schools and universities were the cause of deepening social and economic crises around the world.

The call went out for a dramatic upgrading of the quality of teacher preparation. Some aspects of this were laudable. These included an insistence that teachers should have a high standard of subject content knowledge in their teaching areas and that there should be considerable improvement in practicum-clinical experiences (Price, 1989). The agenda was taken to an extreme in some parts of the world, and especially in England and Wales, where there were calls for a return to an apprenticeship model, with teacher preparation taking place under the control of schools. The view was that it is for political masters to decide on matters to do with content and pedagogy and that teachers are paid simply to carry out changing dictates as they arise. Sutherland (1985, p. 223) succinctly portrayed the mood of the day when she stated:

There seems little impetus to serious consideration of central and general aims. Fashions succeed each other, and teachers – theirs not to reason why – are expected to change content and methods of their work in due conformity, following and climbing on each band-wagon as it comes along.

Little has changed in the intervening years. In other words, most public debate continues to be about how to achieve pre-ordained outcomes in the most cost-effective manner, but very little debate is about the value of pursuing such outcomes in the first instance, and whether or not they are in the best interest of the child. On the other hand, education studies, as a distinct field of study divorced from any practical or professional preparation, has grown greatly in many universities.

Why programmes of teacher preparation should be underpinned by the three principles

It was stated at the beginning of the chapter that this book is based on the following three principles about how teachers should be prepared for, and guided in, their work: teachers should be well versed in the subject matter of the learning areas that they teach; they should know how to teach; and they should engage in reflection not only on their work at the classroom level, but also on education more broadly. So far, considerations have focused on elaborating on each of these principles. Attention now turns to outlining how they are derived from a view that they should underpin programmes of pre-service and on-going teacher preparation in order for teaching to be considered a profession and teachers to be considered professionals.

The notion of what constitutes a professional cannot be understood in isolation from the concept of a profession, which has Christian roots going back many hundreds of years. A person who had 'professed' had taken the vows of a religious order. Traditionally, there were only the three recognized professions of divinity (and, related to it, university teaching), law and medicine. Anyone seeking entrance to these three professions automatically took holy orders. Thus, it is hardly surprising that Christian notions of care and service to others are integral to most definitions of a profession today.

Nevertheless, there is a lot of confusion around the exact meaning of the term 'profession'. Also, it is often applied indiscriminately in the literature to many occupations. Furthermore, opting to use the term does not ensure that the status of a profession will be achieved. These and related issues are dealt with comprehensively in the extensive literature on the criteria that determine if a particular occupation constitutes a profession (Busher and Saran, 2015) and in the literature on the meaning of such associated terms as 'professional', 'professionalization', 'professionality' and 'professionalism'.

Specifically in relation to teaching, McKernan (2004) brought great order to the field. He identified a number of criteria of a professional, from which eight can be distilled. These are as follows: 'qualifications', 'theoretical knowledge', 'commitment to a code of ethics', 'commitment to service', 'self-autonomy', 'commitment to recurrent teacher development', 'membership of a professional group' and 'commitment to reflection'. This book is concerned with the last of these, and particularly as it relates to reflection on education more broadly than just at the classroom level. Before moving on to this focus, however, each of the other seven needs to be considered briefly.

Regarding 'qualifications', a minimum requirement for a professional teacher should be a university degree in one's principal subject teaching area(s), along with a diploma in education studies which certifies competency in teaching and teaching-related skills. This requirement could be met by first of all obtaining a university degree in one or more academic subject areas, followed by enrolment in a diploma course. Alternatively, one could enrol in a teacher preparation programme where both areas are dealt with concurrently.

Meeting this criterion of qualifications is directly addressed by the first of the three main principles underpinning the central argument of this book about how teachers should be prepared for, and be guided in, their work, namely that they should be well qualified academically in the subject matter of what they teach. The next six can be seen as being related to the second principle, namely, that teachers should receive preparation in how to teach. On this, much has been said in this chapter already about the need for the work of teachers to be underpinned by theoretical knowledge. While this knowledge should certainly be related to pedagogy, it should also focus on bringing about a 'commitment to a code of ethics'. This criterion is founded on the reality that teachers are placed in positions of trust and responsibility with regard to the students they teach. Accordingly, they should be governed by a code of ethics drawn up and monitored by the members of the profession. Such a code is common in the medical and legal professions, and is becoming more common in education.

Alongside, and as part of, the acquisition of theoretical knowledge, one should develop a 'commitment to service'. Regarding this fourth criterion, McKernan (2004) has pointed out that professional educators who view work in the context of education institutions, community and society can be termed 'extended' rather than 'restricted' professionals. Furthermore, he argues, teachers need to be extended professionals not only because of their role as leaders in education in influencing curriculum development, pedagogical practice and the professional development of teachers, but also because they need to work in a manner that shows they care.

The fifth criterion is that of 'self-autonomy'. This criterion has already been dealt with in some detail already in considering the position of Stenhouse (1975). His position, it will be recalled, is that teachers need to have a large store of deep knowledge about teaching and learning that is flexible enough to allow them to make professional judgements and decisions on issues affecting their work in the classroom and in other education-related areas. The sixth criterion, a 'commitment to recurrent teacher development', is intimately related to that of self-autonomy in that one needs to maximize the possibility that one's decision making in classroom and classroom-related activities is always made in the light of the most recent scholarly and evidence-based developments. This is also to subscribe to the view that, over time, teachers develop cognitively, technically and socially.

The final two criteria, namely, being a member of a professional group and having a commitment to reflection, relate primarily to the third main principle underpinning the argument of this book, namely, that teachers should be prepared for engagement in reflection about education more broadly than at the classroom level and be guided in their work by such reflection. The first of these, namely, being a member of a professional group, is important as it provides teachers with opportunities to share ideas, concerns and issues with a community of fellow scholarly practitioners. Membership can also serve to improve and enhance the image and status of teachers to the level that they come to be perceived by themselves and society as professionals

The final criterion, namely, having a commitment to reflection, is the focus of the remainder of this book. It is a matter that has been dealt with to some extent in relation to considerations on the role of theoretical knowledge in helping teachers to consider the adequacy and appropriateness of any prescribed pedagogical practices for the particular contexts in which they work. This particular aspect of reflection is promoted to a great extent in many teacher preparation programmes and is often justified by referring to the views of Schon (1983, 1987). Indeed, many institutions still outline what they do in such Schonian terms as 'promoting the wisdom of practice', 'reflection-in-action' and 'reflection-on-action' (Russell, 2014). The general concern of advocates is that teacher preparation should go beyond drawing upon deterministic models of teaching and learning, which are often technocratic, routine and recipe-oriented and produce teachers with utilitarian perspectives. Rather, they argue, what is needed is an approach which promotes the reflective capacities of student teachers and serving teachers.

The position being adopted in this book is in harmony with the latter perspective. At the same time, it is not the central focus of later considerations. That focus, rather, is on the importance of promoting reflection amongst pre-service and serving teachers to assist them in reflecting on education more broadly than just at the classroom level. The argument for this approach was made convincingly back in 1968 by Stanley (1968), who argued that for teachers to be professionals they need to be involved, through genuine participation, not just in the teaching of their subject specialties, but in the planning and determination of the total programme of both the school and the nation. This is important, Stanley argued, so that practitioners' views, as well as those of central-level bureaucrats and leaders, can inform decision making. It is also important, he held, in order to minimize the possibility that plans worked out at the top level are skewed and altered in their application because teachers have not shared in their formulation and a shared understanding of what is involved may not exist.

The argument, then, is that teachers must be able to reflect intelligently on issues that involve the relationship of the school to the social order, as well as on education policy, the curriculum, teaching and learning, leadership and teacher preparation. One problem, however, is that a cursory look at the literature on 'reflection' reveals that it is a term which has a great range of meanings. A good starting point in cogitating this is to recall Dewey's (1933) argument that there is a need to move teachers away from a perception of the everyday reality as given, clearly defined and in need of no further verification beyond its simple presence. In contrast to 'routine action', namely, action which is prompted by tradition, authority, official pronouncements and circumstances, 'reflective action' incorporates active, persistent and careful consideration of any belief or supposed form of knowledge in the light of the grounds that support it and the further consequences to which it leads (Dewey, 1933). In addition, reflection involves a state of doubt, hesitation, perplexity and mental difficulty in which thinking originates, and an act of searching, hunting and inquiring to find material that will resolve the doubt and settle and dispose of the perplexity (Dewey, 1933).

While Dewey's definition of the reflective act is most helpful, it does not, from the point of view of teacher preparation, delineate the focus of reflection. Van Manen's (1977) analysis of 'levels of reflectivity', which has echoes in the recent work of Mulcahy *et al.* (2015) does, however, provide us with such a focus. He identified three levels of reflectivity, each of which describes different criteria for choosing among alternative courses of action. Level one is reflection at the level of 'technical rationality'. This relates to the second major principle underpinning the general focus of this book, namely, that teachers should know how to teach. What is meant here is that, while the primary emphasis in 'technical rationality' within the teaching context is on the efficient and effective application of knowledge in education for the purpose of attaining given ends, reflection at this level is concerned with questioning the appropriateness of various courses of action in the classroom (but does not enquire about purpose). This is most definitely not to argue against teaching student teachers practices that concentrate on technical aspects of teaching. Rather, it is to hold that the nature of the teaching should be such that the practices also become open to the possibility of being turned back upon themselves so as to establish through dialogical approaches the veracity of their own means.

The principal focus in the remainder of this book relates to the second and third levels of reflection promoted by Van Manen. The second level involves the clarification of the assumptions that are the basis of practical action. Here the interest is with the moral, ethical and value considerations in the education enterprise. Engagement in reflection at this level involves deciding the worth of competing education goals and experiences, not just harnessing energies for their attainment. Such activity is to be highly recommended because it provides a safeguard against teachers learning to view set curricula and set methods as the upper and outer limits of what is possible, and developing structures and habits of thought which could retard continued learning from teaching.

Van Manen's third level of reflection is that of 'critical reflection'. Reflection at this level focuses upon the way in which goals and practices in education can become systematically and ideologically distorted by structural forces and constraints at work in various sectors of society, including education settings. It involves paying attention to the wider organizational, social and political factors influencing instruction and the curriculum. To put it another way, the promotion of reflection at this level is concerned with encouraging teachers to reflect on the influence which school and teacher culture has on them and, in particular, to reflect on any difficulties they face as a result of conflict between personal values and institutional pressures to conform. It involves them in a critique of domination and of repressive forms of authority. It is also appropriate for the purpose of promoting a view of problem solving in education as being not just an individual matter but a social matter also, that teachers be encouraged to reflect on how they might, as members of a professional community, engage in appropriate action.

To conclude, the case has now been made as to why students of education studies, student teachers, practising teachers, education leaders and policy should be prepared for, and be guided in, their work through engagement in reflection about education at the broad societal level. This brings us to one final question: what mental apparatus do teachers need to have in order to be able to engage in this task. Crucial in this regard is the importance of having at their disposal a wide range of concepts (and theories, models and typologies developed from them) which they can use to structure their thinking, organize facts and ideas, and raise critical questions; these are their 'tools for thinking with'. Historically, as has already been pointed out, such concepts have been provided either in courses in the foundation disciplines of education (and especially in the four core foundation disciplines of history of education, philosophy of education, psychology of education and sociology of education) or in interdisciplinary courses centred on the five problem areas in education identified by Broudy and colleagues. Notwithstanding the fact that courses of both types are still very common throughout much of the USA and are central to the social, historical and philosophical foundations of education courses that constitute part of the core of teacher preparation programmes in Finland (Sahlberg, 2011), it is likely that a return to provision along these lines throughout much of the English-speaking world is unlikely for the near future.

The remainder of this book can be used to offer a different approach which could form the basis of a compulsory unit or programme of work for both pre-service and practising teachers, as well as being informative for students of education studies, leaders, policy makers, parents and politicians. It consists of a selection of key themes in the field. The first set of themes illuminates various aspects of the social context of education. This is followed by five other sets, each organized largely in terms of each of the areas identified by Broudy and colleagues, namely, education policy, curriculum, teaching and learning, leadership in education and teacher preparation. The book concludes with a section that considers a set of international developments in education. The key influence in making the decision to include this section was Alexander's (2011, p. 27) point that by 'making the strange familiar' we 'make the familiar strange' and 'thus increase our understanding of our own society'.

References

Ainscow, M. (2006). From special education to effective schools for all: A review of progress so far (pp. 146–159). In L. Florian (Ed.), *The Sage Handbook of Special Education*. New York: Sage.

Alexander, R. (2011). *Culture and Pedagogy: International Comparisons in Primary Education*. Oxford: Blackwell Publishing.

Ball, D. L. and McDiarmid, G. W. (1995). *The Subject-matter Preparation of Teachers. Issue Paper 89–4*. National Centre for Research on Teacher Education, East Lansing, MI. http://files.eric.ed.gov/fulltext/ED310084.pdf.

Ball, D. L., Thames, M. H. and Phelps, G. (2008). Content knowledge for teaching. What makes it special? *Journal of Teacher Education*, Vol. 59, No. 5, pp. 389–407.

Bloom, A. (1987). *The Closing of the American Mind*. New York: Simon and Schuster.

Borko, H. and Putnam, R. (1996). Learning to teach (pp. 673–708). In D. Berliner and R. Calfee (Eds), *Handbook of Educational Psychology*. New York: Macmillan.

Bridges, D. (2007). Evidence-based reform in education: A response to Robert Slavin. *European Educational Research Association Annual Conference*, Ghent, 19 September.

Broudy, H. S., Parsons, M. J., Snook, L. A. and Szoke, R. D. (1967). *Philosophy of Education: An Organization of Topics and Selected Sources*. Chicago, IL: University of Illinois Press.

Busher, H. and Saran, R. (Eds). (2015). *Managing Teachers as Professionals In Schools*. London: Routledge.

Calman, R. C. (2010). *Exploring the Underlying Traits of High-performing Schools*. Toronto: Education Quality and Accountability Office.

Carnegie Corporation (1986). *A Nation Prepared: Teachers for the 21st Century. The Report of the Task Force on Teaching as a Profession*. New York: The Carnegie Corporation.

Clarke, S. and O'Donoghue, T. A. (Eds). (2013). *School-level Leadership in Post-conflict Societies: The Importance of Context*. London: Routledge.

Clarke, S. and O'Donoghue, T. (Eds). (2015). *School Leadership in Diverse Contexts*. London: Routledge.

Cochran-Smith, M. (2005). The new teacher education: For better or for worse. *Educational Researcher*, Vol. 34, No. 7, pp. 3–17.

Cochran-Smith, M. and Zeichner, K. (2009). *Studying Teacher Education: The Report of the AERA Panel on Research and Teacher Education*. Mahwah, NJ: Lawrence Erlbaum Associates.

Darling-Hammond, L. (2006). Constructing 21st century teacher education. *Journal of Teacher Education*, Vol. 57, No. 3, pp. 300–314.

Darling-Hammond, L. and Bransford, J. (2005). *Preparing Teachers for a Changing World: What Teachers Should Learn and Be Able to Do*. San Francisco, CA: Jossey Bass.

Dewey, J. (1933). *How We Think*. Boston: D. C. Heath.

Eisner, E. (1983). The art and craft of teaching. *Educational Leadership*, January, 5–13.

Gardiner, D., O'Donoghue, T. A. and O'Neill, M. (2011). *Constructing Education as a Liberal Art and as Teacher Preparation at Five Western Australian Universities: An Historical Analysis*. New York: Edwin Mellen Press.

Grossman, P., Wilson, S. and Shulman, L. (1989). Teachers of substance: Subject-matter knowledge for teaching (pp. 23–36). In M. C. Reynolds (Ed.), *Knowledge Base for the Beginning Teacher*. Elmsford, NY: Pergamon Press.

Henrich, J., Heine, S. J. and Norenzayan, A. (2010). Most people are not weird. *Nature*, Vol. 466, No. 7302, pp. 29–30.

Hirsch, E. D. (1987). *Cultural Literacy: What Every American Should Know*. Boston, MA: Houghton-Mifflin.

Hirst, P. H. (1974). *Knowledge and the Curriculum*. London: Routledge and Kegan Paul.

Holmes Group (1986). *Tomorrow's Teachers: A Report of the Holmes Group*. http://eric.ed.gov/?id= ED270454.

Hopkins, D. (1993). *A Teacher's Guide to Classroom Research*. Buckingham: Open University Press.

Horn, M. B. and Evans, N. (2013). A factory model for schools no longer works. *Milwaukee-Wisconsin Journal Sentinel*, 29 June 2013, np.

James, W. (1958). *Talks to Teachers on Psychology: And to Students on Some of Life's Ideals*. New York: W. W. Norton.

Kansanen, P. (2003). Teacher education in Finland: Current models and new developments (pp. 85–108). In B. Moon, L. Vlasceanu and L. C. Barrows (Eds), *Institutional Approaches to Teacher Education within Higher Education in Europe: Currents Models and New Developments*. Bucharest: UNESCO. http:// citeseerx.ist.psu.edu/viewdoc/download?doi=10.1.1.129.2075&rep=rep1&type=pdf#page=82.

Kind, V. (2009). A conflict in your head: An exploration of trainee science teachers' subject matter knowledge development and its impact on teacher self-confidence. *International Journal of Science Education*, Vol. 31, No. 11, pp. 1529–1562.

Lawn, M. and Furlong, J. (2011). The disciplines of education: Between the ghost and the shadow (pp. 1–12). In J. Furlong and M. Lawn (Eds), *Disciplines of Education: Their Role in the Future of Education Research*. London: Routledge.

Lockheed, M. E. and Verspoor, A. M. (1991). *Improving Primary Education in Developing Countries*. Oxford: Oxford University Press.

Luke, A., Cazden, C. B., Coopes, R., Klenowski, V., Ladwig, J., Lester, J., Macdonald, S., Phillips, J., Spina, N., Shield, P. G., Theroux, P., Tones, M. J., Villegas, M. and Woods, A. (2013). *A Summative Evaluation of the Stronger Smarter Learning Communities Project. 2013 Report*. Brisbane/Canberra: Queensland University of Technology and Department of Education, Employment and Workplace Relations.

McKernan, J. (2004). *Curriculum Action Research: A Handbook of Methods and Resources for the Reflective Practitioner*. London: RoutledgeFalmer (digital edition).

Mulcahy, C. M., Mulcahy, D. E. and Mulcahy, D. G. (2015). *Pedagogy, Praxis and Purpose in Education*. New York: Routledge.

National Commission on Excellence in Education (1983). *A Nation at Risk: The Imperative for Educational Reform*. www2.ed.gov/pubs/NatAtRisk/index.html.

O'Donoghue, T. A. and Clarke, S. (2010). *Leading Learning: Process, Themes and Issues in International Perspective*. London: Routledge.

Organization for Economic Co-operation and Development (2008). *TALIS 2008 Technical Report: Teaching and Learning International Survey*. Paris: OECD. www.oecd.org/dataoecd/16/14/44978960.pdf.

Price, D. (1989). The practicum: A recent review of the literature. *The South Pacific Journal of Teacher Education*, Vol. 17, No. 2, pp. 13–26.

Roehrig, G. (2015). A review of teachers' pedagogical content knowledge and subject matter knowledge for teaching earth system concepts. *Journal of the Korean Earth Science Society*, Vol. 32, No. 5, pp. 494–503.

Rohstock. A. and Trohler, D. (2014). From the sacred nation to the unified globe: Changing leitmotifs in teacher training in the Western world, 1870–2010 (pp. 111–131). In R. Bruno-Jofré and J. S. Johnston (Eds), *Teacher Education in a Transnational World*. Toronto: University of Toronto Press.

Russell, T. (2014). Paradigmatic changes in teacher education: The perils, pitfalls and unrealized promise of the reflective practitioner (pp. 158–186). In R. Bruno-Jofré and J. S. Johnston (Eds), *Teacher Education in a Transnational World*. Toronto: University of Toronto Press.

Sahlberg, P. (2011). *Finnish Lessons: What Can the World Learn from Educational Change in Finland*. New York: Teachers College Press.

Schon, D. A. (1983). *The Reflective Practitioner: How Professionals Think in Action*. New York: Basic Books.

Schon, D. A. (1987). *Educating the Reflective Practitioner: Towards a New Design for Teaching and Learning in the. Professions*. San Francisco, CA: JosseyBass.

Sears, D. O. (1986). College sophomores in the laboratory: Influences of a narrow data base on social psychology's view of human nature. *Journal of Personality and Social Psychology*, Vol. 51, No. 3, pp. 515–530.

Shulman, L. S. (1986). Those who understand: Knowledge growth in teaching. *Educational Researcher*, Vol. 15, No. 2, pp. 4–31.

Shulman, L. S. (1987). Knowledge and teaching: Foundations of the new reform. *Harvard Educational Review*, Vol. 57, No. 1, pp. 1–22.

Simola, H. (2005). The Finnish miracle of PISA: Historical and sociological remarks on teaching and teacher education. *Comparative Education*, Vol. 41, No. 4, pp. 455–470.

Stanley, W. O. (1968). The social foundations subjects in the professional education of teachers. *Educational Theory*, Vol. 18, No. 3, pp. 224–236.

Stenhouse, L. (1975). *An Introduction to Curriculum Research and Development*. London: Heinemann Educational Books Ltd.

Sutherland, M. B. (1985). The place of theory of education in teacher education. *British Journal of Educational Studies*, Vol. 33, No. 1, pp. 222–234.

Van Manen, M. (1977). Linking ways of knowing with ways of being practical. *Curriculum Inquiry*, Vol. 6, No. 3, pp. 205–228.

Part I
The social context of education

2 The functions of education

It is essential that educationists be clear as to the purpose of education. This proposition will be returned to time and again in subsequent chapters, and in a manner that illustrates that the nature of what that purpose might be is not something on which there is always agreement. A useful point at which to commence cogitation on the matter is to consider the range of functions of education identified over the course of history, without at this point necessarily subscribing to any, some or all of them. To do so is to highlight a functionalist perspective on education. This major school of thought within sociology, with its distinctive view on education, is to be distinguished from others, including conflict theory and interpretivist theory.

The fundamental idea which underpins the functionalist perspective is that education serves many important functions in society. For example, in many cultures the school acts to socialize young people and prepare them for life in society by providing them with academic content knowledge and also by teaching them their society's moral values, ethics, politics, religious beliefs, habits and norms. It is also quite common for schools to provide occupational training. Another common function of schooling yet again is social control; to put it in its most simple form, schools can operate to keep young people off the streets and out of trouble.

A text drawing attention to the matters outlined so far, entitled *Rethinking the School: Subjectivity, Bureaucracy, Criticism* (Hunter, 1994), was produced by Hunter back in 1994. In it, he argued that 'the school system is a highly impure, tactically impoverished institution, assembled from different spheres of life and serving a mixture of spiritual and worldly ends' (Hunter, 1994, p. xii). Historically, as Hunter saw it, this means that schooling has had, since its initial development and dramatic growth, a range of intersecting functions.

Freebody (2014) has summarized the main outlines of Hunter's position and extrapolates from it a notion that schools may have at least the following functions:

- a pastoral function;
- a skilling and human capital function;
- a regulative function;
- a function of individual expression;
- a cultural-heritage function;
- a political function.

Before considering each of these functions of schooling, it is important to state that not all of them may be identified in every society. Also, they may compete amongst themselves for policy and community attention.

A pastoral function

This function is concerned with providing young people with a caring and humane environment in which to learn and develop. Within schools the approach is generally known as pastoral care. It arises out of a long tradition in many cultures of providing emotional and spiritual support at the individual level (Flanagan and Thornton, 2014). For many decades, it was particularly associated with priests, pastors, chaplains and other religious leaders. While the role continues at present to be played by many, including teachers, it has also led to the emergence of the professional pastoral carer who has been trained to provide support for students (Doehring, 2006). Usually it involves listening, supporting and encouraging. Also, it tends to be associated primarily with health education, social education, moral education, behaviour management and emotional support.

A skilling and human capital function

This function is concerned with using schools to help produce a skilled and competent workforce. The fundamental idea is that investment and effort in schools should directly enhance economic productivity (Kartick *et al.*, 2015). On this, economists distinguish between investment in physical capital and investment in human capital. Investment in both, they argue, will result in increased productivity.

Schools usually address the skilling and human capital function in a number of ways. They can, for example, involve students in different activities, providing specialized training by way of preparation for various occupations. Often schools are also involved in identifying and developing each student's aptitudes and abilities and in evaluating his or her performance, with the intention of providing direction regarding vocational paths that could be taken (Brewer, 2015). Equally, schools can seek to prepare students for work by developing within them an appreciation of the value to be obtained from it.

A regulative function

Schools can serve a regulative function by seeking to prepare students in a manner that helps to perpetuate domestic and civic order. To this end, they can seek to help students to acquire a personal identity through interaction with each other and with their teachers. This, in turn, requires that they be taught the knowledge, language and skills required for social interaction. While the academic curriculum can play a major role in this regard, so also can the 'hidden curriculum', through which students learn social rules and expectations from responses to their interactions (Myles *et al.*, 2013). For example, through experiencing rewards and punishments, they can learn to follow timetables and instructions, to meet deadlines, to be quiet when required and to know when to wait to express an opinion. Such skills are valued highly by employers in many industries.

A function of individual expression

In many societies it is considered that having freedom of speech represents one's ultimate freedom to be oneself. Indeed, so highly is this principle valued in some countries that freedom of speech has constitutional and legal protection (Sadurski, 2001). Furthermore, it is recognized that schools should encourage freedom of speech amongst young people. Along with justifications being provided for this position on human rights' grounds, there are also arguments that exploring and expressing personal goals can lead to the development of creative thinking, courage, self-confidence and self-assurance (Craft, 2005).

A cultural-heritage function

One of the oldest of the functions of schooling is that of conserving those aspects of a nation's culture deemed most valuable by its population. This includes conserving the nation's traditions and values, and ensuring that they are passed on from one generation to the next. Social scientists call this the process of culturization. Through engaging in the process, there is also the possibility that schools can play a part in creating culture by encouraging intellectual inquiry, critical thinking and the generation of new ideas.

A political function

The home and various other institutions function in many societies to produce loyal citizens. The school is one such institution. It can play a political function by involving young people in activities to help them learn their society's core values. It can also go a stage further through providing formal political education. This education in some contexts consists of learning respect for one's country through engagement in such activities as singing the national anthem and saluting the national flag. In other contexts, it can also involve formal instruction aimed at learning about the society's political institutions and way of life, and the justifications for the forms it takes (Hanf, 2011).

The hope is that, in fulfilling a political function, schooling can play an important role in unifying the population of a nation. The teaching of a common language is often considered to be crucial in this process, the belief being that it helps to promote communication broadly and thus develop understanding and the building of national identity. This function can also be considered to be an integrative one (Byrman, 2008). Particular attention is given to it in countries with great social and cultural diversity.

Emile Durkheim and education

Emile Durkheim (1858–1917) was a French sociologist, social psychologist and philosopher. Blackledge and Hunt (1991) have summarized his functionalist explanation of education. The prime function of education, Durkheim held, is not to develop the individual's abilities and potentialities for their own sake. Rather it is to develop those abilities and capacities that society needs. To this end, it has two main functions, as outlined below.

The specialization function of education

All societies need a certain amount of specialization. In other words, specialization in the division of labour is necessary to maintain society. Therefore, one of the functions of education is to prepare people for various occupations.

The general function of education

Each society needs some basic similarity of thought, values and norms among its members if it is to continue. This is provided through the general function of education, which requires that schools arouse in the child:

- a certain number of physical and mental states that the society to which he or she belongs considers should not be lacking in any of its members;
- certain physical and mental states which the particular group (caste, class, family, profession) considers ought to be found among all those who make it up (Blackledge and Hunt, 1991).

Education's function of fitting people into society is accomplished in the process of socialization. The alternative to a socialized person is someone in a state of 'anomie'.

Education fulfils its general function by:

- providing the norms and values the child needs;
- providing a cognitive framework in terms of which the child can come to understand the world and acquire knowledge.

This involves creating a stable and structured environment in which these things are clearly defined and where conformity to them is demanded by those in authority; 'since all are subjected to the school regime, education will build up the necessary consensus for society to continue' (Blackledge and Hunt, 1991, p. 14).

Finally, Durkheim held that, to function effectively, society must ensure that there is equality of opportunity. Should it fail to provide this, social conflict will follow.

Issues for discussion

1   At the beginning of this chapter it was pointed out that what is presented is based on a functionalist perspective on education and that this is to be distinguished from other positions, including conflict theory and interpretivisit theory.

- Identify the basic principles that underpin conflict theory and interpretivist theory.
- Try to work out what each theory tells us about how schools operate.

2   The concept of 'anomie' was mentioned in the chapter.

- What are the basic ideas to which this concept relates?
- How might schooling function to promote anomie?
- How might schooling function in relation to communities experiencing the state of anomie?

3   A range of functions identified by Hunter that schooling plays in society were outlined.

- Is it possible that Hunter overlooked any functions?
- Have you considered the religious function that schools play in some societies and in certain education systems?

4   What is your understanding of what 'the hidden curriculum' is?
    Could you identify ways in which you experienced it when you were a pupil in school?

5   There are alternative ways of looking at the different functions identified by Hunter. For example, the following alternative view on 'the regulative function of schooling' has been identified by Fletcher (1984, p. 46):

> Since education has to provide for various levels of potentiality and aptitude, and the fulfilling of tasks differing widely in their required degrees of skill and complexity, it is clear that no educational system can be a simple uniform structure. It must provide different types of education and instruction for different levels of capacity with reference to different ends. At some point or other, soon or late, different levels, different capacities and responsibilities, different directions of inclination and occupation, have to be recognized and provided for.... The same point applied not only between trades and professions, but also within them.... A hierarchy of discipline, responsibility and authority is involved.

He concluded that the entire provision of education, instruction and training within any society must always be, therefore, of a differential nature and, thus, that equality of treatment is impossible.

- Can you think of alternative perspectives on any of the other functions of schooling?
- Do you accept Fletcher's position that education must always be differential?
- Do you accept his position that equality of treatment is impossible in education?

6   Many take an alternative view on the political function of schooling to that mentioned already. They accept that the universalization of education is promoted as being a central tool in bringing about social equality. The reality, however, they hold, is that schooling can work to reinforce existing social hierarchies and even to create new ones. While they recognize that it can enable a degree of upward social mobility for some from disadvantaged backgrounds, overall, they argue, it serves to maintain socio-economic inequality and perpetuate the dominance of existing elites.

- Do you agree with this view?
- If not, why not?
- If you do agree with it, how does it manifest itself in relation to:
    o   access to schooling;
    o   the structure of the education system;
    o   the processes involved in the curriculum and teaching?

(continued)

7   Are you familiar with the concept of 'cultural capital'?
    How does it capture the way in which education is structured to maintain inequality, including through schooling?

8   You will recall that one of the functions identified for education is that of promoting individual self-expression.
    What level of importance do you think is attached to this in your own society?

9   Have you ever considered that speech and self-expression do not hold the same degree of importance in the more collectivistic cultural contexts, including in much of East Asia, to what they hold in Western countries? Here thoughtful and self-disciplined silence is often valued above speech. Also, speech is practised with relatively great caution because of the potential negative social implications it can have (Kim and Markus, 2002; Kim and Sherman, 2007).
    What implications might this have in situations where pupils from such a background are being taught in schools like those in which you teach?

10 Durkheim clearly disagrees with educationists who think that there are natural moral values and ways of thinking in children. He would oppose the view that education must develop the children's potentialities, except in so far as these are needed by society. Discuss this proposition.

References

Blackledge, D. and Hunt, B. (1991). *Sociological Interpretations of Education*. London: Routledge.
Brewer, J. M. (2015). *The Vocational-Guidance Movement. Its Problems and Possibilities*. London: Forgotten Books.
Byrman, M. (2008). *From Foreign Language Education to Education for Intercultural Citizenship*. New York: Languages for Intercultural Communication and Education.
Craft, A. (2005). *Creativity in Schools: Tensions and Dilemmas*. London: Routledge.
Doehring, C. (2006). *The Practice of Pastoral Care: A Postmodern Approach*. Louisville, KY: Westminster/John Knox Publishing.
Flanagan, B. and Thornton, S. G. (2014). *The Bloomsbury Guide To Pastoral Care*. London: Bloomsbury Continuum.
Fletcher, R. (1984). *Education in Society: The Promethean Fire*. Harmondsworth: Penguin Books.
Freebody, P. (2014). Geoffrey Sherrington and the history of Australian education: Ideas of use in a needy world. *Journal of Educational Administration and History*, Vol. 46, No. 2, pp. 125–133.
Hanf, T. (2011). *The Political Function Of Education In Deeply Divided Countries*. Munster, Germany: Nomos Publishing.
Hunter, I. (1994). *Rethinking the School: Subjectivity, Bureaucracy, Criticism*. St Leonards, NSW: Allen and Unwin.
Kartick, R., Roberts, R. and Ershad Ali, M. (2015). *Education, Human Capital and Development*. New York: Nova Science Publishers.
Kim, H. S. and Markus, H. R. (2002). Freedom of speech and freedom of silence: An analysis of talking as a cultural practice (pp. 432–452). In R. Shweder, M. Minow and H. R. Markus (Eds), *Engaging Cultural Differences: The Multicultural Challenge in Liberal Democracies*. New York: Russell-Sage Foundation.
Kim, H. S. and Sherman, D. K. (2007). Express yourself: Culture and the effect of self-expression on choice. *Journal of Personality and Social Psychology*, No. 92, pp. 1–11.
Myles, B. S., Trautman, M. L. and Schelvan, R. (2013). *The Hidden Curriculum for Understanding Unstated Rules in Social Situation for Adolescents and Young Adults*. Avalon, NSW: Autism Asperger Publishing Company.
Sadurski, W. (2001). *Freedom of Speech and Its Limits*. Rotterdam: Kluwer.

3   Education versus training

The previous chapter considered a range of possible functions which education can serve in society. One could argue, however, that the notion of education adopted within that frame might more appropriately be termed schooling. This is because the term schooling can often be used without one necessarily having the quality of the practice in mind. Realization of this can be brought home forcefully on cogitating the distinction between 'education' and training' made by Lawrence Stenhouse. The nature of what he had in mind when making the distinction will now be outlined.

Stenhouse's distinction between education and training

Lawrence Stenhouse was a distinguished British curriculum theorist. In his early years he worked in the UK at the University of Durham Institute of Education and at Jordanhill College of Education, before taking up a position with the Schools Council and the Nuffield Foundation, directing what became an internationally well-known Humanities Curriculum Project. In 1970 he moved again, this time to become Director of the Centre for Applied Research in Education at the University of East Anglia. One of his major contributions to education thought was to distinguish between education and training, or, to be more specific, to distinguish between 'training', 'instruction', 'initiation' and 'induction'. Each of these 'functions of the school', as Stenhouse termed them (using 'function' in a somewhat different sense to how it has been used in the previous chapter), is now explained.

Training

On training, Stenhouse (1975, p. 80) stated: 'Training is concerned with the acquisition of skills, and successful training results in capacity in performance. Examples are making a canoe, speaking a foreign language, typing, baking a cake and handling laboratory apparatus.' He pointed out that training takes place in a number of institutions, including the armed forces and industry. He also recognized that a certain amount of training needs to be provided by schools. An example he gave is that of learning to play a musical instrument at the elementary stages. Further, he recognized that when it comes to the training processes in which schools are engaged it is appropriate that what is sought should be stated in the form of behavioural objectives, which are clear statements of what exactly the student should be able to do as a result of his or her training. This matter is returned to in detail in Chapter 14.

Instruction

On instruction, Stenhouse (1975, p. 80) stated: 'Instruction is concerned with the learning of information and successful instruction results in retention.' Examples are 'retention of the table of chemical elements, of dates in history, of the names of the countries of Europe, of German irregular verbs, and of the recipe for making pastry'. Again, Stenhouse held that what is sought here can also be stated in the form of behavioural objectives. This, as he put it (Stenhouse, 1975, p. 81), is because 'retention can readily be tested behaviourally and at different levels; for example, recall and recognition'.

Initiation

On initiation, Stenhouse (1975, p. 80) stated: 'Initiation is concerned with familiarization with social values and norms and successful initiation leads to a capacity to interpret the social environment and to anticipate the reaction of one's actions.' To some extent these social values and norms are 'picked up' at school through the manner in which regular, often daily, practices are carried out, and through one's interactions with peers and teachers. A certain amount of formal curriculum time is also often spent in school familiarizing students with social values and norms.

Induction

On this, Stenhouse (1975, p. 80) stated: 'induction stands for introduction into the thought systems – the knowledge – of the culture and successful induction results in understanding as evidenced by the capacity to grasp and to make for oneself relationships and judgements'. Many people, he concluded, might, quite correctly, substitute the word 'education' for 'induction'. As he saw it, through training, initiation and induction, especially when guided by behavioural objectives, we can produce individuals who will be 'relatively predictable, limited and uncreative' (Stenhouse, 1975, p. 82). The business of education, on the other hand, 'is to make one freer and more creative' (Stenhouse, 1975, p. 82). To put it another way, Stenhouse saw the primary aim of education as being the development of individuality through a creative and critical engagement with culture (Ruddock, 1995). In particular, he argued that education enhances the freedom of individuals by inducting them into the knowledge of their culture as a thinking system. He concluded by arguing that education as induction into knowledge is successful to the extent that it provides students with tools for thinking with, so that one's education becomes challenging and empowering

Elliott (1995, pp. 54–73) elaborated on the type of argument put forward by Stenhouse that knowledge is not information. Rather, it consists of 'structures to sustain creative thought and provide frameworks for judgment'. From this, it followed for Stenhouse that 'education is a process in which pupils develop their intellectual powers by utilising public structures of knowledge in the construction of personal understandings of life situations' (Elliott, 1995, p. 70). Also, such structures are seen as being intrinsically problematic and contestable in the sense that 'the theories, concepts and principles of which they consist are open to a variety of interpretations' (Elliott, 1995, p. 70).

Elliott (1995, p. 70) expounded on the latter matter, stating that 'within an educational process differing understandings of the same situation may manifest similar intellectual powers'. He went on as follows:

> Educationally speaking, it is not sufficient to transmit inert information about ideas, concepts and theories to students in the form of definitions. In the process of induction the teacher represents them as critical standards (s)he brings to bear on students' thinking about problems in the subject matter. They are embedded in the questions (s)he poses, the evidence (s) he draws attention to, and the tests (s)he asks students to submit their thinking to. Moreover, the teacher should induct students in a manner which gives them access to the problematic and contestable nature of the structure of knowledge ... dialogue between teachers and students and discussion among students are procedural principles governing any educationally worthwhile induction into knowledge then.
>
> (Elliott, 1995, p. 61)

In other words, through acquiring knowledge, both teachers and learners come to a better understanding of the world. This, in turn, enables them to make better personal and professional decisions.

Smith and Lovat (2003) hold that, in Stenhouse's view, all school students need 'training' and 'instruction' in the technical processes necessary to acquire 'basic skills' and 'foundational information'. They go on to argue that the view also is that 'other types of procedures are necessary for the fullness of education to occur' (Smith and Lovat, 2003, p. 129). They explain this as follows:

> After all, being able to set up an easel, splash a little paint and recite certain facts and figures about Rembrandt's life does not constitute an artist. An artist is one who appreciates and understands the aesthetics of art and, ideally, is able to contribute to the world of art in a significant way. Only at these sorts of points can education be deemed to have truly happened. For Stenhouse, these levels of education are catered for through the processes termed 'initiation' and 'induction'. Initiation is the point of socialisation, as it were, into the culture associated with any area of knowledge. Initiation into the areas of knowledge is a subtle process Also, Stenhouse asserts that induction is the point of true education. He argues that induction into knowledge is successful to the extent that it makes the behavioural outcomes of the students unpredictable.

It is not difficult to recognize that if one subscribes to the adoption of such a position then teachers need a great repertoire of teaching and learning practices. In particular, this should include a range of practices aimed at enhancing the development of students as flexible learners (Stenhouse, 1988).

It was his recognition of the latter point that led to Stenhouse placing great stress in his extensive writings on the importance of teacher development. These writings are all underpinned by his central argument that 'there can be no educational development without teacher development' (Stenhouse, 1975, p. 83). In adopting this position Stenhouse was reiterating the view expressed a decade earlier by the famous New Zealand educationist C. E. Beeby (1966), whose central ideas are outlined in the next chapter.

Stenhouse had a particular position on what he meant by teacher development. His starting point, as already pointed out in Chapter 1, was that because each classroom setting is unique, each curriculum and pedagogical proposal needs to be tested and verified by each teacher in his or her classroom, to see if it will work for him or her with his or her students. As he put it, any such proposal 'is not to be regarded as an unqualified recommendation but rather as a provisional specification claiming no more than to be worth putting to the test of practice' (Stenhouse, 1975, p. 142). This implies that teacher development should involve teachers in obtaining the necessary research skills to be able to investigate their own practice and to evaluate it.

Issues for discussion

1   It is arguable that the position promoted by Stenhouse is in a long tradition exemplified by the thinking and works of a number of famous educationists. See what you can find out about the views of the following four people on what it means to receive an education:

   • Cardinal John Henry Newman;
   • Mortimer J. Adler;
   • James Bryant Conant;
   • Robert Maynard Hutchins.

2   Consider your own education. Would you say that you had experiences in harmony with all four of Stenhouse's 'functions of the school'?

   • If not, why might this have been the case?
   • If so, why might this have been the case?

3   Consider the education of those you teach. Would you say they have experiences in harmony with all four of Stenhouse's 'functions of the school'?

   • If not, why might this be the case?
   • If so, why might this be the case?

4   Do you think it is possible to have successful induction without sufficient training, instruction and initiation?
   Think of examples to illustrate you answer.

5   Do you think that creativity is accommodated within Stenhouse's 'functions of the school'?
   In what way might this be so?

6   Have you ever considered that much of what is termed creativity might in fact be spontaneity?

   • What might the differences be between spontaneity and creativity?
   • Might training, instruction, initiation and induction be necessary for creativity?
   • Might this mean that creativity means something different in mathematics as opposed to in literature, or in chemistry as opposed to in history?
   • Might this cause us to question the notion that creativity is a general ability?

7 Rickman (2004, p. 1) addressed the distinction between education and training as follows:

> We need to consider the distinction between education and training. Broadly speaking we are familiar with the distinction. A father is supposed to have said: 'If my daughter told me she was getting sex education in school I'd be pleased. If she told me she got sex training I'd go straight to the police.' Training is about practice, about skill, about learning how to do things. Education is about fostering the mind, by encouraging it to think independently and introducing it to knowledge of the physical and cultural world. It's about theory, understanding and a sense of values. There is, of course, some overlap. Practice may require some theory and education may require some skills, such as reading and writing. To teach literature, for example, is obviously part of education as it provides insights, mental enjoyment and an appreciation of beauty; it may also improve your eloquence in selling cars but that's a fringe benefit. It is, however, important to hold on to the different roles the two play in human life because politicians and, indeed, educators obscure the distinction and talk of education when they mean training.

Do you agree with this point of view?

- What are the implications for the classroom teacher?
- What are the implications for those who design the curriculum?
- What are the implications for universities?
- What are the implications for colleges of further and higher education?

References

Beeby. C. E. (1966). *The Quality of Education in Developing Countries*. Cambridge, MA: Harvard University Press.

Elliott, J. (1995). In the shadow of the Education Reform Act (pp. 54–73). In J. Ruddock (Ed.), *An Education that Empowers: A Collection of Lectures in Memory of Lawrence Stenhouse*. Clevedon, Avon, UK: Multilingual Matters.

Rickman, P. (2004). Education versus training. *Philosophy Now*. https://philosophynow.org/issues/47/Education_versus_Training.

Ruddock, J. (Ed.). (1995). *An Education that Empowers: A Collection of Lectures in Memory of Lawrence Stenhouse*. Clevedon, Avon, UK: Multilingual Matters.

Smith, D. and Lovat, T. J. (2003).*Curriculum: Action on Reflection*. Tuggerah, NSW: Social Science Press.

Stenhouse, L. (1975). *An Introduction to Curriculum Research and Development*. London: Heinemann Educational.

Stenhouse, L. (1988). Artistry and teaching: The teacher as focus of research and development. *Journal of Curriculum and Supervision*, Vol. 4, No. 1, pp. 43–51.

4 Stages of education development

The focus of many individuals and groups interested in the development of education is on linear quantitative expansion of education systems. While such a focus is important, there is also a need to consider the quality both of what is taught and of how it is taught. One of the first educationists to draw attention to this was C. E. Beeby (1966) in his book *The Quality of Education in Developing Countries*. Published in 1966, the ideas outlined in Beeby's work are as relevant now in promoting reflection (Guthrie, 2011) as they were when they first appeared. They are also helpful in facilitating discussion on the quality of education and its development not only in 'developing' countries (the particular focus of Beeby's book), but also in 'developed countries'.

Beeby's model of stages of educational development

Beeby provided a model of stages of how education develops which is based on four basic propositions:

1   Historically, primary schooling evolved in four stages: the Dame School Stage, the Stage of Formalism, the Stage of Transition and the Stage of Meaning.
2   Movement through the stages was usually sequential.
3   The key to schools being able to move through the stages has been the ability of their teachers to promote change.
4   The ability of teachers to promote change, while requiring confidence, has fundamentally been a function of their general and professional education.

The characteristics of teachers in each stage

1   Teachers in the Dame School Stage are ill-educated and ill-trained. They have a very low level of teaching subject-matter knowledge and place a great emphasis on memorizing.
2   Teachers in the Stage of Formalism are ill-educated but have received teacher training. They are highly organized, stick to a rigid syllabus, place a major emphasis on the 3Rs, subscribe to 'one best way' of teaching and stick to the use of one textbook. Discipline is tight, memorizing is heavily stressed and the emotional life of students is largely ignored. Examinations and inspection are also heavily stressed.

3   Teachers in the Stage of Transition are better educated and better trained than those in the first two stages. They are also more efficient at achieving the same goals as those in the Stage of Formalism. Their use of syllabi and textbooks is less restrictive. They still have to deal with final school-leaving examinations, which often restrict experimentation. Again, very little takes place in the classroom to cater for the emotional and creative life of the child.

4   Teachers in the Stage of Meaning are well educated and well trained. They:

- emphasize meaning and understanding in their teaching;
- cater for individual differences and creativity;
- engage pupils in activity methods and problem solving;
- utilize a wider curriculum which has a greater variety of content;
- emphasize internal rather than external tests;
- adopt a relaxed and positive approach towards discipline;
- emphasize the emotional and aesthetic life as well as the intellectual life;
- establish close relations with the community and better buildings;
- deem good facilities to be essential for engaging in quality work.

Movement through each stage

Beeby held that as a school system moves through the stages, schools become less rigid (with fewer external controls such as those provided by examinations and inspections), teachers become less formal in teaching style, discipline becomes less authoritarian, and syllabi and textbooks become less prescriptive. Corresponding to these changes, learning becomes more meaningful, the classroom more pupil-centred and the school more self-directed. Beeby also held that all school systems have to pass through these stages, adding that while 'a system may be helped to speed up its progress, it cannot leapfrog a stage or major portion of a stage' (Beeby, 1966, p. 69).

Teacher ability was seen by Beeby as the key to change from stage to stage (Beeby, 1966, pp. 35–47). He identified the following five ways in which this ability could be limited:

1   lack of clear goals in the system affecting teachers' thinking;
2   lack of both understanding and acceptance by teachers of reforms;
3   teachers, as products of a system needing to be changed, not being prone to innovate;
4   isolation of teachers in their classroom slowing down diffusion of innovations;
5   a wide range of ability of teachers making diffusion rates uneven.

Beeby's view was that educational quality would improve as teachers moved from being ill-educated and untrained at the Dame School Stage to being well-educated and well-trained at the Stage of Meaning. At all levels this requires improvements in the general education of teachers and in the amount and nature of their professional education.

The following overview on Beeby's work has been provided by Renwick (1998, pp. 343–344):

It was within the education sector, especially among administrators and those involved in teacher education and training educational administrators in developing countries, that *The Quality of Education in Developing Countries* made its main impact. There, it had a tonic effect. It addressed issues of great practical concern to them using a language that they understood, and it did so with sparkling clarity and on the authority of an internationally acclaimed educational administrator. Above all, it gave them arguments to use in advocating higher levels of national commitment to the professional education of primary teachers and supporting services. It was thus more as a teaching aid and as a source of justifying argument, than as a generator of research aimed at testing his theory, that Beeby's *The Quality of Education in Developing Countries* made its mark.

Renwick went on to argue that what characterized all of Beeby's writings in his capacity as a professional advisor to various national governments was his ability to grasp and articulate what had to be done in the circumstances of the moment to improve the quality of an education system.

Advantages of Beeby's model

1   When Beeby's book appeared, it was very positively reviewed. On the whole, his model was seen as a much-needed attempt to create a theoretical framework for considering how to promote the development of education.
2   It provides a very useful framework for allowing us to have conversations about how any particular system of education is currently positioned, and about whether it is stable, or moving upwards or downwards through the stages. Cogitating this can lead one to engagement in more sophisticated analyses.
3   As one of the founding figures in UNESCO, and an analyser of education in many developing countries, Beeby had a major influence on the World Bank and succeeded in shifting the thinking of its staff in the early 1980s so that the quality of schooling became an overriding concern for them (Barrett *et al.*, 2006, pp. 4–8).
4   Beeby's model can be used to illuminate some of the thematic aspects of education. In particular, it can provide the basis for initial considerations of a set of categories for analysing instructional procedures in the classroom, while recognizing that one can then progress to considering more sophisticated categories.

Disadvantages of Beeby's model

Guthrie (2011) considers Beeby's model to have the following disadvantages:

1   The notion that Western styles of teaching represent educational progress is at the centre of the model. The criterion of judgement is Western and culture-bound. While it is true that education is values-based, we should be quite clear as to whose values apply in different cultural settings.
2   Stage of Meaning teaching may be inappropriate at a particular point in time for the following reasons:

    • Classroom conditions may not be appropriate for some teaching styles.
    • Teachers may have insufficient time to innovate.
    • Examinations may emphasize learning inconsistent with innovations.
    • Educational administrators may be unable to provide appropriate organizational support, particularly during extension phases.
    • Costs of reform may be prohibitive.

3   We have to make sure that culturally based and often false assumptions about teaching styles do not remain unexamined and untested.

This latter point is considered below in more detail.

Watkins (2000) has provided some examples which help to illustrate point number 3 above. Regarding memorizing, he states that, without understanding, it can lead at best to very limited outcomes. However, for Confucian-tradition learners the repetition involved is important in deepening understanding by discovering new meaning. This is unlike the situation with the Western students he studied, who tended to use repetition to check that they had really remembered something. Watkins has also highlighted the misperception of Western observers regarding how Chinese teachers use group work. The usual Western approach, he stated:

> is to split the class up into pairs or small groups, say of four to five, and then have members of each group discuss an issue or work on a problem together at the same time as other groups ... many Western teachers try to involve students in the class through simultaneous pupil talk. Large class sizes are seen as a constraint on this teaching method. By way of contrast, Chinese teachers often use sequential talk for the purpose of involvement ... two pupils may come to the front of the class to perform a dialogue which has been prepared in advance to the teacher and the rest of the class.... What makes this approach work in the context of the Chinese classroom is that the rest of the class consider they learn through listening to the teacher or their peers.
>
> (Watkins, 2000, p. 169)

Watkins also points to the role of questions in the classroom. Whereas Western teachers expect questions to be asked by students during the process of learning 'to fill in gaps in their knowledge, or to aid understanding of the reasoning involved', Confucian-tradition students tend to wait to ask questions until they have learnt independently of the teacher. The reason for this, he states, is that students consider that questions should be based on knowledge. Finally, he points out that while there is a belief amongst many teachers from a Western tradition that children learn through being creative, teachers from Confucian traditions may see creativity as a slow process that depends on solid basic knowledge (Watkins, 2000, p. 171).

Issues for discussion

1   Do you think that Beeby's theory may apply to education in 'developed' as well as in 'developing' countries'?

2   If you accept Beeby's model, how long do you think it could take to move an education system from one stage to the next?

3   Do you think Beeby was correct in saying that no education system can skip a stage?

   •   Why might this be so?
   •   Can you think of any instance in which it might not be so, or where it was not so?

(continued)

4   Where do you think the educational system of your own country is currently located in terms of Beeby's stages?
     If this represents progression, why do you think this has taken place?
     If it represents regression, why do you think it has taken place?

5   One aspect of Beeby's theory is that he does not consider what forces might hold back an education system or, on the other hand, accelerate it through the stages.
     What do you think these forces might be?

6   Regarding constraining factors, a significant one in some developing countries is post-colonialism. Colonialism can be defined as a situation in which the colonizer rather than the colonized holds power for purposes the colonizer defines. A colonial education system, then, is one in which the residents of the area do not determine the nature of schooling. Rather, the amount and type of education, and to whom it is available, are decided by 'foreigners'.
     Thomas and Postlethwaite (1984) have identified three variations of colonialism:

     Classical colonialism: This consists of a people being ruled by a distant overseas government whose representatives determine key political, economic and social issues, including the issue of what kinds of schooling will be offered.
     Internal colonialism: This consists of one subgroup in a self-governing society dominating another subgroup. An upper social class may control the society's political and economic life and determine as well the kinds of educational opportunities available to lower social classes. Or one powerful ethnic group may determine what sorts of education will be offered their own members and what sorts will be offered members of other ethnic groups. Or the division between dominant and subordinate groups may be based on religious affiliation.
     Neo-colonialism: This consists of a politically independent people of a developing nation continuing to be bound, voluntarily yet often through necessity, to a former colonial power. Neo-colonialism constitutes the deliberate policies of the industrialized nations to maintain their domination. It may function through foreign-aid programmes, technical advisers, publishing firms or other means.

     Identify a post-colonial education system. Regarding your selection ask yourself:

     • Who determines the purposes of schooling?
     • From what culture are the purposes derived?
     • Whose welfare is served by the purposes?
     • Who determines the administrative structure?
     • From what culture does the structure derive?
     • Who decides what system will be used for recruiting, training and promoting educational personnel?
     • Who determines the nature of the curriculum and teaching methods?
     • What are the cultural sources of the curriculum and the teaching methods?
     • Whose welfare is served by the curriculum?

References

Barrett, A., Chawla-Duggan, R., Lowe, J., Nikel, J. and Ukpo, E. (2006). *The Concept of Quality in Education: Review of the International Literature on the Concept of Quality in Education*. Working Paper No. 2. Bristol: EdQual.

Beeby. C. E. (1966). *The Quality of Education in Developing Countries*. Cambridge, MA: Harvard University Press.

Guthrie, G. (2011). *The Progressive Education Fallacy in Developing Countries*. Dordrecht: Springer.

Renwick, W. L. (1998). Profiles of great educators: Clarence Edward Beeby. *Prospects*, Vol. 28, No. 2, pp. 334–348.

Thomas, R. M. and Postlethwaite, T. N. (1984). *Schooling in the Pacific Islands*. Oxford: Pergamon Press.

Watkins, D. (2000). Learning and teaching: A cross-cultural perspective. *School Leadership and Management*, Vol. 20, No. 2, pp. 16–173.

5 Education and national development

The study of the relationship between education and national development has interested educationists for a long time. Many of those engaged with this area premise their considerations on the assumption that there is a positive relationship between an educated population and national development. They also assume that education can be used to fight poverty and address other forms of underdevelopment. This leads them to argue that education should be seen as a public good that is worthy of the allocation of public money and that it needs to be publicly controlled.

Overall, as Harber and Davies (1997) have put it, education can be seen to have a contribution to make to development within a number of different contexts in society. This contention is now considered in relation to those UNESCO-identified contexts in which education can contribute to sustainable development (UNESCO, 2015). It also considers the basic ideas of four dominant theories regarding how development can take place. It then outlines a very different view, namely, that promoted by the government of Bhutan.

Contexts in which education can contribute to societal development

According to UNESCO (2015), education for sustainable development should promote such competencies as critical thinking, imagining future scenarios and making decisions in a collaborative way.

The economic context

UNESCO's Millennium Development Goals, adopted in 2000 (UNESCO, 2015, p. 1), include the following quantitative targets for addressing extreme human deprivation around the world:

- halving extreme poverty;
- reducing child and death rates;
- reducing maternal death rates;
- countering environmental degradation.

Achieving these targets, it is held, would not only lead to an improved quality of life for individuals and communities, but also to an increase in economic development.

UNESCO also holds that there are clear linkages between education, poverty reduction and sustainability. Education that is relevant and purposeful, it is argued, has the power to transform people's lives, equipping them with skills needed to improve their livelihoods

The context of violence

UNESCO holds that living in an environment of peace and security is fundamental to human dignity and development. Therefore, it argues, those providing teaching and learning for sustainable development must take cognizance of social, economic, environmental and cultural perspectives. In particular, it is held that by '"learning to live together", learners acquire knowledge, values, skills and attitudes for dialogue, cooperation and peace' (UNESCO, 2015, p. 9). UNESCO concludes that education can help develop the capacity to respect differences and diversities as well as build social tolerance.

The health context

UNESCO defines health in relation to the environmental and human characteristics of people's daily lives and the links between them. It also holds that awareness and education are powerful ways to drive behavioural change related to health, that health promotion is the process of enabling people to increase control over and improve their health and that the goal of universal education cannot be achieved while the health needs of all remain unmet. It concludes that 'education should enable learners to adopt caring and supportive attitudes to others as well as protective and health-seeking behaviours for themselves' (UNESCO, 2015, p. 8).

The cultural context

UNESCO holds that the cultures of the world have created a rich and varied tapestry that has 'expanded choices, nurtures a variety of skills, human values and worldviews and provides wisdom from the past to inform the future'. Accordingly, it argues that education for societal development should be locally relevant and culturally appropriate 'if people are to live together peacefully, tolerating and accepting differences amongst cultural and ethnic groups' (UNESCO, 2015, p. 8). It also cautions against cultural industries commodifying culture for outsiders. Because of this possibility 'cultures must be respected as the living and dynamic contexts within which human beings find their values and identity' (UNESCO, 2015, p. 8).

The gender context

UNESCO claims that gender-based discrimination in education is 'both a cause and a consequence of deep-rooted disparities in society' (UNESCO, 2015, p. 7). Amongst the factors identified as undermining the ability of women and girls to exercise their rights are the following:

- poverty;
- geographical isolation;
- ethnic background;

- disability;
- traditional attitudes about their status;
- traditional attitudes about their role.

The following have also been identified as 'harmful practices' by UNESCO (2015, p. 7):

- early marriage;
- early pregnancy;
- gender-based violence;
- discriminatory education laws, policies, contents and practices.

These are deemed to be dangerous in so far as they can act to prevent millions of girls from enrolling, completing and benefitting from education. Consequently, UNESCO concludes, gender must be integrated at all levels of education, from early childhood to higher education, in formal and non-formal settings, and from planning infrastructure to training teachers.

Theories of education for development

A number of theories exist regarding how development takes place and the role of education in the process. A brief overview of four of these – human capital theory, modernization theory, correspondence theory and liberation theory – is now outlined. This overview is based on the extensive exposition provided by Phillips and Schweisfurth (2011).

Human capital theory

The basic premise of this theory is as follows:

> Investment in human beings is a way of increasing the overall economic production of a nation. Education is assumed to be a good means of doing this, instilling skills, knowledge and motivations for economic productivity. This contributes to the wealth of individuals, leading to higher wages and salaries, for example, and in agrarian societies, more efficient farming techniques.
>
> (Phillips and Schweisfurth, 2011, pp. 69–70)

Phillips and Schweisfurth (2011) conclude by stating that a whole nation's economic development is then seen to be dependent upon these skills, knowledge and motivations for productive behaviours in the whole population. In this way, education is believed to be a sound investment both for the individual and for the nation (Becker, 2009).

Modernization theory

The basic premise of this theory is as follows: 'Development is conditional upon members of a society holding "modern values". The prevalence of these values facilitates working behaviours and personal priorities that allow industrialization and economic growth to take place' (Phillips and

Schweisfurth, 2011, p. 71). Modern values include a 'sense of control over one's destiny', 'motivation to work for success', 'respect for evidence', 'punctuality', 'acceptance of diversity' and 'belief that everyone should be treated according to a set of principles'. Schooling, according to this view, 'is seen to inculcate modern values in learners by virtue of the "hidden curriculum" that is an integral part of the bureaucratic nature of school routines' (Phillips and Schweisfurth, 2011, p. 72).

Correspondence theory

This theory questions the assumption that education is a medium of positive change. Phillips and Schweisfurth (2011, p. 74) summarize it as follows:

> Opportunities in school mirror those in life. Working-class children often receive a different education from those of the middle- and upper-class homes, as a result of settlement patterns, selective entry, private education opportunities or streaming within schools. The different forms of education prepare them for their role in life – in correspondence with their backgrounds. Children from the poorer homes learn pre-vocational and vocational skills, while children of the elite learn confidence and independence of thought, preparing them to take charge. Thus the class system is reproduced.

Phillips and Schweisfurth (2011, p. 74) conclude by stating that 'rather than gearing towards national development for everyone, it is seen to perpetuate the status quo and ensure the dominance of those already living at the high end of the development spectrum'.

Liberation theory

While not rejecting the fundamentals of correspondence theory, liberation theory is not as fatalistic. It accepts that education can play a role in oppression by dulling people's minds and reinforcing the status quo. At the same time, it 'prioritizes the moral obligation to side with the oppressed of the world, and to seek development through freedom from domination' (Phillips and Schweisfurth, 2011, p. 73). It argues that 'the right kind of education can serve to "conscientize" the oppressed', giving them 'the opportunity and skills of analysis, through dialogic approaches to learning, to awaken critical consciousness and ultimately to reconstruct society along more democratic and fair lines' (Phillips and Schweisfurth, 2011, p. 73).

A contrasting view from Bhutan

Walcott (2011, p. 253) has posited on development as follows:

> Development is seen as the path to, and outcome of, modernisation ... it implies improvement in terms of material benefits, but at the cost of cultural values, environmental degradation, increased rural and urban disparities and income inequalities and ethnic uneasiness.

The set of undesirable outcomes identified in this quotation can be seen to be inherently fractious with a revered set of Bhutanese cultural values (Bisht, 2012). These values are rooted in traditional Buddhist doctrine represented and proudly protected by the concept of 'gross national happiness' (GNH).

Bhutan is a small nation situated between two of the largest on earth. Due to its remoteness and historical lack of direct involvement in European affairs, it avoided participation in both world wars despite a history of interaction with British India and the signing by the first Bhutanese king, Ugyen Wangchuck, of the Treaty of Punakha in 1910, which guaranteed Bhutan's continuing internal independence in exchange for the forfeiting of its foreign relations to the British administration (Ura, 2005, p. 3). With the support of India, Bhutan joined the United Nations in 1971 and introduced the discourse of GNH in 1972 (Ura, 2005). From this time onwards the Bhutanese political elite increasingly made clear the desire to preserve the Bhutanese Drukpa majority's Buddhist cultural identity and values.

The Bhutanese monarchy and its recently established parliament continue to strive to embed and proliferate the values embodied by the GNH framework throughout Bhutan's public institutions (Ura *et al.*, 2012). The efforts made in this regard are especially evident in the reforms undertaken within Bhutan's education institutions as the nation moved beyond the predominant and spiritually and civic-minded monastic schools of the pre-1959 era, into the hitherto largely unknown world of the secular, academically oriented 'modern' public schools it administers today. These efforts shaped the formation of the following five major ideological pillars which constituted the first conceptions of the GNH Index (Ura, 2005):

- economic self-reliance;
- conservation of Bhutan's unique environment;
- maintenance of equitable development across all rural and urban areas of the nation;
- decentralized and transparent exercise of political power;
- preservation of local languages, beliefs, customs, skills, trades and institutions.

These pillars can be seen to be directly responsive to perceived shortcomings of neo-liberal institutional responses to fostering economic development within nations desiring to participate in global economic networks.

Education is conceptualized within the GNH philosophy as having four strands:

- *Literacy* – a citizen's ability to read and write in either English, Dzongka or Nepali;
- *Educational qualification* – the achievement level of a citizen in either traditional monastic schooling, contemporary non-secular schooling or non-formal education;
- *Social and cultural issues* – a citizen's knowledge of Bhutanese folk tales and songs, local festivals, the constitution and the intricacies of HIV transmission;
- *Buddhist values*.

Bhutan's approach to designing and administering its public education system and curriculum through the lens of the aspirations and the concepts constituting the GNH Index has resulted in what is commonly known in the country as a 'holistic' approach to education. This is a hybrid of academic, spiritual and civic education that seeks to promote a balance between academic learning and other uniquely Bhutanese areas of interest. Overall, the aim, as Walcott (2011 p. 254) has put it, is to attempt to foster within Bhutanese students the 'prioritisation of personal satisfaction based on lack of attachments, over the pursuit of material prosperity'. It is officially held that the associated locally produced curricular priorities based upon the delivery of locally valued knowledge that eschews standardization and competition seem to fit well with Bhutan's social, political and geographical realities. These are deemed to be far more suitable than if a Western-styled curriculum were simply purchased, imported and imposed upon the nation's population. Overall, the Western conception that creating an environment most conducive to the accumulation of material wealth will allow for happiness to somehow naturally flourish has been profoundly challenged.

Issues for discussion

1   It has been pointed out by UNESCO (2015, p. 8) that 2005–2014 was named the United Nations Decade in Education for Sustainable Development. This global movement was set in train to attempt to transform education policy, investment and practice. Amongst the key processes underpinning its Education for Sustainable Development (ESD) frameworks and practices were the following:

  • processes of collaboration and dialogue (including multi-stakeholder and intercultural dialogue);
  • processes which engage the 'whole system';
  • processes which innovate curriculum as well as teaching and learning experiences;
  • processes of active and participatory learning.

  What, in your view, is involved in engaging in each set of processes outlined above?

2   The following has also been pointed out by UNESCO (2015, p. 8):

  'Learning' for ESD refers to what has been learnt and is learned by those engaged in ESD, including learners, facilitators, coordinators as well as funders. Often learning is interpreted as the gaining of knowledge, values and theories related to sustainable development but, as this review indicates, ESD learning also refers to:

  • learning to ask critical questions;
  • learning to clarify one's own values;
  • learning to envision more positive and sustainable futures;
  • learning to think systemically;
  • learning to respond through applied learning;
  • learning to explore the dialectic between tradition and innovation.

  Consider what each of these types of learning means for yourself and your students.

3   Consider the following propositions of De Oliveira Andreotti and Stein (2015, p. 1):

  a   Poverty and 'underdevelopment' are represented as apolitical and ahistorical phenomena. This denies the complicity of 'developed' nations in the production and maintenance of poverty – first, through the initial dispossession and extraction of resources that accompanied colonization, and later through the implementation of global policies that economically and ideologically favoured their interests.

(continued)

b   Mainstream development presumes a single linear path of human progress, and the universal value of Western knowledge, liberal democracy and a capitalist economy as a means to achieve it. In contrast, non-Western knowledge is viewed as particular, anachronistic or backward. This knowledge may be tokenistically celebrated or positioned as a barrier to 'developing' countries' 'advancement', but either way is rarely understood as the basis for viable alternative approaches to development.

c   Development during the Cold War era was modelled on the same European Enlightenment tenets that were once used to justify colonization. Thus, mainstream development maintains the myth of Europe's civilizational supremacy, which in turn positions non-European peoples as inferior 'others'. Development is understood as a continuation of the 'civilizing mission' of colonization, which also helps to ensure the maintenance of Western geopolitical and economic advantage.

Do you think that these critiques of the basic assumptions and absences of the mainstream development agenda are justified?

4   Aguirre and Sogge (2006) argue that the less aid developing countries have the better they do. The aid lobby, they hold, claims the opposite, and exhorts a doubling, or even tripling of aid. They go on to argue that if it is aid on the old terms, it will not bring progress. They hold that saying that the world is richer than ever and implying that development can simply be purchased is a monumental deception as it ignores the primordial need for countries to foster their own capacity for development.

- What do you think Aguirre and Sogge mean by 'aid on the old terms'?
- Why might they be justified in saying that it is a 'monumental deception' to think that 'development can be purchased'?
- How might countries 'foster their own capacity for development'?

5   A variety of arguments have been put forward both in favour of and against the provision of education aid to developing countries.
Do some background research on each set of arguments and discuss them in the light of what you have read.

References

Aguirre, M. and Sogge, D. (2006). *Crisis of the State and Civil Domains in Africa*. Madrid: FRIDE.

Becker, G. S. (2009). *Human Capital: A Theoretical and Empirical Analysis with Special Reference to Education*. Chicago, IL: University of Chicago Press.

Bisht, M. (2012). Bhutan's foreign policy determinants: An assessment. *Strategic Analysis*, Vol. 36, No. 1, pp. 57–72.

De Oliveira Andreotti, V. and Stein, S. (2015). *Higher Education, Development, and the Dominant Global Imaginary*. www.academia.edu/11499513/Higher_Education_Development_and_the_Dominant_Global_Imaginary_2015_.

Harber, C. and Davies, L. (1997). *School Management and Effectiveness in Developing Countries*. London: Cassell.

Phillips, D. and Schweisfurth, M. (2011) *Comparative and International Education: An Introduction to Theory, Method, and Practice*. London: Bloomsbury.

UNESCO (2015). *Education for Sustainable Development*. Paris: UNESCO. www.unesco.org/new/en/education/themes/leading-the-international-agenda/education-for-sustainable-development/.

Ura, I. (2005). *The Bhutanese Development Story*. Thimphu: Centre for Bhutan Studies. www.bhutan studies.org.bt/publication Files/Monograph/.

Ura, I., Alkire, S., Zangmo, T. and Wangdi, I. (2012) *A Short Guide to Gross National Happiness Index*. Thimphu: Centre for Bhutan Studies. www.grossnationalhappiness.com/wp-content/uploads/2012/04/Short-GNH-Index-edited.pdf.

Walcott, S. M. (2011). One of a kind: Bhutan and the modernity challenge. *National Identities*, Vol. 13, No. 3, pp. 253–265.

6 Globalization and internationalization of education

'Globalization' has been defined as an 'outcome of various structural processes that manifest in different ways' and 'produce entrenched and enduring patterns of worldwide interconnectedness' (Rizvi and Lingard, 2010, p. 24). Such a definition embraces the interdependence that Dabbagh and Bannan-Ritland (2005) state exists between technological, economic, political and socio-cultural outcomes of globalization. At the same time, there has over the last decade been unprecedented debate about globalization's complexity and ambiguity, particularly in regard to education (Bates, 2011; Brown and Lauder, 2011).

The notion of the internationalization of education is less contentious; it has been defined as 'the process of integrating an international perspective in the teaching/learning, research and service functions' (Knight, 2001, p. 229). Such a definition implies that internationalization of education is a partly planned process and an integrated phenomenon that is usually agreed upon by one, or more, partners. The planned process of internationalization relies on policy, organization and resources for enactment. Also, there is a general consensus that globalization and internationalization of education are inextricably linked and affected by technology and change. Using globalization as the focus of attention, this chapter considers linkages between it and internationalization.

Rather than define globalization, some describe different types:

- Globalization has six forms: economic, political, cultural, demographic, managerial and environmental (Bottery, 2006).
- Globalization is 'the acceleration of interregional contacts in speed, in increased volume, and in widening range' (Stearns, 2003, p. 154).
- Globalization consists of a flow of technology, economy, knowledge, people and ideas across borders (Knight, 2001).
- Globalization incorporates the movement of socially constructed global ideologies (Marginson and Rhoades, 2002; Rizvi and Lingard, 2010).

There are also those who discuss globalization as a global culture, or as Westernization or Americanization, suggesting a homogenization of values (Currie *et al.*, 2003). The following are a number of examples in this regard:

- Wylie (2011) argues that the process of globalization promotes the hegemonic interest of the West.

- Rizvi and Lingard (2000) discuss how Western interests are transmitted through global forces and can result in uneven benefits that have the ability to create greater social stratification.
- Dabbagh and Bannan-Ritland's (2005) description captures the concern that globalization is both politically and economically motivated.

Others, instead of describing types of globalization, or the process of globalization, have attempted to measure the rate and dynamics of the phenomenon in terms of economic, political, technological, cultural and social changes (Andersen and Herbertsson, 2005). An example of such an attempt is the policy of the Geneva Centre for Security (2008), outlined in its work entitled *Globalization Matrix*.

Considerations above are illustrative of the many images of globalization that have been presented within the literature in economic, political, social and cultural terms (Currie *et al.*, 2003; Peters, 2003). Less attention has been given to globalization and education policy, curriculum and pedagogy (Hayden and Thompson, 2008; Winter, 2012; Yates and Grumet, 2011). An exception is to be found in the work of Taylor and Henry (2000), who have recognized that globalization has an impact on the education sphere in specific contexts that are intertwined and porous.

Marginson and Rhoades (2002) coined the concept of a 'glo-na-cal agency heuristic' to help capture the dynamic interactions between different contexts at global, national and local levels. The following points have been made regarding each of these levels:

- Globalization at a macro-level is influenced by technological, economic, political and social change (Knight, 2001).
- Globalization at a meso-level is often affected by a nation's individual history, traditions, culture and priorities (Ruddy, 2008).
- At the local level, 'place and space matters' and forces of globalization are 'felt' (Green, 2009, p. 390).

In terms of defining 'global' and 'international', the education literature defines global relations as super-territorial (Scholte, 2005) or supra-national (Vidovich, 2007), whereas international relations occur across borders, involving bilateral or multilateral exchanges between several nations. 'Internationality' relates to one or more nations, whereas 'globality' transcends geography (Currie *et al.*, 2003; Scholte, 2005). According to Yang (2002), both constructs are interconnected and interdependent.

Core themes in the literature on education in relation to both globalization and internationalization

This section of the chapter is based on a summary of an exposition by Ledger *et al.* (2014) on education in relation to both globalization and internationalization.

Contexts

Globalization was initially conceived of as a macro-level phenomenon but, over time, the meaning shifted to include localized contexts (Green, 2009). The construct of a 'glo-na-cal agency heuristic' (Marginson and Rhoades, 2002), where global, national and local perspectives are identified, captures this shift. Overall, the literature exposes the complex interplay of global and local dimensions. It also underscores the importance of studying local contexts when analysing global trends (Zajda, 2005).

Power

Globalization is also a powerful influence on the structural arrangements and ideologies that dominate life in schools. In this, it has the capacity to cause tensions, both unprecedented and unpredictable (Apple, 1979), since the cultural life of schools is influenced by a combination of local, national and global demands (Caffyn, 2011; Yates and Grumet, 2011). Also, global ideologies, products and forces can be in conflict with local cultural demands and desires. As a result, power inequities and relationships are affected. When a clash of cultures occurs between international and local forces, interpersonal and intercultural relationships can be fractured in a manner that can result in conflicts or compromises (Caffyn, 2011).

Technology

The range of technologies being employed in schools is diverse. It includes:

*   knowledge portals;
*   tele-learning;
*   virtual classrooms (Levin and Schrum, 2012).

Schools can use technology to provide one-on-one web-based personalized instruction for their students, seeking to connect them to educational products and programmes around the world. At the same time, technological advances in a globalized world have the ability to both marginalize and be inclusive. For example, while technology allows international students to remain connected with their family and friends in their home country, it can, at the same time, disconnect them from the local culture and population (Allen, 2002).

Global organizations as vehicles to transmit ideologies

Globalization and internationalization can facilitate the transmission of ideologies through a range of such global organizations as:

*   the United Nations;
*   the World Bank;
*   the International Monetary Fund;
*   the OECD.

A variety of international educational 'brands' has also emerged over the years that seek support and favour from these large global organizations. They include:

- the Cambridge Local Examinations Syndicate (UK);
- International School Services (USA);
- Yew Chung Education Foundation (China);
- International Schools Association (USA);
- The European Council of International Schools (EU).

Such institutions have the capacity to promote the transmission of Western ideologies, language and cultural desires (Hill, 2007). They include what is commonly referred to as 'international mindedness', 'global citizenship' and 'cosmopolitanism', or what Zhao (2010) has termed 'global competencies'. These social constructs are embedded in education policies and discourses related to international organizations and schools.

Globalization has been associated with the ascendancy of a market ideology in education over the last three decades, particularly in regard to international education and schooling. The impact of globalization has seen international schools' networks develop into both the product and the process for internationalizing education (MacDonald, 2006). This network of international schools has been referred to as 'a franchised outlet' (Cambridge, 2002; Hayden and Thompson, 2008; Wylie, 2011) that readily distributes international education to a wide range of locations. The franchise guarantees a high profile, a positive reputation and a 'brand proposition' that help schools attract customers (Bates, 2011; Cambridge, 2002). The relationship is also regulated by quality assurance mechanisms, accreditation processes and support organizations comparable with how most franchised businesses are regulated.

Issues for discussion

1 Smith (2008, p. 1) has commented as follows:

> We have witnessed a fundamental attack on the notion of public goods and upon more liberal ideas of education. Learning has increasingly come to be seen as a commodity or as an investment, rather than as a way of exploring what might make for the good life or human flourishing. Teachers' and educators' ability to ask critical questions about the world has been deeply compromised. The market ideologies they have assimilated, the direction of the curricula they are required to 'deliver', and the readiness of the colleges, schools and agencies in which they operate to embrace corporate sponsorship and intervention have combined to degrade their work to such an extent as to question whether what they are engaged in can rightfully be called education.

- Separate out each of the contentions in this quotation.
- Do you agree with each of them in the light of what you know about internationalization and globalization?
- Are there any with which you disagree? Why?

(continued)

---

2   Regarding the position outlined above, Smith (2008, p. 1) holds that we can:

> seek to undermine the narrowing and demeaning processes that pass under the name of education in many systems. Alternative ways of educating that look to well-being and participation in the common life have been well articulated. Whether they can be realized is down in significant part to our courage as educators, and our ability to work with others with a similar vision.

- Would one be justified in engaging in such an undermining exercise?
- Do you think that anyone could engage in this in effective ways? What might they be?
- Can you identify any examples of the kind of 'alternative ways of educating' to which Smith is likely to be referring?

3   Khan (2015, p. 1) holds that an aspect of globalization that countries in the developed world encounter is:

> the assimilation of immigrants into their education system. Though apparently this may seem as an exchange of cultures that could be beneficial for the maturation of a pan-culture, it is nevertheless dominated by the norms of the host culture with an emphasis on integration and conformity.

- Do you agree with this contention in relation to the situation in your own country?
- If so, why do you think this is the case? Do you think it is justified?
- If not, why do you think this is the case?
- Can you characterize the situation in this regard in relation to any other countries?

4   Khan (2015, p. 1) also holds that while globalization has resulted in the involvement of such international development organizations as UNESCO and UNICEF in education in developing countries, their programmes act to create a coordinated global education system. A resulting drawback, he states, is that indigenous forms of education are being replaced throughout the world and the focus is on preparing students exclusively for an urban existence.

- Do you agree with this position? Why?
- If you do agree with it, is the situation necessarily an unwelcome one? Why?
- Might it be possible to preserve indigenous forms of education and prepare students for an urban existence without doing so exclusively?
- If it is possible, how might it be organized?

References

Allen, K. (2002). Atolls, seas of culture and global nets (pp. 112–135). In M. C. Hayden, J. J. Thompson and G. Walker (Eds), *International Education in Practice: Dimensions for National and International Schools*. London: Kogan Page.

Andersen, T. and Herbertsson, T. T. (2005). Quantifying globalization. *Applied Economics*, Vol. 37, No. 10, pp. 1089–1098.

Apple, M. W. (1979). What correspondence theories of the hidden curriculum miss. *The Review of Education*, Vol. 5, No. 2, pp. 101–112.

Bates, R. (Ed.). (2011). *Schooling Internationally: Globalisation, Internationalisation and the Future for International Schools*. Oxford: Routledge.

Bottery, M. (2006). Education and globalization. Redefining the role of the educational professional. *Educational Review*, Vol. 58, No. 1, pp. 95–113.

Brown, C. and Lauder, H. (2011). The political economy of international schools and social class formation (pp. 39–58). In R. Bates (Ed.), *Schooling Internationally: Globalisation, Internationalisation and the Future for International Schools*. Oxford: Routledge.

Caffyn, R. (2011). International schools and micropolitics: Fear, vulnerability and identity in fragmented space (pp. 59–82). In R. Bates (Ed.), *Schooling Internationally: Globalisation, Internationalisation and the Future for International Schools*. Oxford: Routledge.

Cambridge, J. (2002). Recruitment and deployment of staff: A dimension of international school organization (pp. 158–169). In M. Hayden, J. Thompson and G. Walker (Eds), *International Education in Practice: Dimensions for National and International Schools*. London: Kogan Page.

Currie, J., DeAngelis, R., deBoer, H., Huisman, J. and Lacotte, C. (2003). *Globalizing Practices and University Responses: European and Anglo-American Differences*. Westport, CT: Greenwood Publishing Group.

Dabbagh, N. and Bannan-Ritland, B. (2005). *Online Learning: Concepts, Strategies, and Application*. Upper Saddle River, NJ: Pearson/Merrill/Prentice Hall.

Geneva Centre for Security (2008). *Globalization Matrix*. Geneva: Centre for Security.

Green, B. (Ed.). (2009). *Understanding and Researching Professional Practice*. Rotterdam: Sense.

Hayden, M. and Thompson, J. (Eds) (2008). *International Schools and International Education: Improving Teaching, Management and Quality*. London: Kogan Page.

Hill, I. (2007). International education as developed by the International Baccalaureate Organization (pp. 25–38). In J. Thompson, M. Hayden and J. Levy (Eds), *The SAGE Handbook of Research in International Education*. London: Sage.

Khan, S. H. (2015). *The Effects of Globalization on Education*. www.academia.edu/6755602/Effects_of_Globalisation_on_Education.

Knight, J. (2001). Monitoring the quality and progress of internationalization. *Journal of Studies in International Education*, Vol. 5, No. 3, pp. 228–243.

Ledger, S., Vidovich, L. and O'Donoghue, T. (2014). *Global to Local: Curriculum Policy Processes: The Enactment of the International Baccalaureate in Remote International Schools*. The Netherlands: Springer.

Levin, B. and Schrum, L. (2012). *Leading Technology-rich Schools: Award-winning Models for Success*. New York: Teachers College Press.

MacDonald, J. (2006). The international school industry: Examining international schools through an economic lens. *Journal of Research in International Education*, Vol. 5, No. 2, pp. 191–213.

Marginson, S. and Rhoades, G. (2002). Beyond national states, markets, and systems of higher education: A glonacal agency heuristic. *Higher Education*, Vol. 43, No. 3, pp. 281–309.

Peters, M. A. (2003). Education policy in the age of knowledge capitalism. *Policy Futures in Education*, Vol. 1, No. 2, pp. 361–380.

Rizvi, F. and Lingard, B. (2000). Globalization and education: Complexities and contingencies. *Educational Theory*, Vol. 50, No. 4, pp. 419–426.

Rizvi, F. and Lingard, B. (2010). *Globalizing Education Policy*. London: Taylor and Francis.

Ruddy, A. (2008). *Internationalisation: Case Studies of Two Australian and United States Universities*. PhD thesis, Murdoch University, Perth.

Scholte, J. A. (2005). *Globalization: A Critical Introduction*. London: Palgrave Macmillan.

Smith, M. K. (2008). Globalization and the incorporation of education. http://infed.org/mobi/globalization-and-the-incorporation-of-education/.

Stearns, P. (2003). Treating globalization in history surveys. *The History Teacher*, No. 36, pp. 154–172.

Taylor, S. and Henry, M. (2000). Globalization and educational policy-making: A case study. *Educational Theory*, Vol. 50, No. 4, pp. 487–503.

Vidovich, L. (2007). Removing policy from its pedestal: Some theoretical framings and practical possibilities. *Educational Review*, Vol. 59, No. 3, pp. 285–298.

Winter, C. (2012). School curriculum, globalisation and the constitution of policy problems and solutions. *Journal of Education Policy*, Vol. 27, No. 3, pp. 295–314.

Wylie, M. (2011). Global networking and the world of international education (pp. 21–38). In R. Bates (Ed.), *Schooling Internationally: Globalisation, Internationalisation and the Future for International Schools*. Abingdon: Routledge.

Yang, R. (2002). *The Third Delight: Internationalization of Higher Education in China*. London: Routledge.
Yates, L. and Grumet, M. (Eds). (2011). *Curriculum in Today's World: Configuring Knowledge, Identities, Work and Politics World Yearbook of Education 2011*. Oxford: Routledge.
Zajda, J. I. (2005). *International Handbook on Globalisation, Education and Policy Research: Global Pedagogies and Policies*. Dordrecht: Springer.
Zhao, Y. (2010). Preparing globally competent teachers: A new imperative for teacher education. *Journal of Teacher Education*, Vol. 61, No. 5, pp. 422–431.

Part II
Education policy

7   Key foci of policy analysis

There are a number of approaches to the definition of the term 'policy' and to describing systematically what is involved in the policy process. Early definitions emphasized decision making. Later definitions also emphasized goal-oriented rather than random or chance activity. Harman's (1984, p. 13) definition embraced both orientations:

> Policy refers to the implicit or explicit specification of courses of purposeful action being followed or to be followed in dealing with a recognised problem or matter of concern and directed towards the accomplishment of some intended or desired set of goals.

This definition also accommodates the notion that policies may differ in scope; they may refer to specific single issues, such as school attendance, or they may have a bearing on a wide range of related topics.

Three dimensions of education policy

It is helpful in examining education policy to see that it can be identified as having three dimensions.

Policy related to access

To focus on education policy in terms of its access dimension is to be concerned with strategies and measures that influence, promote or facilitate access to, and participation in, education, including schooling.

Policy related to process

To focus on education policy in terms of its process dimension is to concern oneself with what goes on in the heart of any education system. This can relate to what goes on in the individual school or classroom, and includes considering the quality of the curriculum and instruction, the physical and instructional environment of the school and other determinants of quality.

Policy related to structure

To focus on education policy in relation to structure is to concern oneself with issues relating to the national and local organization of the education system, the details of management and funding, and the articulation mechanism governing the links between different sectors of the system.

It would be somewhat unusual to have a policy stated only about, or operating in any one of, the three dimensions outlined above. What is more usual is to be able to identify two or all three of them and to examine how they are interrelated in various ways.

Analysis *of* policy and analysis *for* policy

Ham and Hill (1993, p. 4) distinguished between 'analysis of policy' and 'analysis for policy', stating: 'This distinction is important in drawing attention to policy analysis as an academic activity concerned primarily with advancing understanding, and policy analysis as an applied activity concerned mainly with contributing to the solution of social problems.' If one engages in both forms of analysis then one usually engages first of all in an analysis of policy. Approaches to this activity are outlined in the next chapter. Hogwood and Gunn (1981) also identified a research area they termed 'evaluation study', which is located in the border area between both approaches. This area of study is sometimes referred to as that of 'impact studies' since the concern is with analysing the impact policies have on a population.

In an 'analysis for policy making', data are marshalled in order to assist policy makers to make decisions. The data may derive from reviews carried out as part of a regular monitoring process by government, or it may be provided by academic policy analysts applying their knowledge to practical problems. The analysis can involve:

- attempts to improve the functioning of government through the reallocation of functions and tasks;
- efforts to enrich the basis for policy choice through the developing planning systems and new approaches to the appraisal of options.

There can also be policy advocacy during analyses for policy. This can involve the analyst in promoting particular options and ideas in the policy process, either individually or with others, often through pressure groups.

Substantive and procedural education policies

Anderson (1979) distinguished between these as follows.

Substantive policies

These are concerned with 'the nature and substance of educational provision and include any policy that directly embodies an educational aim, purpose or rationale' (Codd, 1993, p. 84).

Procedural policies

These are concerned with 'administrative structures and include any policy that determines how educational provisions are to be controlled or distributed' (Codd, 1993, p. 84).

Substantive policies can, according to Anderson (1979), be 'regulatory', 'distributive' or 'redistributive'.

Regulatory policies

These involve 'the imposition or the removal of rules or limitations controlling the actions of various agents within the education system' (Codd, 1993, p. 84).

Distributive policies

These are 'those in which resources are allocated to assist particular groups, and where those seeking benefits are not in direct competition with one another' (Prunty, 1984, p. 5).

Redistributive policies

These involve deliberate efforts 'to shift the allocation of wealth, income, property or rights among broad classes or groups of the population' (Anderson, 1979, p. 130).

Some other key concepts

Considine (1994, 2005) offers the following additional key concepts which are helpful in understanding policy:

- Policy is a deceptively simple term which conceals some very complex activities. All political actors espouse policies, decry the policies of others or mutter in discontent at things omitted from what should have been.
- When governments announce a public stance in regard to some contemporary issue they are said to have adopted a policy.
- Any firm decision to grant entry to a programme or turn off access to a valued good is termed a policy stance.
- When public officials commit public resources to a programme to support some members of society, these too are called policies.

Policy then may be expressed as any or all of the following three things:

a   clarifications of public values and intentions;
b   commitments of money and services;
c   granting of rights and entitlements.

What these very different actions have in common is that they are each part of the public exercise of power. Therefore, policy involves various groups of policy actors working continuously through available institutions to articulate and express the things they value.

Differences between public and private policy

Considine (1994, 2005) also outlined the following differences between public and private policy.

Differences because of the nature of government authority

- Governmental authority is quite unlike that found in the private sphere. This is because of the need for governments to gain continuing popular support for their actions.
- Authority is a specific form of activity in which those engaged in a relationship acknowledge the existence of legitimate power.
- When the source of legitimate power is invested in an institution, it becomes a critical gateway through which values and resources must pass in order to survive or prosper.

Differences because of values

In private transactions people may choose different values to guide them. Markets use money as the measure of value. In families and other close relationships, values may be based on affection, common interest or beliefs. In the public sphere, values must ultimately be located within a framework of rights.

Policy actors

Considine (1994, 2005) also makes the following points on policy actors:

- While policy is always an expression of governmental authority, policy makers may come from anywhere.
- Policy makers are not just those key politicians and bureaucrats who have command of the institutions which must give approval to any decision or programme. They include any individual or group able to take action on a public problem or issue.
- Anyone engaged in policy analysis must define who has influence, who is excluded and who achieves what is defined as being desirable.

Policy process

Considine (1994, 2005) also makes the following points on the policy process:

- We can separate official and non-official actions from the continuing process of which the action is a part.
- Sometimes a crisis will occur for which there is no precedent. More usually, however, what is taking place is a struggle for certainty through modifying and adjusting the existing situation.
- Modifications and adjustments will only make little sense to the observer when considered in terms of what has preceded them, and also in the context of the social and political context in which they are taking place.

• The task of researchers is to try to understand the rules of what is an on-going set of episodes driven by policy makers.

The internationalization of education policy – the Bologna Process

Education systems in Europe have been undergoing profound changes over the last number of years. New actors and new procedures for policy making have emerged and have a strong effect on today's education systems. In particular, international initiatives and programmes, of which the Programme for International Student Assessment (PISA) study for secondary education and the Bologna Process for higher education are the most prominent, have provided the trigger for many countries to engage in major education change.

The Bologna Process emerged from a series of ministerial meetings and agreements between European countries, the aim being to ensure comparability in the standards and quality of higher education qualifications. The European Higher Education Area was created through the Bologna Accords. In 1999, the Bologna Declaration was signed by education ministers from 29 European countries, most of them being within the European Community.

Under the Declaration, qualifications were defined in terms of statements of what students know and can do on completion of their degrees. The qualifications' framework is largely as follows:

• first cycle: 180–240 ECTS credits, usually leading to the awarding of a bachelor's degree;
• second cycle: 90–120 ECTS credits, usually leading to the awarding of a master's degree;
• third cycle: usually leading to the award of a doctoral degree.

In most cases, the bachelor's degree course is of 3–4 years' duration (full-time), the master's degree course is of 1–2 years' duration (full-time) and the doctoral degree course is of 3–4 years' duration (full-time). The naming of the degrees may vary from country to country. One academic year corresponds to 60 ECTS credits, which are equivalent to 1,500–1,800 hours of study.

Overall, the Bologna approach is driven by economic considerations, with a Europe-wide standardization of the degree structures being seen as facilitating ease of mobility and cutting down costs. However, the Bologna Process does not have the status of European Union legislation. Also, the Bologna Declaration is not a treaty or convention. Overall, participation and cooperation are voluntary; there are no legal obligations for the signatory states. As a result, most countries do not currently fit the framework as there is great resistance to moving away from their own time-honoured systems.

Issues for discussion

1   The one thing most writers on education policy agree on is that the term 'policy' is highly contested. Accordingly, it has many definitions. These range from a static and simple view of policy as a text that is implemented with total fidelity, to a more dynamic and complex view incorporating process. An overview of these differing definitions is presented below. Consider each of the following definitions in terms of its advantages and disadvantages:

   • Policy is an operational statement of values.
   • Policy is a plan of action or statement of ideals.
   • Policy is who gets what, when and how.
   • Policy is an active and contested process involving daily practice, consultation, negotiation, bargaining, resistance and decision making.
   • Policy is a document embodying a contract or formal authorization.
   • Policy is whatever governments choose to do or not do.
   • Policy is what is enacted as well as what is intended.
   • Policy is both text and action – words and deeds.
   • Policy is a decision, or set of decisions, made by a person or group or political party, concerning a goal to be sought and a means to obtain it.

2   Select three broad education policy areas that interest you.

   • Are there any international policy documents on each of these areas that have been produced by bodies like the OECD, UNESCO, Education International or the European Union?
   • What does it suggest should happen, when, how and why?
   • What is discouraged, either implicitly or explicitly?
   • Whose values are represented in this approach?
   • Whose values are not valued?

3   Is there a specific national policy document in your own country that interests you?

   • If so, why?
   • Is it possible to have different interpretations of the policy makers' intentions regarding how the policy should be understood?

4   Are you familiar with any non-government education policies?

   • Identify one produced for religious education systems.
   • What are the distinguishing features of this policy?
   • Is it possible to have different interpretations of the policy makers' intentions regarding how the policy should be understood?

5   Are you familiar with any education policies produced for 'alternative' education systems?
    What are the distinguishing features of this policy?

6   Are you familiar with any education policies produced by an individual school, college
     or university?
     What are the distinguishing features of this policy?

References

Anderson, J. E. (1979). *Public Policy Making*. New York: Holt, Rinehart and Winston.

Codd, J. (1993). Equity and choice: The paradox of New Zealand educational reform. *Curriculum Studies*, Vol. 1, No. 1, pp. 75–90.

Considine, M. (1994). *Public Policy: A Critical Approach*. Melbourne: Macmillan.

Considine, M. (2005). *Making Public Policy: Institutions, Actors, Strategies*. Cambridge, UK: Polity Press.

Ham, C. and Hill, M. (1993). *The Policy Process in the Modern Capitalist State*. Hemel Hempstead, UK: Harvester Wheatsheaf.

Harman, G. (1984). Conceptual and theoretical issues (pp. 13–29). In J. R. Hough (Ed.), *Educational Policy. An International Survey*. London: Croom Helm.

Hogwood, B. and Gunn, L. (1981). *The Policy Orientation*. Strathclyde: Centre for the Study of Public Policy, University of Strathclyde.

Prunty, J. (1984). *A Critical Reformulation of Educational Policy Analysis*. Victoria: Deakin University Press.

8   Education policy orientations

Jones (2013) in her primer, *Understanding Education Policy*, has identified a framework of four education orientations. These are as follows:

- the conservative orientation;
- the liberal orientation;
- the critical orientation;
- the post-modern orientation.

While the fourth of these, namely, the post-modern orientation, is as valid as the other three, it is different in that it can often be identified only when prescribed policies are being adopted by teachers and others, as opposed to being identifiable in actions that lead up to, and in policy documents that are meant to guide, what is to take place. Since the concern here is with the latter focus, attention is given only to the first three of Jones' orientations. At the same time, the three are presented as four because it is felt that a sub-set of the liberal orientation is the neo-liberal orientation and that it can be considered as a separate orientation in its own right. The fundamental principles of each of these four orientations is now considered.

Four orientations to policy

The conservative orientation

Jones (2013, p. 30) summarizes this orientation as follows:

> Schools and teachers take an authoritarian approach and inculcate students with the dominant values, beliefs and practices of the time. Students are merely passive recipients of this knowledge and constructed as the 'empty vessel' or 'blank slate' to be filled with knowledge.

She goes on to state that within this perspective education is viewed as preparation for work and the discourses within educational policies stemming from it 'focus on shaping students to fit current social, civic, religious, and vocational conventions. Classroom pedagogy is seen as ideally characterised by the undisputed authority of the teacher and the unproblematic transmission of authorised knowledge' (Jones, 2013, p. 30). Jones (2013, p. 30) concludes by stating that 'methods include lectures or sermons, viewing of texts, enforcing of behavioural rules and pledges'.

The liberal orientation

Jones (2013, p. 34) points out that this orientation has been linked to 'human capital theory' and the shift in post-industrial societies, where preparation for a single career has been replaced 'by multifarious "up-skilling" of individuals to allow for a competitive, flexible and insecure workforce'. She goes on as follows:

> Within this orientation, schools and teachers act as facilitators of students' development of knowledge and skills; particularly relating to academic inquiry and personal decision-making. This orientation is concerned with the preparation of the 'whole student' for 'life' rather than simply for employment ... liberal education embraces engagement of the affective and intellectual domains. Classroom pedagogy is characterised by democratic settings where the teacher's position is as a facilitator of active inquiry by students and an emphasis on understanding the reasons for social phenomena.
>
> (Jones, 2013, p. 34)

She concludes by pointing out that associated classroom methods include class discussion, writing personal reflections, expression of feelings and opinions, debate, role-play, testing knowledge and practising skills.

The neo-liberal orientation

Jones (2013, p. 36) notes that, while this orientation can be considered within the liberal orientation, it should be differentiated 'from general "progressive" and "Victorian" liberal perspectives with the assumption of a clear separation of the state and the autonomous individual (and insistence on the pre-availability of choice)'. She goes on to say that it sees the 'weak state' as intentionally positive in trying to engineer the market for efficiency purposes. Simply put, she argues, neo-liberal agendas centre on further separating state and citizen as a pre-condition for greater choice. She elaborates as follows:

> Deriving from public-choice theory, the neo-liberal framing sees bureaucratic control as necessarily peppered with inefficiencies caused by the self-interest of bureaucrats. Yet such self-interest is argued as a potentially positive force if properly harnessed, as with within the free market where the self-interest of consumers of the education product can be freely explored in a way that stimulates the competitiveness of autonomous schools (leading to school improvements) and maximises profits.
>
> (Jones, 2013, p. 36)

She concludes by stating that 'education is seen as, for the most part, a "natural" private good that should be marketized, despite its potential for national and even global public goods and outcomes' (Jones, 2013, p. 37) and that equality in this orientation is 'equality of opportunity (for the pursuit of competitive excellence in the liberal sense), not of outcomes (in the critical sense)' (Jones, 2013, p. 37).

The critical orientation

This orientation is linked to such movements as class-system reforms, post-colonialism and attempts to address issues of the marginalization of particular social and cultural groups. Jones (2013, p. 40) states that it sees whole-school reforms as being necessary to achieve its ends. She elaborates thus:

> Teachers aim to engage students more actively in social issues and action, and students are ideally empowered to promote alternative principles, question deep-seated social values and unjust practices, and undertake actions to lead to a more equitable society. Education is understood as having the potential to revolutionise society ... challenging marginalisation and established social orders.
>
> (Jones, 2013, p. 40)

She goes on to say that the view of classroom pedagogy within this orientation is student-centred and action-based, and is characterized by high levels of collaboration between teacher and students. Traditional authorities can be directly called into question, with teaching 'employing ideological critique of mainstream notions from a marginalised perspective and the use of alternative sources and accounts' (Jones, 2013, p. 40).

Issues for discussion

Regarding the conservative orientation

1 Recall the structural-functionalist approach to education policy considered in Chapter 2. How does it relate to the conservative education policy orientation?

2 Can you identify some solid reasons why schools and teachers should inculcate students with the dominant values, beliefs and practices of the time?

   - Does it necessarily follow that this needs to be done by adopting an authoritarian approach?
   - Does it necessarily follow that students should not be given opportunities to question the reasons you identified above?
   - What possible questions could be raised regarding these reasons?
   - What might the consequence be of not adopting a conservative orientation?

Regarding the liberal orientation

3 Recall what you considered about 'human capital theory' and education in Chapter 5. Relate what you recall to the liberal orientation.

4 The liberal orientation assumes it is possible to prepare individuals so that they can be part of a flexible workforce.

   - How do you think this might take place?
   - Can you see any problems with it?
   - Can you mount any objections to it?

5 Do you consider that the conservative orientation and the liberal orientation are mutually exclusive, or can they co-exist?

Regarding the neo-liberal orientation

6 How would you define neo-liberalism?

- What are the consequences for schooling of adopting a neo-liberal agenda?
- What are the consequences for other aspects of education of adopting a neo-liberal agenda?
- What advantages can you see in adopting such an agenda?
- What disadvantages can you see in adopting such an agenda?
- Do you consider that the neo-liberal orientation can sit comfortably alongside a conservative orientation and the liberal orientation?

Regarding the critical orientation

7 Is the critical orientation to be seen in any way in your educational system?

- If so, how does it manifest itself?
- Is it opposed in your education system?
- If so, how does this manifest itself?
- Should it be adopted as an orientation in all education systems?
- Can you see any advantage in it being the only orientation?
- Can you see any disadvantage in it being the only orientation?
- Do you think that schools can take part in action that can, in any meaningful way, lead to a more equitable society?

Reference

Jones, T. (2013). *Understanding Education Policy: The Four Education Orientations' Framework*. Dordrecht: Springer.

9   Models for analysing education policy

The previous chapter outlined four major orientations to policy. They can be identified in policy texts and in analyses of practice. This observation begs the question: How does one go about the task of identifying these and other orientations, and possible relations between them, in a system-atic scholarly manner in relation to any particular policy or sets of policies? This chapter addresses the matter by outlining a number of models for engaging in policy analysis of this type in the education field. It opens by centring initially on the work of Stephen Ball. It then goes on to outline two related models, namely, one developed by Taylor and colleagues (1997) and the other developed by Vidovich.

A model for educational policy analysis centred on the work of Stephen Ball

A model for an analysis of education policy was put forward by Ball and associates in the early 1990s. It was developed in a number of publications (Ball and Bowe, 1992; Ball, 1994a, 1994b) and further delineated in response to several critiques (Gale, 1999; Henry, 2001). The principal features of Ball's framework include the following:

- the idea of a policy cycle and its three inherent contexts (influences, text production and practice);
- the concept of a trajectory study, which advocates an analysis of the policy process across the three contexts;
- its flexibility in approaches to analysis, reflected in the idea of a 'toolbox' for analysis rather than a single theory.

Analysts such as Hogwood and Gunn (1981) have referred to the difficulty of defining policy and to the argument that traditional 'public administration' models of policy often simplify the policy process into a 'top-down' linear pathway or a cycle. Ball's conceptualization of policy and policy analysis addresses this by focusing on what he calls a messy complexity and serendipity where a clear definition of policy and particular stages becomes impossible. Rather than leading to a study adopting a traditional linear concept of policy following a top-down structure, this is a view of policy analysis as a 'trajectory study', a cross-sectional analysis across five contexts, which are not necessarily successive.

The five principal contexts identified by Ball (1994a) are:

- the context of influence;
- the context of policy text production;
- the context of practice;
- the context of outcomes;
- the context of policy strategies.

Each context represents an area of contest and tension as different parties within the policy process struggle to bring their interests, ideologies or points of view to the fore.

The context of influence

This refers to the various sources of the policy: the causes and background issues and the factors that give the policy process its gestation, initiative and direction.

The context of policy text production

This refers to the struggle over the actual text of the policy, traditionally considered to be the central feature of the linear policy process. Again, this context is represented as a struggle of interests.

The idea of policy as text borrows ideas from literary theory. It involves a conceptualization of policy as a text to be read in as many ways as there are readers. In particular, there are:

- 'writerly texts', which are clearly directive, can be interpreted relatively simply and are relatively uncontested;
- 'readerly texts', which are more ambiguous and open to a wide range of interpretations. Here the practitioner, as reader, is able to bring his or her own understandings to the text, thus leading to a wide range of possible consequences in the practice of the policy.

The context of practice

This context should not be confused with the traditional notion of 'policy implementation'. The latter label is now seen as being inadequate as it suggests simply putting into practice the directives of a policy text. Ball and his associates went to great lengths to show that practice is a significant part of the policy process, as practitioners can bring to bear a multitude of ways of carrying out, reinterpreting, reinventing or resisting the policy text.

The context of outcomes

This relates to issues of 'social justice, equity and individual freedom' (Ball, 1994a, p. 26).

The context of political strategies

This refers to political and social inequalities arising from policy consequences. It recognizes that issues of power and social justice can arise because of the plurality of contexts and multiple trajectories inherent in the policy process.

The model of Taylor and colleagues

Taylor *et al.* (1997), like Ball, made an appeal for greater empirical study in policy analysis. They suggested a model which largely reflects Ball's position, but also made important modifications to it. Also, the model focused more on the role of the state and had a greater reliance on critical theory and other perspectives, including feminism.

Taylor *et al.* (1997) identified three areas of policy analysis:

- context;
- text;
- consequences.

These areas are not dissimilar to those outlined by Ball. The first of them, however, differs somewhat from Ball's context of influence; on this, Taylor and colleagues (1997) stressed the importance of understanding the historical, political, social and economic context of any policy, seeing it as an essential ingredient in policy analysis.

Taylor *et al.* (1997), like Ball, stressed the importance of a multidisciplinary approach to policy analysis, and offered feminism as a major feature of their critical perspective which, they argued, can lead to a major concern with issues of social justice. Furthermore, they provided more clarity than Ball on the nature and importance of discourse theory as an approach to policy analysis. Discourse theory leads to an emphasis on the language and meanings contained in the text.

Taylor *et al.* (1997) argued that unravelling the politics of discourse leads to a greater understanding of the three dimensions of a study, namely context, text and consequences. Discourses highlight the various features of the context in which the policy gestates. They also substantiate the struggles of interests and ideologies in the production of the text, and help to unravel the variety of responses that may occur in the implementation of the policy text.

Finally, Taylor *et al.* (1997) stressed the importance of understanding meaning in the analysis of policy; they argued that an important feature of research in the field is to gain an understanding of the meanings that key players at the different levels in the policy process bring to it. Meaning is in part gained from an analysis of the discourses in the documents and texts of, and around, the policy. However, it can also be gained from the understandings communicated by interviewing key players.

The model of Vidovich

Vidovich (2002, 2007, 2013) synthesized the ideas of Ball, Taylor and others into yet another model for education policy and practice. She retained Ball's notion of a trajectory study, but offered further detail, elaboration and development to facilitate the conducting of empirical policy studies. By synthesizing modernist approaches (which stress the importance of the state in the policy process) and post-modernist frameworks (which have been criticized for underplaying the role of the state with an emphasis on the consequences), Vidovich produced a model which provides a highly relevant and detailed framework for designing research projects.

Vidovich's framework, as mentioned above, retains the three principal contexts of Ball's model – the context of influence, the context of policy text production and the context of practice – and assumes the cross-sectional basis of a 'trajectory study' (Ball, 1994a). However, she has made the following modifications:

- There is a clear recognition of global influences, which is a feature and a result of the improved communications, information technology and ideological shifts in the last three decades of the twentieth century.
- Greater recognition is given to state-centred constraint, thus emphasizing the importance of state-mandated policies which have been an important feature of education policy in some countries more than others. At the same time, Vidovich (2002) is careful to stress the difference between state-controlled policy and state-centred policy. The first gives too much primacy to a limited conceptualization of the modern state and its influence over the whole policy process, conceived as 'top-down', whereas the second recognizes the significance of the state by emphasizing the often central role taken by governments on policy.
- The linkages between the three contexts and the different levels of the trajectory are highlighted.

Vidovich's emphasis on the need to consider different levels of the policy process arose out of cogitating analyses of responses to, and re-workings of, policy texts. She has argued that the contexts of influence and of policy text production may operate at one level – for example, at the macro-level of global influences or federal/national incentives. Equally, the two contexts could be influenced by factors operating at the micro-level. Furthermore, the context of policy text production may operate at another level yet again (for example, the intermediate, or meso-level, of the state). Also, the context of practice can operate at the micro-level (for example, at the school or even at the subject-department level).

Issues for discussion

1 Rizvi and Lingard (2010, p. 44) have argued that policy is 'the authoritative allocation of values'.
   Discuss.

2 Identify a contemporary policy development with which you are familiar. From your general reading and experience, discuss this policy in terms of each of the contexts of the policy trajectory identified by Vidovich.

3 Identify another contemporary policy development with which you are familiar.

   - What are the major debates that are taking place about this development?
   - What concepts are prominent in the debates?

(continued)

- What are the leading issues of contention?
- What is the significance of the development at present?
- Who is writing about the development and what stances are they adopting?

4   Identify a policy initiative you feel needs to be undertaken?

- What is the historical context to this?
- What is the political context to this?
- What is the social context to this?
- What is the economic context to this?
- What are the points at issue?
- Do you think there may be any common ground on the matter?
- What key questions need to be addressed?

5   Select three research papers that have been published in relation to one education policy.

Does the paper indicate a perception of policy as that of a text or document only?

Does the paper indicate a perception of policy as that of value-laden actions?

Does the paper indicate a perception of policy as consisting of processes, including implementation?

To whom might the papers be of interest? Why?

References

Ball, S. J. (1994a). *Education Reform: A Critical and Post-structural Approach*. Buckingham: Open University Press.

Ball, S. J. (1994b). Some reflections on policy theory: A brief response to Hatcher and Troyna. *Journal of Education Policy*, Vol. 9, No. 2, pp. 171–182.

Ball, S. and Bowe, R. (1992). Subject departments and the 'implementation' of national curriculum policy: An overview of the issues. *Journal of Curriculum Studies*, Vol. 24, No. 2, pp. 97–115.

Gale, T. (1999). Trajectories: Treading the discursive path of policy analysis. *Discourse*, Vol. 20, No. 3, pp. 393–407.

Henry, M. (2001). *Policy Approaches to Educational Disadvantage and Equity in Australian Schooling*. Paris: International Institute for Educational Planning.

Hogwood, B. and Gunn, L. (1981). *The Policy Orientation*. Strathclyde: Centre for the Study of Public Policy, University of Strathclyde.

Rizvi, F. and Lingard, B. (2010). *Globalising Educational Policy*. London: Routledge.

Taylor, S., Rizvi, F., Lingard, B. and Henry, M. (1997). *Educational Policy and the Politics of Change*. London: Routledge.

Vidovich, L. (2002). *Expanding the Toolbox for Policy Analysis: Some Conceptual and Practical Approaches*. Hong Kong: Comparative Education Policy Research Unit, Department of Public and Social Administration, City University of Hong Kong.

Vidovich, L. (2007). Removing policy from its pedestal: Some theoretical framings and practical possibilities. *Educational Review*, Vol. 59, No. 3, pp. 285–298.

Vidovich, L. (2013). Policy research in higher education: Theories and methods for globalizing times? (pp. 21–39). In J. Huisman and M. Tight (Eds), *Theory and Method in Higher Education Research (International Perspectives on Higher Education Research, Volume 9)*. Bingley, UK: Emerald Insight.

10 Policy borrowing

For centuries different countries have tried to learn from each other in order to enhance the quality of their educational systems. Time and again, however, politicians, policy makers and educationists have failed in their efforts in this regard. This is partly because they failed to note how apparently well thought-out ideas on education in the past floundered because they involved inappropriate transnational educational knowledge transfer. By such transfer is meant the process which involves the exchange of theories, models and methods for academic or practical purposes among countries. The lesson to be learned is that the possibility of any set of education ideas and practices being adopted successfully for any context is maximized only when attention is paid to the nature of that context (Clarke and O'Donoghue, 2015).

What is meant by context?

Baun *et al.* (2011) point out that education policies can be influenced by a variety of commitments, values and experiences, and that these should be made clear in frameworks for policy implementation. They also contend that anyone using such frameworks should be informed regarding the reality that policies are 'enacted in material conditions, with varying resources' (Baun *et al.*, 2011, p. 588). They conceptualize this situation in terms of four sets of contexts: the 'situated contexts', the 'professional contexts', the 'material contexts' and the 'external contexts'.

Situated contexts

This set of contexts consists of those aspects of context that are 'historically and locationally linked to the school. They include a school's setting, its history and its pupil intake' (Baun *et al.*, 2011, p. 591).

Professional contexts

This set of contexts includes 'values, teacher commitments and experiences, and "policy management" in schools' (Baun *et al.*, 2011, p. 591).

Material contexts

This set of contexts refers to such matters as staffing, budget, buildings, available technology and surrounding infrastructure.

External contexts

These are conceptualized as pressures and expectations that arise as a result of the influence of broader local and national policies. They include such matters as local authority support, inspectors' reports, league table positions, legal requirements and responsibilities, as well as the relationship that any particular school has with other schools.

The tradition within comparative education of paying attention to context

During the nineteenth century, as nation states began to emerge in Western Europe and North America, and national systems of primary school education were created, educators began to travel to other nations to seek out, as they saw it, the best ideas and insights from abroad to improve their education systems at home (Wolhuter *et al.*, 2007; Fraser and Brickman, 1968). Equally, the European and American models of education were exported to colonial dependencies. The Japanese were also active borrowers in the field (Clarke and O'Donoghue, 2015).

At the same time, some powerful cautionary voices were raised. Sir Michael Sadler, British historian, educationist and university administrator, stressed that national education systems could only be understood by first of all understanding the national contexts in which they functioned. He made his case as follows:

> We cannot wander at pleasure among the educational systems of the world, like a child strolling through a garden, and pick off a flower from one bush and some leaves from another, and then expect that if we stick what we have gathered into the soil at home, we shall have a living plant. A national system of education is a living thing, the outcome of forgotten struggles and difficulties, and 'of battles long ago'. It has in it some of the secret workings of national life.
>
> (quoted in Higginson, 1979, p. 49)

Put simply, Sadler argued convincingly that it could be folly to borrow an educational practice or innovation which evolved in one national context and try to transplant it into a different societal context.

Sadler's position either implicitly or explicitly influenced the thinking of various world-leading comparative educationists in the twentieth century (Wolhuter *et al.*, 2007). Nevertheless, in many situations policy makers were either blind to their insights or took the decision to ignore them. Thus, a process of uncritical transnational knowledge transfer continued, accompanied by failure after failure in what was being sought (Kumar, 1979; Useem and Useem, 1980). This matter can be illustrated by the following examples from the experience in one part of the world, namely, the South Pacific Island nations:

- the failure of a number of projects for the development of social studies curricula for nine nations because they were incompatible with contextual assumptions about learning (LeSourd, 1990; Thaman, 1991);
- the failure of curricula designed by overseas 'experts' emphasizing teaching for understanding rather than rote learning, and pupil participation rather than lecture methods, because teachers and school leaders were not engaged in efforts aimed at discovering their views on what was needed by way of preparation to facilitate successful implementation;
- teachers' and school leaders' resistance to embracing new approaches to teaching because external examinations continued to dominate the educational system and they felt that any change might jeopardize pupils' chances of getting high scores (Mangubhai, 1984; Thomas, 1984);
- the failure of a very well-designed and trialled primary science programme for Melanesian schools because there was a lack of equivalence between students' conceptualizations and the concepts on which the programme had been focusing;
- the failure of a 'general teaching programme' which attempted to provide an integrated multi-subject approach in the first two grades of high school in Papua New Guinea by, in Beeby's (1966) terms, demanding 'stage of meaning' thinking and practices from school leaders and teachers who were only in 'the stage of formalism'.

Nevertheless, during the 1970s, with the emergence of dependency theory, the rise of Third World consciousness and the increasing cultural awareness of some Western social scientists, heed began to be taken again of the wisdom of the likes of Sadler.

Developments since the 1980s

During the 1980s new group of academics highlighted Sadler's position once again, albeit through using a new set of metaphors. Hargreaves (1993, p. 149), for example, argued as follows on why educational innovations frequently fail quite disastrously:

> in grafting new ideas onto schools, we do it with so little knowledge about the nature of the everyday world of teachers, pupils and schools that our attempted grafts (and various forms of major and minor surgery) merely arouse the 'anti-bodies' of the host which undermine our attempts to play doctor to an educational patient.

He went on to state that 'only when we understand the precise nature of the host body can we design our innovatory grafts with any confidence that they will prove to be acceptable' (Hargreaves, 1993). This was an echoing of the argument of Carron and Chau (1996), Fullan (1982), Little (1988) and Rondinelli *et al.* (1990) that to introduce change that promises more success and less failure, the world of the people most closely involved in implementation must be understood.

Unfortunately, some of the developments of the past two decades, which have involved greater centralization than hitherto many aspects of education have, as has already been stated in Chapter 1, led to calls once again for the invention and discovery of sure-fired prescriptive models in all aspects of education which would lead to easily generalizable solutions in each of them. Associated with this is the expectation that the successful implementation of these solutions necessitates that leaders at the school level be appropriately 'trained'. Over ten years ago Smith and Lovat (2003, p. 95) argued against this view when applied to school principals. Notwithstanding increasing control from education systems, principals, they held, need to be able to help their staff take account of the importance of context and 'create decision-making space so that they can exercise autonomy and critical professional judgment in, at least, their own classrooms'. Others found it necessary to make similar statements in relation to teachers in statements like the following:

> to plan creatively, and effectively, teachers need to have wide-ranging knowledge about their students, their interests and abilities; the subjects being taught; alternative ways to teach and assess understanding; working with groups; the expectations and limitations of the school and community; how to apply and adapt materials, texts and multimedia; and how to pull all this knowledge together into meaningful activities and experiences.
>
> (Woolfolk and Margetts, 2007, p. 458)

Issues for discussion

1   Have you experienced any education practices that have led to problems because of the failure of teachers to take cognizance of certain realities?

2   Have you experienced any education practices that have led to problems because of the failure of students to take cognizance of certain realities?

3   Are you familiar with the TIMS and PISA tests, and their results?
    What might we be able to learn from the results of countries that do exceptionally well in these tests that can be applied in our own countries?
    About what sorts of related issues might we want to be careful?

4   Do considerations in this chapter imply that there is nothing one can learn for one's own education system from examining the practices in another country?
    What benefits might actually be gained from such an examination?

5   Why do you think politicians and policy makers persist with the uncritical borrowing of educational ideas and practices gained from examining one country and ignore the sorts of arguments outlined in this chapter?

References

Baun, A., Ball, S. J., Maguire, M and Hoskins, K. (2011). Taking context seriously: Explaining policy enactments in the secondary school. *Discourse: Studies in the Cultural Politics of Education*, Vol. 32, No. 4, pp. 585–596.

Beeby. C. E. (1966). *The Quality of Education in Developing Countries*. Cambridge, MA: Harvard University Press.

Carron, G. and Chau, T. N. (1996). *The Quality of Primary Schools in Different Development Contexts*. Paris: International Institute for Educational Planning, UNESCO Publishing.

Clarke, S. and O'Donoghue, T. (Eds). (2015) *School Leadership in Diverse Contexts*. London: Routledge.

Fraser, S. E. and Brickman. W. W. (Eds). (1968). *A History of International and Comparative Education: Nineteenth Century Documents*. Glenview, IL.: Scott, Foreman.

Fullan, M. (1982). *The Meaning of Educational Change*. New York: Teachers College, Columbia University.

Hargreaves, D. (1993). Whatever happened to symbolic interactionism? (pp. 135–152). In M. Hammersley (Ed.), *Controversies in Classroom Research*. Buckingham: Open University Press.

Higginson, J. H. (1979). *Selections from Michael Sadler: Studies in World Citizenship*. Liverpool: Dejall and Meyorre International Publishers.

Kumar, K. (1979). *Bonds without Bondage: Explorations in Transcultural Interactions*. Honolulu: University Press of Hawaii.

LeSourd, S. J. (1990). Curriculum development and cultural context. *The Educational Forum*, Vol. 54, pp. 205–216.

Little, A. (1988). *Learning from Developing Countries*. London: University of London Institute of Education.

Mangubhai, F. (1984). Fiji (pp. 167–202). In R. M. Thomas and T. N. Postlethwaite (Eds), *Schooling in the Pacific Islands: Colonies in Transition*. London: Pergamon Press.

Rondinelli, D., Middleton, J. and Verspoor, A. (1990). *Planning Education Reforms in Developing Countries: The Contingency Approach*. London: Duke University.

Smith, D. and Lovat, T. J. (2003). *Curriculum: Action on Reflection*. Tuggerah, NSW: Social Science Press.

Thaman, K. H. (1991). Towards a culture-sensitive model of curriculum development for the Pacific countries. *Directions: Journal of Educational Studies*, Vol. 13, pp. 1–13.

Thomas, R. M. (1984). American Samoa and Western Samoa (pp. 67–110). In R. M. Thomas and T. N. Postlethwaite (Eds), *Schooling in the Pacific Islands: Colonies in Transition*. London: Pergamon Press.

Useem, J. and Useem, R. H. (1980). Generating fresh research perspectives and study designs for transnational exchange among the highly educated. DAAD Research and Exchange. Proceedings of the German-American Conference at the Wissenschaftszentrum, Bonn, pp. 24–58, November.

Wolhuter, C. C., Lemmer, E. M. and de Wet, N. C. (Eds). (2007), *Comparative Education: Education Systems and Contemporary Issues*. Pretoria: Van Schaik.

Woolfolk, A. and Margets, K. (2007). *Educational Psychology*. Sydney: Pearson Education Australia.

11 Policy changes in higher education

The origins of the modern university can be traced back to the monastic and cathedral schools in medieval Europe (Wolhuter et al., 2007). The cathedral school of Paris is sometimes considered to be where the modern university originated; in 1080 AD the Pope gave the students and masters a charter giving them freedom from interference by the ecclesiastical authorities. This guaranteed their freedom of scholarly inquiry and of teaching and learning. The result was the establishment of the University of Paris (Wolhuter et al., 2007). From then onwards the number of universities in Europe increased rapidly.

The evolution of the modern university took a major leap forward in the early nineteenth century. After the defeat of Prussia by Napoleon, the Prussian King founded the Von Humboldt University in Berlin in 1810 to serve the development of the state (Wolhuter et al., 2007). This university differed from others in that, along with its teaching activities, it developed a major research agenda. The latter included both basic research (knowledge for the sake of knowledge) and applied research (research concerned with the solution of problems experienced by society). After the unification of Germany in 1871, this model spread throughout the rest of the country and from there to much of Europe and to North America.

The university, with its intertwined activities of teaching and research, came to fulfil a number of functions in society. These included:

- the training of highly skilled and knowledgeable people;
- the conducting of basic and applied research to solve problems experienced by society;
- being a conscience of society by critiquing both government and civil society, something that was possible as the institution in most countries was free from government control (Wolhuter et al., 2007).

A wave of developments in universities took place in the late 1950s and 1960s as more people moved into the higher education sector in professional capacities (Frank and Gabler, 2006; Wolhuter et al., 2007). These included:

- the rapid expansion of higher education after World War II;
- the rapid increase in enrolments;
- the more heterogeneous nature of the student population;
- the increasing funding governments had to allocate to higher education;

- the demand for more precise planning of higher education, and for technically competent individuals who were thoroughly familiar with the complexities of the collegiate situation to carry
out the planning activities.

With regard to curriculum organization, Wolhuter *et al.* (2007) have also noted two basic changes
that occurred:

1   the division of year courses into smaller units, originally into semester (six-month) lengths, but
later into even smaller units (modules of a quarter or term or six-week lengths);
2   vocationalization and the movement towards more pragmatic-oriented courses. In some cases
this led to a marginalization of such traditional basic disciplines as history, sociology and
physics.

There are those who hold that the latter change is a risky one for universities if they take seriously
their mission of pushing back the frontiers of science and also if they take cognisance of those who
argue that the traditional academic disciplines are the most economical, most logical and most
clear way of ordering and managing knowledge about the natural and social environment.

Towards the end of the twentieth century, the proud tradition of university autonomy began to
face a series of challenging societal trends (Wolhuter *et al.*, 2007) due to:

- the population explosion in developing countries;
- the technological, communications and information revolutions;
- globalization;
- multiculturalism;
- the demise of the nation state;
- democratization;
- economic liberalization and privatization.

While these trends have created many unprecedented opportunities for higher education, they also
pose a number of serious challenges.

Some current challenges in the university sector

In 2013 the Boston Consulting Group (BCG) (2013) surveyed the higher education landscape and
identified five long-term trends. While they concentrated their work on the US scene, the trends are
also instructive for considering developments in other countries. These were summarized by them
as follows.

Revenue from key sources is continuing to fall, putting many institutions at severe financial risk

Enrolment is the main driver of tuition and fee revenue. But enrolment has been flat or declining in
recent years, a trend that could cause a painful readjustment for institutions accustomed to
stronger enrolment growth.

Demands are rising for a greater return on investment in higher education

By some measures, the return on investment is high: college graduates have much higher earnings and lower unemployment rates, on average, than people with a lower-level degree or diploma. The gap is even greater between the expected earnings of graduates holding a four-year bachelor of arts degree and those with a master's or professional degree. The rate at which this gap is growing suggests that many students must continue their education past college to reap the full benefit of their degree.

Greater transparency about student outcomes is becoming the norm

At a time when only 59 per cent of first-time students at institutions offering four-year undergraduate programmes graduate within six years, colleges and universities are increasingly being challenged to be accountable for student outcomes. For instance, more and more, employers are demanding competencies that are closely linked to the needs of the workplace.

New business and delivery models are gaining traction

Institutions are providing alternatives to traditional degrees, including accelerated three-year degrees, industry accreditations and 'low cost degrees' made possible by colleges accepting credits earned in high school. Competency-focused course 'bundles' are also emerging, which provide certifications relevant to vocations and supplement a degree. Also, there has been an increase in online programmes, particularly hybrids that blend online and face-to-face learning.

The globalization of education is accelerating

Students are increasingly mobile. The best and brightest are travelling to the developed world's major universities for higher education. Top universities that once vied locally and nationally for students now face global competition from other top-tier universities.

Some current developments in university curriculum policy

Significant policy developments are taking place in relation to what some curriculum theorists (Gleeson, 2010) term the 'whole curriculum'. This relates to:

- the range of curriculum objectives sought;
- the nature of associated values and beliefs;
- the extent to which various objectives are prescribed for some, or for all;
- the pattern of components into which the 'whole' curriculum is divided and how lecturers and students are grouped in relation to this;
- the content, pedagogical approaches and modes of assessment outlined;
- the methods used to evaluate the success of the work.

A variety of 'whole' curriculum policy initiatives in higher education over the past decade have been highlighted in the academic literature (Vidovich *et al.*, 2012). These include:

- the deconstruction of the traditional university subject through modularization and the cross-curricular key generic skills movement and competence-based developments (De la Harpe and Thomas, 2009);
- contestations over core knowledge in particular disciplines;
- the establishment of US-style graduate schools in some European countries (Powell and Green, 2007);
- the spread to overseas universities of the strongly embedded US civic engagement practice (Watson 2007);
- initiatives on internationalizing the curriculum (Jones and Brown, 2007).

Lattuca (2006, p. 59) contends there is some consensus among the signatories to the European Bologna accords 'that educational preparation for employment need not be geared to a specific profession but may also take the form of preparation for postgraduate studies'.

The argument is that in a rapidly changing society where specific competencies have become obsolete, employers increasingly recognize the value of generic competencies with well-developed analytical and problem solving skills, leading to an interest in promoting 'general' education' at the undergraduate level. Altbach (2011, p. 131) concurs, defining 'general education' as that which provides 'a broad background in the disciplines along with critical thinking skills'. The international dimension has also been highlighted, with Knight (2011) maintaining that as universities have matured in their approach to internationalization they have put a lot of effort into developing strategic alliances and networks with clear purposes and outcomes.

With the control of curriculum policy in universities shifting from individual academics (who design and teach a course), to university administration (Vidovich *et al.*, 2012), decisions are becoming more 'high stakes' in terms of meeting government and employer accountability requirements, to attract the 'best' students from around the world, and to respond to the growing recognition of the importance of higher education in a knowledge era (Grumet and Yates, 2011).

A particularly radical curriculum policy direction being taken in some research-intensive universities outside of the USA (radical in terms of their history) at the undergraduate level resonate with both the European Bologna model and the emphasis in the USA on a 'general' and 'liberal' undergraduate education, while also being suggestive of new paradigms (Vidovich *et al.*, 2012). The universities that are taking this route share the following related radical curriculum policy transformations:

- a focus on internationalizing the curriculum;
- an increase in curriculum breadth and depth through placing a stronger emphasis than previously on research, communication skills, community service and study abroad components;
- a commitment to students engaging with a range of disciplines to obtain a 'well-rounded' education;
- a major emphasis on interdisciplinarity and integrating knowledge across different disciplines.
- policy flows between the universities undertaking the reforms.

Two distinct reform patterns are discernible within the universities involved: separated generalist undergraduate programmes from specialist and professional education at the postgraduate level, and generalist compulsory core programmes which run in parallel with specialist and professional education at the undergraduate level.

Issues for discussion

1   What is an appropriate mix, in your view, between face-to-face and online teaching?
    Which is best at fostering critical thinking and social learning?
    What importance do you attach to such learning in university courses?

2   What is the extent, do you think, of the emphasis given in universities to programmes in science and technology?
    What does the future hold for courses in humanities and social sciences?

3   Should university programmes help every student acquire the values he or she needs in order to live as responsible citizens, regardless of the degree in which one is enrolled?
    If so, how might this be undertaken?

4   Should a university promote a strong sense of identity and community amongst its students?
    How can this be done when so many universities now serve heterogonous student populations?

5   Should universities provide a wide variety of programmes and course options at the undergraduate degree level, or should what is offered be general degrees in the sciences, social sciences and humanities?
    If the latter, should these be discrete or should there be some degree of overlap between them?

6   Ask yourself with regard to any universities you know, if the state:

    • decides which programmes and courses will be taught;
    • determines which research projects universities will conduct;
    • decides how many students each university shall admit to which programmes;
    • determines the curricula of courses;
    • decides on the trustworthiness of qualifications, programmes and even institutions by means of quality audits;
    • decides which institutions will continue to exist.

7   Preston (2015, p. 14) contends as follows: 'Academics say that the curriculum in the humanities is under attack as universities focus on the more profitable areas of science, technology, engineering and maths. Higher education as a public good is in peril.'
    He then raises the following questions for discussion:

    • Can education in the humanities survive the assault?
    • What will become of universities – for centuries the custodians of knowledge, curiosity and inspiration?

8 Have you any idea how much cultural industries contribute to the national economy in your country? Find out what it is and discuss the implications for the promotion of the humanities in schools and universities.

9 If everything of value has to be monetized, what happens when education becomes a commodity?

10 Speaking in relation to the Australian context, James Allan, professor of Law at the University of Queensland has adopted a very hard-hitting position regarding the management and administration of Australian universities. On this, he states (Allan, 2014a, np):

> In Australia, unlike anywhere else, virtually every issue is decided from the centre: how and when to mark, whether job candidates must have PhDs, what electronic course descriptions must say. The rules are made by people who know nothing about law. We have a managerialist mania, partly because of excessive reporting rules the commonwealth imposes, partly self-imposed. Then there's the attitude to grants. Imagine two academics who publish the same articles in the same journals. One applies for no grants. The other spends much time applying for grants and requires the services of the university grant-getting bureaucracy but gets big money from the Australian Research Council. Both produce the same outputs but the grant-getting academic will be treated as a god. The other will be lucky to get a promotion. Treating inputs as though they were outputs is bonkers. Would you buy a car based on how much government money the car manufacturer got?
>
> All those international rankings of universities also mean next to nothing. They measure only the hard sciences by using criteria such as the number of Nobel laureates (30 per cent of the score on one well-known ranking), the number of papers in *Nature* and *Science*, and citations. For business, law or arts students, indeed for anyone not doing a doctorate, the rankings are worthless.

Do you think this statement of Allan is justified in relation to the situation in your own country (including if it happens to be Australia)?
For a more extensive exposition on Allan's position, see his work entitled 'Why our universities are failing' (Allan, 2014b).

References

Allan, J. (2014a). Fix low quality campuses: Managerialist mania. *The Australian*, 29 August, np.

Allan, J. (2014b). Why our universities are failing. *Quadrant Online*, 8 April, np.

Altbach, P. (2011). Globalization and the university: Realities in an unequal world (pp. 122–139). In J. Simons and P. Altbach (Eds), *International Handbook of Higher Education*. Dordrecht: Springer.

Boston Consulting Group (2013). Five trends to watch in higher education. *BCG Perspectives*. www.bcg perspectives.com/content/articles/education_public_sector_five_trends_watch_higher_education/?chapter=2.

De la Harpe, B. and Thomas, I. (2009). Curriculum change in universities. *Journal of Education for Sustainable Development*, Vol. 3, No. 1, pp. 75–85.

Frank, D. and Gabler, J. (2006). *Reconstructing the University*. Palo Alto, CA: Stanford University Press.

Gleeson, J. (2010). *Curriculum in Context*. New York: Peter Lang.

Grumet, M. and Yates, L. (2011).The world in today's curriculum (pp. 239–247). In L. Yates and M. Grumet (Eds), *Curriculum in Today's World*. London: Routledge.

Jones, E. and Brown, S. (2007). *Internationalising Higher Education*. London: Routledge.

Knight. J. (2011). Internationalization: Concepts, complexities and challenges (pp. 207–227). In J. Simons and P. Altbach (Eds), *International Handbook of Higher Education*. Dordrecht: Springer.

Lattuca, L. (2006). Curricula in international perspective (pp. 39–64). In J. Forest and P. Altbach (Eds), *International Handbook of Higher Education*. New York: Springer.

Powell, S. and Green, H. (2007). *The Doctorate Worldwide*. Maidenhead: Open University Press.

Preston, A. (2015). Education. *The Observer*, 29 March, pp. 14–17.

Vidovich, L., O'Donoghue, T. and Tight. M. (2012). Transforming university curriculum policies in a global knowledge era: Mapping a global-local research agenda. *Educational Studies*, Vol. 38, No. 2, pp. 283–295.

Watson, D. (2007). *Managing Civic and Community Engagement*. Maidenhead: Open University Press.

Wolhuter, C. C., Lemmer, E. M. and de Wet, N. C. (Eds). (2007). *Comparative Education: Education Systems and Contemporary Issues*. Pretoria: Van Schaik.

Part III
Curriculum

12 Orientations to curriculum

An immense amount has been written over the centuries about the purpose of the curriculum. In very general terms four orientations can be distilled out of this corpus of work. They are as follows: academic rationalism, cognitive processes, self-actualization and social reconstruction.

The academic rationalist orientation to curriculum

The central argument of this orientation is that the major function of the school curriculum is to enhance the individual's intellectual abilities in subject areas most worthy of study (Barone, 2010). This usually refers to such academic disciplines as history, chemistry, English, biology and geography. The view is that these subjects are considered to be the depositories of accumulated wisdom which has been systematically organized into fields of study and bodies of knowledge over the years.

Usually academic rationalists also argue that:

- development through the subjects should be many sided, without early specialization;
- a curriculum should in some sense be balanced between the humanities and the sciences;
- such a curriculum would provide a sound basis for students to become effective members in adult society.

Academic rationalists tend to reject the notion of general competencies. For example, they do not see 'creativity, 'problem solving' and 'analysing' as generic attributes. Rather, they speak of thinking creatively as a historian as being different from thinking creatively as a scientist. Similarly, they see problem solving in mathematics as being very different from problem solving in political science.

The educationist and psychologist Jerome Bruner (1966), in advocating the academic rationalist approach, stressed the importance of adopting a spiral curriculum. This is an approach to organizing curriculum content in each learning area such that pupils are introduced to the most powerful ideas within the area, not additively, but by presenting the same fundamental ideas in different, more complex modes of representation repeatedly. He stressed that this should involve the use of:

- enactive (acting out) approaches to teaching;
- iconic (making things) approaches to teaching;
- symbolic (representing, particularly using language) approaches to teaching.

He also argued that, whenever possible, all three approaches should be used.

The cognitive processes orientation to curriculum

This orientation holds that the curriculum should be primarily concerned with providing students with the necessary skills to help them learn how to learn and with the opportunities to employ and enhance their intellectual faculties (Janesick, 2003). Unlike the academic rationalist orientation, that of cognitive processes is based on a view that the human mind is capable of acquiring such generic competencies as the ability to:

- visualize;
- extrapolate;
- synthesize;
- conceptualize;
- analyse;
- evaluate;
- deal with ambiguity;
- solve problems;
- think creatively.

The curriculum, then, should be organized in a manner that facilitates their acquisition and enhances what is acquired (Brady and Kennedy, 2013; Print, 1993).

John Dewey (1938) placed great emphasis on the curriculum being essentially concerned with developing one's problem solving abilities. Central to this is his notion of engagement in reflective thinking. On this he identifies:

- the Pre-Reflective Situation – this is where one experiences obscurity, doubt, conflict or disturbance of some sort;
- the Reflective Situation (see below);
- the Post-Reflective Situation – this is where engagement in reflective thinking and action has transformed the situation into one that is clear, coherent, settled and harmonious.

The Reflective Situation consists of:

- suggestions – in which the mind leaps forward to a possible solution:
- problem formulation – an intellectualization of the difficulty or perplexity that has been felt into a problem to be solved, a question for which the answer must be sought;
- hypothesis – the use of one suggestion after another, as a leading idea or hypothesis, to initiate and guide observation and other operations in collection of factual material;
- hypothesis elaboration – the mental elaboration of the idea or supposition;
- testing the hypothesis by overt or imaginative action.

In order to engage in the reflective process one needs appropriate knowledge, sound judgement, sensitivity, imagination and the ability to reason.

The self-actualization orientation to curriculum

The basis of this orientation is to be found in the work of humanistic psychologists. Their main concern is with enhancing personal growth (Janesick, 2003). They hold that the curriculum should provide opportunities to enhance the individual's self-concept in order to achieve self-actualization. Those who subscribe to this orientation emphasize the importance of the curriculum being organized in such a manner that learners are provided with intrinsically rewarding experiences to enhance personal development. They also place a major emphasis on the teacher providing a supportive environment to enhance what is essentially self-learning, and acting as a facilitator, a resource person, a supporter and an understanding adult.

Carl Rogers (1969), a major exponent of this position, argued that teachers should provide a non-threatening environment in the school and the classroom and also engage in activities to help the student to become a fully functioning person. This involves:

- creating a climate of trust and openness in which self-direction can occur;
- being non-judgemental;
- conveying respect for students.

He also argued that the provision of extrinsic awards should be eschewed for such intrinsic rewards as acceptance, understanding and empathy.

The social reconstructionist orientation to curriculum

Social reconstructionists argue that the needs and betterment of society should take priority over those of the individual. They also hold that most curricula are organized in a manner that supports the status quo rather than trying to effect social reform and produce a more just society. As they see it, the school should promote social change (Flinders, 2004). For some of them, this does not necessarily require a radical overhaul of the curriculum. Rather, in the teaching of social studies and English, the teacher can address such topics as environmental issues, world peace, political corruption, racial prejudice, religious values and ethnic culture. In other words, controversial issues would be introduced when teaching existing school subjects. Also, these issues should be dealt with in such a manner that the student comes away encouraged to intervene actively to shape changes aimed at trying to ensure the world becomes a more democratic place.

A major exponent of this position was Paulo Freire (1970). His fundamental idea is that humans are conscious beings endowed with the capacity to understand themselves and the world they inhabit, and to act in the light of that understanding. Also, the environment they act upon is not only the physical environment but also the social environment in which they live. Both should be structured, he argued, so as to promote the well-being and progress of all of its members. We should cooperate in building together a society in which the freedom of each of us is respected and promoted. By our activity we can humanize the world and in doing so transform ourselves.

Education, Freire argued, should entail the development of human beings as human beings and give us the knowledge we need to be truly human. But knowledge alone is not enough. We must act in the light of that knowledge. Reflection and action combined are necessary for the true life of human beings. Also, the teacher–student relationships must be such as would encourage this, not hinder it.

Freire rejected what he called 'the banking system of education', which emphasized the teacher dispensing information and the student merely receiving it. Education should, rather, be problem-posing. Both teacher and student should approach each problem with open minds, reflect on it as individuals, discuss it and share their views on it, see the difficulties and explore the possible answers. They may agree or disagree on a solution to the problem. The important thing is that both are thinking and acting for themselves, and sharing and cooperating with each other.

It is arguable that there is room within existing curricula for adopting the type of approach advocated by Freire. Within various learning areas opportunities can be found to engage students in critical questions (Smyth, 2011). These include questions like the following on the manner in which historical and contemporary issues are portrayed in school texts and the media:

- What is happening here?
- What do I know about what is happening here?
- How are these practices historically derived?
- Are there any themes or patterns to what is occurring?
- What is the significance of these regularities?
- What are the contradictions?
- Why is this happening?
- Who says this is the way things ought to happen?
- Whose interests are being served by things happening this way?
- Whose interests are denied or silenced?
- Who, therefore, exercises power here?
- How might things be changed?
- What are the personal and structural impediments to change?

Individuals who adopt this sort of lens can help students to develop a commitment to seeing the world and the way it is in concrete, practical and socially just and unjust terms.

Issues for discussion

1 Regarding all four orientations, do you consider they are mutually exclusive?
   If so, why?

2 Could all four orientations be accommodated in a curriculum?
   If so, how?

3 Even if all four could not be accommodated in a curriculum, could more than one of them be accommodated?
   If so, how and why?

4 Do each of the orientations suggest that the curriculum should have some concern with the maintenance of a basic level of physical well-being, including physical education and hygiene?
   If not, should it?

5   Regarding Dewey's ideas on problem solving, do you think his approach can be adopted for the solving of moral problems?

6   What do you know about the Italian social theorist Gramski?

- What is your understanding of his concept of 'hegemony'?
- How might hegemonic processes operate in the classroom and lecture hall?

7   Explore Freire's notion of 'conscientization'.

References

Barone, T. (2010). Academic rationalism (pp. 2–3). In C. Kridel (Ed.), *Encyclopedia of Curriculum Studies*. New York: Sage.

Brady, L. and Kennedy, K. (2013). *Curriculum Construction*. Sydney: Pearson.

Bruner, J. (1966). *Towards a Theory of Instruction*. Cambridge, MA: Belknap Press.

Dewey, J. (1938). *Experience in Education*. New York: Macmillan.

Flinders, D. J. (2004). Teaching for cultural literacy: A curriculum study (pp. 285–296). In D. J. Flinders and S. J. Thornton (Eds), *The Curriculum Studies Reader*. New York: RoutledgeFalmer.

Freire, P. (1970). *Pedagogy of the Oppressed*. New York: Herder and Herder.

Janesick, V. J. (2003). *Curriculum Trends: A Reference Handbook*. Santa Barbara, CA: ABC-CLIO Inc.

Print, M. (1993. *Curriculum Development and Design*. Sydney: Allen and Unwin.

Rogers, C. R. (1969). *Freedom to Learn*. Columbus, OH: Charles E. Merrill.

Smyth, J. (2011). *Critical Pedagogy for Social Justice (Critical Pedagogy Today)*. London: Continuum.

13 Approaches to curriculum planning

The notion of systematically planning the curriculum is relatively recent when considered in relation to the full duration of the history of education. This chapter outlines some of the principal models. These are considered in relation to their principal exponents and the chronological order in which they evolved.

The McMurrys and Herbartism

Charles A. McMurry (1857–1929) and his brother Frank (1862–1936) taught in elementary schools in the USA (McNeil, 1985). They attended the University of Jena in Germany in the 1890s where they became influenced by the pedagogical theory of Johann F. Herbart. The convention is to speak about Herbart's ideas as 'Herbartism'. They consist of a rationalized set of psychological positions applied to instruction.

A major assumption in Herbartism is that only large units of subject matter are able to arouse and keep alive the child's deep interest (Herbart, 1895). Related to this are:

- the doctrine of concentration: the mind can be wholly immersed in one interest to the exclusion of all else;
- the doctrine of correlation: one subject is made the focus of attention but one sees to it that this subject receives support from related subjects.

Herbart also identified five essential steps in instruction:

1　preparation in consciousness of the related ideas from prior experience that will arouse interest in the new material and prepare the pupil for its rapid understanding;
2　presentation of the material in concrete form unless there is already ample sensory experience. It must also be related to the students' past experiences, such as reading, conversing and experimenting;
3　association, to analyse and compare the new and the old, thus evolving a new idea;
4　generalization, to form general rules, laws or principles from the analysed experience, developing general concepts as well as sensations and perceptions;
5　application, to put the generalized idea to work in other situations, to test it and to use it as a practical tool.

The McMurrys recognized in Herbartian pedagogy a systematic method for selecting, arranging and organizing the curriculum. They laid out their ideas by considering three main questions, as follows.

What subject matter has the greatest pedagogical value?

Initially, they saw literature as most useful in bringing the aesthetic and intellectual together (McMurry and McMurry, 1897; McMurry, 1903). They saw geography as the subject with the greatest potential to unify all other subjects on the curriculum. Also, they saw literature and history as being the best ones to teach to develop students' character. In their later years they saw the worth of such 'new' subjects as nature study, science, industrial arts, health, agriculture, civics and modern languages as also being valuable on the curriculum (McNeil, 1985).

How is subject matter related to instructional method?

On this, McNeil (1985) has summarized the position of the McMurrys as follows:

- They believed that there are formal elements of method and concepts for each school subject.
- They insisted that the child learn to think with these elements just as the specialist did in these fields and that the learner develop a consciousness of the right method of thinking in each subject.
- They stressed the importance of organizing studies in relation to the child's mode of thought.

How can the curriculum be organized?

On this, McNeil (1985) has also summarized the position of the McMurrys as follows:

- Knowledge from different subjects should be coordinated into a single project or unit of study.
- Pupils should become absorbed in pragmatic life problems or units of study – for example, the problem of securing a pure milk supply.
- Each project or series of projects should reveal the scope and meaning of a larger idea, which brings into simple perspective and arrangement a whole vast grouping of minor facts.
- A well-defined continuity of thought should be kept steadily developing from grade to grade. The growth of institutions, for example, could be one element chosen to effect continuity over the span of several years of study.

Franklin Bobbitt (1876–1936)

Bobbitt was given the task of developing a curriculum for the Philippines following the Spanish-American War at the end of the nineteenth century. He was forced to abandon his initial effort on realizing he was imposing a curriculum that would have been ideal for many parts of the USA but not necessarily for another country. This prompted him to ask himself how one should systematically go about 'making a curriculum'. As a result, he developed 'scientific curriculum making' (Bobbitt, 1918).

Bobbitt lived in the age of industrialism, scientific methods and scientific techniques. He laid out his ideas in *How to Make a Curriculum* (Bobbitt, 1924). His method, which was guided by an assumption that education is to prepare us for the activities that ought to make up a well-rounded adult life, and which McNeil (1985) has summarized, is as follows.

Step 1

Separate the broad range of human experience into major fields – for example, Language, Health, Citizenship, Social, Recreation, Religious, Home, Vocation. The whole field of human experience should be reviewed in order that the portions belonging to the schools may be seen in relation to the whole.

Step 2

Break down the fields into the more specific activities. This involves finding out what activities are crucial to one or more of the categories of human experience. To do this, Bobbitt drew heavily on what in his time was the new technique of job analysis (a list of duties and/or a list of methods for performing duties).

Step 3

Derive objectives, i.e. statements of the abilities that are required to perform the activities. In *How to Make a Curriculum* he presented over 800 major objectives in ten fields of human experience. He also realized that each of the objectives could be broken down further into its component parts.

Step 4

- Eliminate objectives that can be accomplished through the normal process of living.
- Emphasize objectives that will overcome deficiencies in the adult world.
- Avoid objectives opposed by the community.
- Avoid objectives where the practical constraints are such that they are unlikely to be achieved.
- Differentiate between the objectives for some and for all.
- Sequence the objectives, indicating how far pupils should progress each year in attaining the general goals.

Step 5

Lay out the kinds of activities, experiences and opportunities involved in attaining the objectives. Details for the day-to-day activities of children at each age or grade level must be laid out. These activities make up the curriculum. As project work and part-time work at home and in the community are introduced, there must be cooperative planning. Teachers, nurses, play activity directors and parents together should plan the detailed procedures of the courses. Their plans should then be approved by the principal, superintendent and school board.

Ralph Tyler (1902–1994)

Tyler (1949) outlined his ideas in his famous book *Basic Principles of Curriculum and Instruction*. From this work we get the well-known Tyler model:

- What educational purposes should the school seek to attain? (State Objectives)
- What educational experiences can be provided that are likely to attain these purposes? (Select Learning Experiences)
- How can these educational experiences be effectively organized? (Organize Learning Experiences)
- How can we determine whether these purposes are being attained? (Evaluation)

These ideas are often reduced to the 'Objectives, Content, Method, Evaluation' model. This is now such a taken-for-granted model in lesson planning and curriculum programming that it is easy to assume it has always been used.

Tyler was also concerned with asking how can we state the objectives in a form helpful in selecting learning experiences and in guiding teaching. His position was that an objective should specify:

- the content to be learned – knowledge, skills, attitudes;
- the processes and skills that the learners are to engage in and develop in dealing with that content;
- what pupils will be able to do after completing the course.

This approach was exemplified by him in the following statement of an objective: 'Pupils will be able to write an account of daily life in a typical Elizabethan farmhouse, showing sympathetic insight into the concerns and experiences of the people living there (Tyler, 1949, p. 3).

Hilda Taba (1902–1967)

Taba extended Tyler's model (McNeil, 1985). She continued with a linear approach but argued for the following sequence of activities to be followed so that there would be more information input at each stage:

- diagnosis of needs;
- formulation of objectives;
- selection of content;
- organization of content;
- selection of learning experiences;
- organization of learning experiences;
- determining what to evaluate and how to do it.

Mager and Beach's Vocational or Training Model

Training, as has been argued already in Chapter 3, implies narrower purposes than education. Mager and Beach (1967) proposed a training model for formulating proposed outcomes. It has two main functions:

- to reveal particular manpower needs or occupations which the institutions or programmes should serve;
- to determine the specific competencies that must be taught in order for learners (trainees) to take their place within the target occupations.

The following is an overview of McNeil's (1985) summary of the process.

Determining occupational targets

Many countries release detailed area manpower requirements for hundreds of key occupational categories, reflecting for each category current employment, anticipated industry growth and personnel replacement.

Determining the objectives for training programmes of courses

Job description and task analysis procedures are used. A job description is a paragraph or two listing the tasks involved and any unusual conditions under which those tasks are carried out. All classes of tasks are listed. A task analysis involves one asking:

- What tasks are required on this job?
- How frequently are they required?
- What skills and information is the graduate of the training programme expected to bring to each task?

The analysis is undertaken through:

- observation – which shows what the employees do;
- questionnaires and interviews – which reveals what employees say they do;
- critical incident techniques – which also indicate what people say they do.

Mager and Beach define a task as a logically related set of actions required by a job objective. Tasks are identified by going through the following steps:

- Step 1 – list all tasks that might be included in the job.
- Step 2 – for each of these tasks an estimate is made of:
  - frequency of performance;
  - relative importance;
  - relative ease of learning.

- Step 3 – detail the task by listing what the person does when performing each of the tasks.
- Step 4 – by subtracting what the student is already able to do from what he or she must be able to do one can obtain the course objectives. Course objectives are not the same as task analyses. They describe the abilities one must have to do the job. Also, one cannot go directly from task analysis to the formulation of objectives for a course. It is necessary to decide which of the skills demanded by the occupation may be better taught on the job or in the course.

Issues for discussion

1 Consider the notion which has been promoted in certain school curricula over the past number of years of engaging students in 'rich tasks'.
   Do you think this can be seen as a contemporary application of a Herbartian notion?

2 Some examination boards require that students be examined in what they term a 'general paper' in their high school leaving certificate examination.
   What do you think this involves?
   To what extent do you think this can be seen as a current application of a Herbartian notion?

3 To what extent can the concept of engaging students in 'cross-curricular themes', especially in the sense that this notion has been promoted in the national curriculum in England, be seen as a current application of a Herbartian notion?

4 Are Bobbitt's ideas so complicated as to make the task he details impossible to carry out?
   When might any group find itself faced with a situation where the application of Bobbitt's ideas might be appropriate?

5 Do Bobbitt's ideas have any significance for practising teachers in education systems which currently operate with curricula that are prescribed centrally?

6 Do you think that the origin of the 'outcomes-based education' movement in Australia, USA and the UK, the 'target-oriented' curriculum in Hong Kong and the 'desired curriculum outcomes' movement in Singapore can be found in Tyler's approaches to curriculum?

7 What are your views on the criticism of the vocational curriculum development approach that it prepares people for work as it is, rather than as it should be?

References

Bobbitt, F. (1918). *The Curriculum*. Boston, MA: Houghton Mifflin.
Bobbitt, F. (1924). *How to Make a Curriculum*. Boston, MA: Houghton Mifflin.
Herbart, J. (1895). *The Science of Education. Its General Principles Deducted From Its Aims*. Boston, MA: D. C. Heath and Company.
Mager, R. F. and Beach, K. M. (1967). *Defining Vocational Instruction*. Palo Alto, CA: Fearon Publishers.

McMurry, C. (1903). *The Elements of General Method*. New York: Macmillan.

McMurry, C. and McMurry, F. (1897). *The Method of the Recitation*. Bloomington, IL: Public School Publishing Company.

McNeil, J. D. (1985). *Curriculum: A Comprehensive Introduction*. Boston, MA: Little, Brown and Co.

Tyler, R. (1949). *Basic Principles of Curriculum and Instruction*. Chicago, IL: University of Chicago Press.

14 Outcomes-based education

The 'Issues for discussion' section in the previous chapter referred to the emergence of the 'outcomes-based education' movement in Australia, the USA and the UK, the 'target-oriented' curriculum in Hong Kong and the 'desired curriculum outcomes' movement in Singapore. The term that is most generally used to capture such developments is the first of those just mentioned, namely, 'outcomes-based education'. This chapter describes the background to the term. It then goes on to outline the major advantages and disadvantages of this approach to curriculum planning as outlined in the academic literature.

Background

The notion of outcomes-based education (OBE), coined by William Spady in 1988, is essentially an extension of the positions of the likes of Bobbitt and Tyler. According to Brandt (1991, np), Spady's approach was 'the latest, though perhaps the most sophisticated' version of the position that 'planning for curriculum and instruction has to start with what students are expected to be able to do'. Spady (1988) challenged the prevalent educational paradigm of his era whereby the school curriculum in the USA tended to be organized in terms of the allocation of particular sets of content to be covered at certain times of the year.

In Spady's alternative model, outcomes are to be pursued until they are achieved regardless of the school calendar. He (Spady, 1988, p. 5) described his theory thus:

> Outcome-Based Education (OBE) means organizing for results: basing what we do instruction-ally on the outcomes we want to achieve, whether in specific parts of the curriculum or in the schooling process as a whole. Outcome-based practitioners start by determining the know-ledge, competencies, and qualities they want students to be able to demonstrate when they finish school and face the challenges and opportunities of the adult world. Then, with these 'exit outcomes' clearly in mind, they deliberately design curriculums and instructional systems with the intent that *all* students will ultimately be able to demonstrate them successfully. OBE, therefore, is not a 'program' but a way of designing, developing, delivering, and documenting instruction in terms of its intended goals and outcomes.

A few years later, Spady and Marshall (1991) identified three different types of OBE:

- Traditional OBE: this approach, they argued, was constrained by unit and course outcomes, and was not consistent with a more overarching outcomes approach.
- Transitional OBE: this was described as a way of moving from a traditional approach to a transformational one.
- Transformational OBE: this and transitional OBE, they claimed, is the superior model, because it represents the highest evolution of the concept, with a guiding vision of the student as a competent future citizen.

With its clearly articulated targets, OBE is seen to complement the new focus on efficiency and standards shaping educational policy in various developed countries since the 1980s. Adopted in the USA from the 1980s, it had grown at a great rate throughout North America by the early 1990s. It is also an approach that strongly influenced the development of the national curriculum introduced in England and Wales in 1988. Equally, it guided curriculum development in such countries as New Zealand, Hong Kong, South Africa, Singapore, Malaysia and Australia.

Advantages of OBE

Shine and O'Donoghue (2013) have provided the following summary of the advantages of OBE outlined in the academic literature:

- OBE has been praised for strengthening curricula and removing ambiguities in learning by identifying clear goals for students and teachers.
- Supporters have argued that because OBE is not concerned with the process by which learning is achieved, it offers more flexibility than traditional curriculum models. According to Alderson and Martin (2007), the seemingly common-sense philosophy underpinning the approach is difficult to refute. As they put it, it is 'hard to take exception to the notion of schools and teachers focusing efforts on what students learn and on what they achieve' (p. 163).
- Alderson and Martin (2007, p. 179) have also argued that OBE offers the following advantages for teaching and learning:

    [OBE] fundamentally challenges teachers to re-examine what they do as teachers and the way they do it. For those teachers who embrace it, it is liberating. It affirms what many teachers have previously struggled to do individually in the privacy of their classrooms, often against the prescriptions of school systems ... that all students are capable of learning and worthy of teachers' support.

- OBE has also been seen to be more equitable than traditional academic-focused learning where the emphasis is on the content to be imparted rather than the goals to be achieved. Spady's premise that all students would eventually be able to demonstrate the desired outcomes is advocated as being more inclusive than approaches underpinning other curriculum models. The argument is that OBE could eliminate failure, as students who would not reach a target would be deemed to have not completed the outcome, rather than have failed.

Disadvantages of OBE

- Teachers in North America and in England and Wales initially supported OBE. However, this support was to dissipate as many struggled with the onerous preparation and assessment tasks dictated by the associated curricula (Ellerton and Clements, 1994).
- Opponents argue that OBE does not foster, or accommodate, creativity and is particularly unsuited to subjects such as art, literature and music.
- As far back as 1993, OBE was seen to favour performance, rather than knowledge or understanding. On this, McKernan (1993) argued that it trivialized knowledge by reducing it to facts. He elaborated as follows:

> The 'means-ends' OBE stance treats knowledge as instrumental, a position that violates the epistemology of the structure of certain subjects and disciplines. Some activities or educational encounters are worth doing for reasons other than serving some instrumental purpose as means to a predetermined outcome, aim or objective. They may be either intrinsically rewarding, as in the case of understanding concepts like tragedy from a reading of Macbeth, or extrinsically worthwhile, as in the case of being able to create or solve problems as a result of inductive reasoning.
>
> (McKernan, 1993, p. 345)

- Another criticism around since the 1990s is that OBE is too prescriptive, limits the autonomy of both teachers and students, and can be seen as being another technique by which governments can control education while disempowering teachers (Apple, 1995).
- There have been claims that the approach is theoretically weak. One observation made in this regard is the 'overwhelming absence of a theoretically rigorous (and arguably psychometric) research base regarding the benefits to students and teachers of arranging the curriculum in terms of sequential outcome statements' (Lee, 2003, p. 93).
- The fact that students cannot 'fail' under such a system has also been problematic, particularly for parents who lament the loss of clear indicators of their child's performance in relation to other students.
- Teachers have reported that an outcomes style of reporting which removes an emphasis on competition can be demotivating for students (Griffith *et al.*, 2008).

The perceived shortcomings of the OBE model saw it abandoned in various parts of the USA from the mid-1990s in favour of a 'standards' approach. Compared to OBE, the standards model places more emphasis on academic content and the curriculum descriptors provided are more specific and measurable (Donnelly, 2007). The standards model is also seen as being more consistent with the standardized testing that has come to dominate North American education. In England and Wales, an outcomes focus continues to influence the curriculum, but the initial system has been revised in response to considerable opposition from teachers, who complained that the national curriculum was creating much more work, restricting their autonomy and not serving students well (Alexander *et al.*, 2010). In January 2011, it was announced that the existing curriculum would be reviewed and a new national curriculum developed.

Issues for discussion

1   A regular contention is that instructional objectives can be powerful directives in the teaching process.
    Discuss.

2   Can you think of any aims or objectives of education that cannot be reduced to measurable forms of predictable performance?
    Should such aims be abandoned?

3   Can you think of any educational processes in which it would be worthwhile to engage but which cannot be measured?
    How might one assess performance in these areas?

4   Schlafly (1993, np) made the following contentions about OBE:

> OBE is a dumbed-down egalitarian scheme that stifles individual potential for excellence and achievement by holding the entire class to the level of learning attainable by every child. To accomplish this, children are placed in politically correct groups (race, ethnicity, gender, class) for 'cooperative learning' and may be given a group grade instead of individual grades. Cooperative learning researchers admit that the purpose of this strategy is to eliminate grading and competition in the classroom. This is the essence of OBE and explains why all measurable criteria – standardized tests, the Carnegie units, traditional subject-matter and report cards – must be eliminated.
>
> OBE is based on the unrealistic notion that every child in a group can learn to the designated level and must demonstrate mastery of a specific outcome before the group can move on. The faster learners are not allowed to progress, but are given busy work called 'horizontal enrichment' or told to do 'peer tutoring' to help the slower learners, who are recycled through the material until the pre-determined behaviour is exhibited.
>
> If some students take much longer than others to learn a particular objective, then either corrective instruction must be given outside of regular class time, or students who achieve mastery early on will have to waste considerable amounts of time waiting for their classmates to catch up. . . . If OBE were applied to basketball, the basket would have to be lowered so all could score equally.
>
> In order to master all outcomes, children with a particular talent are required to forfeit time in their area of strength. Because no child moves ahead until all demonstrate mastery, the inevitable happens: the faster learners quickly learn to slow their pace in order to avoid extra work, and they just give the answers to the slower learners so the group can move forward. Incentive and motivation are reduced, and boredom and resentment increased. The result is that all students demonstrate 'mastery' of mediocrity, and none can aspire to excellence. Every child loses under this system.

Discuss each of Schlafly's contentions outlined above.

References

Alderson, A. and Martin, M. (2007). Outcomes based education: Where has it come from and where is it going? *Issues in Educational Research*, Vol. 17, No. 2, pp. 161–182.

Alexander, R., Doddington, C., Gray, J., Hargreaves, L. and Kershner, R. (Eds). (2010). *The Cambridge Primary Review Research Surveys*. Oxford: Routledge.

Apple, M. W. (1995). The politics of official knowledge: Does a national curriculum make sense? (pp. 17–33). In M. Olssen and K. Morris Matthews (Eds), *Education, Democracy and Reform*. Auckland: NZARE/RUME.

Brandt, R.(1991). Overview: The outcomes we want. *Educational Leadership*, Vol. 49, No. 2, pp. 1–2.

Donnelly, K. (2007). Australia's adoption of outcomes based education: A critique. *Issues in Educational Research*, Vol. 17, No. 2, pp. 183–206.

Ellerton, N. F. and Clements, M. A. (1994). *The National Curriculum Debacle*. West Perth: Meridian Press.

Griffith, J., Vidovich, L. and Chapman, A. (2008). Outcomes approaches to assessment: Comparing non-government and government case-study schools in Western Australia. *The Curriculum Journal*, Vol. 19, No. 3, pp. 161–175.

Lee, H. (2003). Outcomes-based education and the cult of educational efficiency: Using curriculum and assessment reforms to drive educational policy and practice. *Education Research and Perspectives*, Vol. 30, No. 29, pp. 60–107.

McKernan, J. (1993). Some limitations of outcome-based education, *Journal of Curriculum and Supervision*, Vol. 8, No. 4, pp. 343–353.

Schlafly, P. (1993) *What's Wrong with Outcome-based Education?* Report. www.ourcivilisation.com/dumb/dumb3.htm.

Shine, K. and O'Donoghue, T. (2013). *Schoolteachers in the News: A Historical Analysis of Coverage in The West Australian Newspaper*. New York: Cambria Press.

Spady, W. G. (1988). Organizing for results: The basis of authentic restructuring and reform. *Educational Leadership*, Vol. 46, No. 2, pp. 4–8.

Spady, W. G. and Marshall, K. J. (1991). Beyond traditional outcome-based education. *Educational Leadership*, Vol. 49, No. 2, pp. 68–70.

15 Alternatives to the objectives model for curriculum planning

A number of significant curriculum theorists in the 1960s and 1970s put forward some alternatives to the objectives model of curriculum. These are very persuasive. In recent years they have been revisited and highlighted once again. This chapter outlines some of them. They are considered in relation to their principal exponents and the chronological order in which they evolved.

Hogben's views on curriculum planning

Hogben (1972) addressed some problems and dangers of uncritically adopting behavioural objectives, the precursor of the outcomes-based approach to stating objectives. He recalled the following arguments for formally stating educational objectives in specific behavioural terms:

- They provide clear-cut end points or goals towards which students and teachers can work.
- Their focus on exactly what the student should be able to do facilitates the measurement and evaluation of curriculum outcomes.

He recognized that it is clearly implied that reference to specific subject-matter content should be included in the statement of a behavioural objective and that, where possible, the criteria of acceptable student performance should be included in statements. He then went on to identify the following problems:

1   The demand for highly specific statements of intent leads to the practical difficulty that any curriculum of substance based on such an approach requires the outlining of a huge number of such statements which curricula of any substance must demand.
2   Requiring that all objectives be stated in advance assumes that one is able accurately to predict what the outcomes of instruction will be. The difficulty with this is that 'the particular amount, type and quality of learning that occurs in any classroom is largely unpredictable and, therefore, the outcomes are far too numerous and complex to be covered by any list of objectives set down in advance' (Hogben, 1972, p. 43).
3   A requirement to provide very specific statements of outcomes encourages a bias towards low-level cognitive performance and simple skill.

Hogben concluded with the following five suggestions for the consideration of curriculum designers:

- Course objectives should be stated, but we should not insist that they are all framed in highly specific behavioural terms.
- There are many worthwhile educational outcomes which may not become apparent until months or years after the conclusion of a particular course. We should not be afraid to state these.
- We must be continually on the alert for unexpected or unintended outcomes – both desirable and undesirable.
- In translating broad general curricular goals into more specific language, we should make sure that the sum of the objectives faithfully reflects the full intention of the original goals that generated them.
- We should not allow measurement considerations alone to dictate objectives' formulation and teaching practice. An objective, the achievement of which cannot readily be assessed, need not be unimportant or unrealistic.

Lawton's views on curriculum planning

Lawton (1983) argued that it is not helpful to discuss the education of human beings as if it were the same as the training that Skinner gave to his pigeons. He added that the arguments against the behavioural model do not only concern more creative subjects of the curriculum. He developed this position in relation to science, stating:

> If science is not regarded as a collection of facts, but in the way that Popper has suggested as a series of hypotheses waiting to be refuted, then to teach science in the behavioural object-ives way is to teach anti-science or non-science. According to Popper, the essence of scientific thinking is to realise that we *know* nothing for certain and that science is concerned to construct useful conjectural (and tentative) explanations. To give a very simple example, it was once reasonable to suggest (as a hypothesis) that 'all swans are white' – until a species of black swans was discovered in Australia. 'Swans are white' was a useful hypothesis or even helpful generalisation until it was refuted. But a science teacher who made his pupils learn 'all swans are white' (as a 'fact') was transmitting to his pupils an unscientific attitude.
>
> (Lawton, 1983, p. 21)

But, Lawton concludes, this is precisely what the behavioural objectives model does for most, if not all, of the time; 'he (*sic*), the teacher, "knows" and transmits "the known facts" to the pupils who must memorize them' (Lawton, 1983, p. 21)

Eisner's views on curriculum planning

Eisner's (1969) two main premises are as follows:

- The school is an institution responsible for the transmission of culture, enabling students to acquire those intellectual codes and skills which will make it possible for them to profit from the contributions of those who have gone before. He accepted that to accomplish this task one has to learn an array of socially defined skills, including reading, writing and arithmetic, as they are basic to further inquiry into human culture.

- Schools should also be concerned with enabling children to make a contribution to their culture by providing opportunities for individuals to construe their own interpretation of the material they encounter or construct. A simple repetition of the past, he argued, 'is the surest path to cultural rigor mortis' (Eisner, 1969, p. 14).

He then differentiated between two types of educational objectives which can be formulated in curriculum planning, as outlined below.

Instructional objectives

These are objectives which specify unambiguously the particular behaviour (skill, item of knowledge and so forth) the student is to acquire after having completed one of more learning activities. The 'effective curriculum, when it is aimed at instructional objectives, will develop forms of behaviour whose characteristics are known beforehand and, as likely as not, will be common across students' (Eisner, 1969, p. 15).

Expressive objectives

These do not specify the behaviour the student is to acquire after having engaged in one or more learning activities. Rather, an expressive objective describes an educational encounter:

> It identifies a situation in which children are to work, a problem with which they are to cope, a task in which they are to engage; but it does not specify what from that encounter, situation, problem, or task they are to learn.
>
> (Eisner, 1969, p. 16)

He went on to say:

> The expressive objective is intended to serve as a theme around which skills and understandings learned earlier can be brought to bear, but through which those skills and understandings can be expanded, elaborated, and made idiosyncratic. With an expressive objective what is desired is not homogeneity of response among students but diversity. In the expressive context the teacher hopes to provide a situation in which meanings become personalised and in which children produce products, both theoretical and qualitative, that are as diverse as themselves. Consequently the evaluative task in this situation is not one of applying a common standard to the products produced but one of reflecting upon what has been produced in order to reveal its uniqueness and significance. In the expressive context the product is likely to be as much of a surprise to the maker as it is for the teacher who encounters it.
>
> (Eisner, 1969, p. 16)

He then identified the following examples of expressive objectives:

- to interpret the meaning of *Paradise Lost*;
- to examine and appraise the significance of *The Old Man and the Sea*;
- to develop a three-dimensional form through the use of wire and wood;
- to visit the zoo and discuss what was of interest there.

He concluded by saying that the two types of objectives – instructional and expressive – require different kinds of curriculum activities because 'instructional objectives emphasize the acquisition of the known, while expressive objectives its elaboration, modification, and, at times, the production of the utterly new' (Eisner, 1969, p. 16).

Raths' criteria for worthwhile activities

Raths (1971) proposed that the selection of what should be in the curriculum should be based on the following criteria:

1 All other things being equal, one activity is more worthwhile than another it if permits children to make informed choices in carrying out the activity and to reflect on the consequences of their choices.
2 All other things being equal, one activity is more worthwhile than another if it assigns to students active roles in the learning situation rather than passive ones.
3 All other things being equal, one activity is more worthwhile than another if it asks students to engage in enquiry into ideas, applications of intellectual processes or current problems, either personal or social.
4 All other things being equal, one activity is more worthwhile than another if it involves children with realia (real things).
5 All other things being equal, one activity is more worthwhile than another if completion of the activity may be accomplished successfully by children at several different levels of ability.
6 All other things being equal, one activity is more worthwhile than another if it asks students to examine in a new setting an idea, an application of an intellectual process or a current problem which has been previously studied.
7 All other things being equal, one activity is more worthwhile than another if it requires students to examine topics or issues that citizens in our society do not normally examine and that are typically ignored by the major communication media in the nation.
8 All other things being equal, one activity is more worthwhile than another if it involves students and faculty members in 'risk' taking – not a risk of life or limb, but a risk of success or failure.
9 All other things being equal, one activity is more worthwhile than another if it requires students to rewrite, rehearse and polish their initial efforts.
10 All other things being equal, one activity is more worthwhile than another if it involves students in the application and mastery of meaningful rules, standards or disciplines.
11 All other things being equal, one activity is more worthwhile than another if it gives students a chance to share the planning, the carrying out of a plan or the results of an activity with others.
12 All other things being equal, one activity is more worthwhile than another if it is relevant to the expressed purposes of the students.

Is there room in the curriculum for programmes where outcomes are not clearly specified?

There is a certain tradition in curriculum planning which provides room in the curriculum for discussion-based work without the need for outcomes to be clearly specified (Elliott, 2006). It is a tradition where:

- the teacher is seen as operating a style of discussion-based teaching;
- the pupils examine critical 'evidence' as they reflect upon issues;
- guidance is provided by the teacher, acting as a neutral-chairperson who submits to parliamentary procedures and to neutrality.

The teacher is expected to be committed to such educational values as:

- rationality;
- concern for evidence and sensitivity to others.

He or she should not publicize his or her own views.

Such an approach conceives of both teachers and pupils as learners. It is also based on a view of understanding as something that, while it can never be totally achieved, can be regularly deepened and widened. It is sometimes adopted through discussing controversial value issues.

Stenhouse (1968), for his Humanities Curriculum project, argued that such discussion should be based on the following premises:

- The teacher needs to temper his or her position on value issues by adopting the criterion of procedural neutrality, i.e. teachers regard it as a responsibility not to use their authority position to promote their value beliefs.
- Discussion should be the main teaching strategy.
- Divergence of opinion should be supported.
- The teacher, as a chairperson, should have responsibility for quality and standards in learning through enquiry.

The teacher, Stenhouse also stated, should have responsibility for:

- knowing the materials;
- providing evidence;
- keeping the discussion on a coherent track;
- opening up as wide a range of alternatives on an issue as possible;
- keenly observing group processes.

The sorts of issues that could be discussed are as diverse as the following:

- war;
- relations between the sexes;
- the family;

- the law;
- poverty;
- education;
- people and work;
- living in cities;
- race relations.

Issues for discussion

1   This chapter has focused on alternative, 'procedural' approaches to the objectives curriculum model. Focusing on such approaches, Smith and Lovat (2003, p. 134) ask
you to imagine that you are in a multicultural school or university and you are planning
to teach a unit to your class on the theme of 'Valuing Difference'. They then go on to
pose the following questions:

   a   What principles of procedure might you employ in planning and teaching the unit?
   b   What beliefs and understandings do they reflect?

2   Discuss and summarize the relative strengths and weaknesses of the 'objectives' versus
'procedural' approaches to curriculum planning.

3   Read more of Stenhouse's (1975) thoughts on the 'research' model:
Identify his preferred roles for teacher and student.
If you are a teacher, how well does this accord with the role you were encouraged to
play in your own teacher preparation?

4   Speculate on whether Stenhouse's vision is realistic or too idealistic.

5   Beyer and Apple (1998) have argued that educationists need to be familiar with the
types of curriculum models outlined in this chapter as well as those outlined in the
previous one. They hold that different models can be seen as answers to different questions or as different notions of legitimate answers.
What do you think they mean by this?

6   Beyer and Apple (1998) also hold that familiarity with both types of models is necessary in order that one be able to understand the assumptions underlying curriculum
discussion and what is taken for granted. To have such capacity, they hold, is to have
a curriculum conscience.
Does this idea appeal to you?
If so, why?

References

Beyer, L. E. and Apple, M. W. (1998). *The Curriculum: Politics, Problems and Possibilities*. New York:
SUNY Press.

Eisner, E. (1969). Instructional and expressive educational objectives (pp. 1–18). In W. Popham, E. Eisner
and H. Sullivan (Eds), *Instructional Objectives*. Chicago, IL: Rand McNally.

Elliott, J. (2006). The impact of research on professional practice and identity. *ESRC Thematic Seminar Series*. www.tlrp.org/themes/seminar/gewirtz/papers/seminar8/paper-elliott.pdf.

Hogben, D. (1972). The behavioural objectives approach: Some problems and some dangers. *Journal of Curriculum Studies*, Vol. 4, No. 1, pp. 42–50.

Lawton, D. (1983). The problem of curriculum objectives (pp. 15–23). In D. Lawton, *Curriculum Studies and Educational Planning*. London: Hodder and Stoughton.

Raths, J. D. (1971). Teaching without specific objectives. *Educational Leadership*, April, pp. 714–720.

Smith, D. L. and Lovat, T. J. (2003). *Curriculum: Action on Reflection*. Tuggerah, NSW: Social Science Press.

Stenhouse, L. (1968). The Humanities Curriculum Project. *Journal of Curriculum Studies*, Vol. 1, No. 1, pp. 26–33.

Stenhouse, L. (1975). *An Introduction to Curriculum Research and Development*. London: Heinemann Educational.

16 The curriculum ideas of Kieran Egan

This chapter provides an overview of Egan's (1985, 1986, 1988, 1990, 1992) theory of education development, highlighting the importance he places on engaging children's imaginations in learning and the power of the story form to teach units of work engagingly and meaningfully. He encourages teachers to see lessons and units as good stories to be told, rather than as sets of objectives to be attained. This perspective constitutes an interesting counter view to those who emphasize the 'over-rational' curriculum.

Egan's theory of education development

Egan holds that much of the education research to which teachers are exposed seems to be dominated by psychological theories that lead to knowledge of psychological value and interest but offer only occasional implications for education. He offers an alternative approach based on four stages of development (O'Donoghue and Saville, 1996). At each stage, he argues, we make sense of the world and experience it in significantly different ways. These differences require that knowledge be organized differently to be most accessible and educationally effective at each stage. No stage is solely discrete. Rather, understanding is accumulative, with each layer providing a foundation for further growth.

Egan's stages are as follows.

The mythic stage

This stage occurs between the ages of 4–5 and 9–10 approximately. Egan described the stage as mythic because he believes that young children's thinking shares important features with the kind of thinking evident in the stories of myth-using people. Mythic thinking, he contends:

- provides children with intellectual security. It provides absolute accounts of why things are the way they are. Each story is a complete unit which correlates with young children's inability to grasp a sense of time or of age;
- lacks a clear sense of the world as autonomous and objective. The child's world is full of entities charged with and given meaning by those things that the child knows best. These include love, hate, fear, joy, good and bad.

Mythic stories possess two key elements: the story line or narrative, and the structure of the story. A story has a beginning which excites, a middle which complicates and an ending which resolves. There are powerful concepts within the story. Egan describes them as 'binary opposites'. They include:

- love/hate;
- courage/cowardice;
- good/bad;
- happiness/sadness.

Egan sees that children tend initially to make sense of things in these terms, using only a couple of concepts at one time. Children at this stage love stories and fairy tales and much of their imaginative thought is framed within the story form, which is built on sets of binary opposites.

The romantic stage

The romantic stage occurs from the ages of 8–9 to about 14–15. During this stage the perception that the world is autonomous, separate and fundamentally different from the child begins to develop within a context of reality. Students want to know everything about something. Collections of basketball cards, postage stamps, photographs and life histories of favourite musicians, for example, become important.

Students identify with the struggles towards glory of such characters as Luke Skywalker in *Star Wars*. Egan states that such stories are not real in the sense of seeking to be literally true. Rather, they are concerned always to be possible within the real world. For example, it is important that Luke Skywalker appears real so that a knowledge of his family life and background are important to help put his life into a 'real' context. Also, romantic stories are relatively complicated in their structure and complex in the conceptual struggles they contain.

The philosophic stage

This stage occurs roughly between 14–15 and 19–20 years of age. Students move from a focus on extremes and on the most fascinating 'bits and pieces', on dramatic events, bizarre facts, and heroes and heroines, 'to the strengthening realisation that all the bits and pieces are interconnected parts of some general unit'. They begin to see that they have a place in the real world. They become agents rather than players.

The search for truth and the search for generalities is the major characteristic of this stage. In order to establish these, a certain body of knowledge is essential. Also, the degree of sophistication of the generalities is dependent on the extent of students' general knowledge. The role and importance of the story form diminishes because stories end but reality continues. Within this reality, students are able to separate their serious roles from their leisure activities.

The ironic stage

The ironic stage of development begins at around 19–20 years and continues through adulthood. Its key characteristic is a clear sense of what the mind contributes to knowledge. It represents an appreciation of where we end and the world begins. There are no stories at this stage. Rather, the ironic mind is able to introduce the mythic, romantic and philosophic senses of games and play into everything, guided by aesthetic criteria of appropriateness.

Egan's alternative curriculum model for teachers

Egan questions a few assumptions teachers have long held about children's development. These assumptions, he holds, have resulted in the exclusion of much of the richness of human experience to which young children can have direct access. We commonly hear asserted such claims as 'children learn best from concrete, hands-on experiences'. Egan says we need to ask ourselves the following:

- Do children learn everything best from such experiences?
- Can they learn only from such experiences?
- Are there things that cannot be learned from such experiences?
- Are there things best learned from other kinds of experiences?

Egan believes that by focusing on the imaginative as well as the logico-mathematical, we can develop a more balanced appreciation of children's intellectual capacities and enhance their capacity for learning. He feels that the dominant rational model of curriculum and lesson planning does not allow for unpredictability, spontaneity and creative imagination. Rather, it generates something which is controllable, predictable and pre-specifiable. He argues that the story form provides a more adequate model for planning teaching, one that captures more of the proper character of education.

Imagination in education

Egan suggests that a child's imagination is a most powerful and energetic learning tool. He sees imagination as the capacity to think of things as possibly being so; it is an intentional act of mind; a source of novelty and generativity. The imaginative person has this capacity in a high degree. Thus, Egan argues, imagination should be taken very seriously by educationists.

Following this, Egan talks of teaching as story-telling but not in the sense that children relate and respond to stories. Rather, he means that we can shape our lessons to reflect the basic patterns of the story. In this way, lessons can become meaningful to children rather than being just a collection of seemingly unrelated facts. Because the world of the story is limited in that the context is created and given, the events of a story are able to be grasped and their meaning understood more readily than in other forms of lesson plans. Story provides a powerful means for us to create whole topics for study. By identifying the following features of stories that children find most engaging, Egan is able to develop them into a model for planning teaching.

Story rhythm

Stories are narrative units. At the simplest level there is a rhythm in stories. They have a beginning which sets up an expectation, a middle in which an elaboration or complication of the beginning exists, and an ending in which a resolution is found or a mediation sought. This story form is universal. Anything which does not contribute or fit into this rhythm is irrelevant to the story and should be excluded.

Binary opposites

Egan comments that one of the most obvious structural devices we can see in children's stories is the use of binary opposites. Embedded in the story are conflicts between good and bad, courage and cowardice, fear and security. The characters and events embody these underlying abstract conflicts. It is these binary opposites which help us select and organize the content of the story and which are used to enable the story to move forward. The student associates with the characters, with their self-reliance, courage, persistence, energy and so on and thinks of him or herself as embodying the transcendent qualities inherent in the hero.

Affective meaning

According to Egan, students' imaginations are more readily stimulated by content that engages their emotions than by content that does not. He sees that stories have the power to be affectively engaging. He defines 'affective' meaning as the kind of meaning that is unique to stories. They provide us with affective meaning because their ending provides a resolution to the earlier complications and we know how to feel about what has happened.

Egan's planning frameworks

From Egan's stages of education development, planning frameworks which offer some curriculum alternatives have been developed. These include:

- two models for planning teaching that encourage us to see lessons as good stories to be told rather than sets of objectives to be attained, an approach that puts meaning centre stage;
- an approach that draws on the power of the story form to stimulate children's imagination;
- an approach based around a model of teaching which is primarily concerned with providing children with access to and engagement with rich meaning;
- giving teachers a clear means of deciding what should and should not be included in any given topic.

The two planning models are as follows.

The story form model

This has been developed for use with children at the mythic stage, but it has also been success-fully used with children in the romantic stage of development. The focus can be seen in the use of binary opposites to capture children's interest and engage them in meaningful learning.

Topic selection

What is important about this topic?
Why should it matter to children?
What is affectively engaging about it?

Finding binary opposites

What powerful binary opposites best catch the importance of the topic?

Organizing content into story form

What content most dramatically embodies the binary opposites, in order to provide access to the topic?
What content best articulates the topic into a developing story form?

Conclusion

What is the best way of resolving the dramatic conflict inherent in the binary opposites?
What degree of mediation of those opposites is it appropriate to seek?

Evaluation

How can one know whether the topic has been understood, its importance grasped and the content learned?

The romantic model

This planning framework has been developed for use with students in the romantic stage. The general principles allow for variety in interpretation and implementation.

The characteristics of students at this stage are embodied in the following:

- The framework as principles can be drawn on to guide teaching.
- The power of the story form remains to engage students affectively.
- Extremes and limits of reality enable students imaginative grasp of a topic to be enhanced.
- Heroic qualities are searched for.
- An interest in the pursuit of detail is evident.

The model is as follows.

Identifying transcendent qualities

What transcendent human qualities can be seen and felt as central to the topic?
What affective images do they evoke?

Organizing content into a narrative structure

INITIAL ACCESS

What content, distinct from the students' everyday experience, best embodies the transcendent qualities most central to the topic?
Does this expose some extremes or limits of reality within the topic?

STRUCTURING THE BODY OF THE UNIT OR LESSON

What content best articulates the topic into a clear narrative structure? Briefly sketch the narrative line.

HUMANIZING THE CONTENT

How can the content be shown in terms of human hopes, fears, intentions or other emotions?
What aspects of the content can best stimulate romance, wonder and awe?
What ideals and/or revolts against conventions are evident in the topic?

PURSUING DETAIL

What content best allows students to pursue some aspect of the topic in exhaustive detail?

Conclusion

How can one bring the topic to satisfactory closure, while pointing to further dimensions or to other topics?
How can the students feel this satisfaction?

Evaluation

How can one know whether the topic has been understood, and has engaged the students' imagination?

Egan's theory of education development and associated planning frameworks provide educators with an alternative and effective way of planning and delivering the curriculum. In endeavouring to bring the student's mind and knowledge into sharper focus and in considering the development of the student in the process of education, teachers are challenged to think beyond the dominant curricular objectives approach to teaching to something much more inspiring. The approach suggests that the more knowledge teachers have about a subject, the more easily they will be able to engage their students' imaginations. This requires teachers who are imaginatively energetic and committed to the approach.

Issues for discussion

1   Do you think there is any correspondence between Egan's position and Herbartism? If so, what is it?

2   In his work, Egan argues that the neglect of fantasy and the subjugation of children's imagination are due in large part to a school system that places too much value on the product – an individual who can find his or her place in the culture – and not enough on the process – the development of sense-making capacities that might see past the restrictions of the here and now (Buckley, 1994, p. 43).

   • Why, do you think, we should be concerned about the neglect of fantasy and the imagination in the individual's education?
   • Thinking on the latter question is usually centred on matters to do with emotional development. Give some thought to how it also might be important for future scientists, given the role of hypothesis formation in scientific investigation.

3   Egan began his study of child development by examining and then discarding the constraints placed on the child's education by psychologists such as Piaget.

   [The] rejection of the constraints that have led educators to conceive of the child only in terms of cognitive abilities, to the detriment of the affective, is one of the most appealing features of Egan's theory. But he takes too much about the child's imagination for granted, as if it were just common sense.

                                                                                      (Buckley, 1994, p. 35)

   Discuss.

References

Buckley, J. (1994). A critique of Kieran Egan's theory of educational development. *Journal of Curriculum Studies*, Vol. 26, No. 1, pp. 31–43.

Egan, K. (1985). Imagination and teaching. *Teachers College Record*, Vol. 87, No. 2, pp. 155–166.

Egan, K. (1986). *Teaching as Storytelling. An Alternative Approach to Teaching and Curriculum in the Elementary School.* London, Ontario: The Althouse Press.

Egan, K. (1988). *Primary Understanding. Education in Early Childhood.* London and New York: Routledge.

Egan, K. (1990). *Romantic Understanding. The Development of Rationality ad Imagination, Ages 8–15.* New York and London: Routledge.

Egan, K. (1992). *Imagination in Teaching and Learning.* Chicago, IL: University of Chicago Press.

O'Donoghue, T. and Saville, K. (1996). The power of the story form in curriculum development: An exposition on the ideas of Kieran Egan. *Curriculum*, Vol. 17, pp. 24–35.

Part IV
Teaching and learning

17 Learning and the conditions that enhance learning

There has, for quite some time, been a certain lack of clarity in much of what has been written regarding learning-centred education. One reason for this stems from the failure to differentiate between learning theory and the conditions that enhance learning. This chapter, based on an exposition by O'Donoghue and Clarke (2010), opens with a brief statement on the distinction. It goes on to provide a short outline of some influential theories of learning. A particularly popular approach at present, namely, constructivism, is then considered.

Learning and the conditions that enhance learning

Barrow (1984, p. 98), in considering learning and the conditions that enhance learning, established a very important foundation for his position, stating: 'Learning theory describes what happens when learning takes place, rather than why or how it takes place. It seeks to offer an explanation of what goes on in the process of learning.' To this, he added that 'to learn is to acquire knowledge, not previously possessed, of propositions or skills'. He went on:

> So far as the meaning of 'learning' goes it does not matter whether this acquisition of knowledge is accidental, deliberately imposed from with-out, or sought after. Nor does the length of time one retains the knowledge cause any serious problem, though one would hope that what is learned is retained for some time, and might quibble about the case of somebody who forgot as soon as he [sic] had 'learned'.
>
> (Barrow, 1984, p. 98)

Fontana (1981, p. 147) argued along similar lines in holding that 'learning is a relatively persistent change in an individual's possible behaviour due to experience'. In this definition, as Barrow (1984, p. 99) has pointed out, 'reference to experience is designed to contrast with changes in behaviour that come about automatically through maturation and physical development'.

Some theories of learning

A principal concern of educators is with the conditions that enhance learning rather than with learning theory per se. Nevertheless, theories of learning have been helpful, especially in helping us to understand particular teacher–student interactions in the classroom and lecture hall. Some of these theories are now detailed.

Gagne's theory of learning

Gagne's (1970) classified eight types of learning:

- signal learning (making a conditioned response to a non-specific type of stimulus);
- stimulus–response learning (a specific response is elicited by a stimulus);
- chaining (the ability to join two or more stimulus–response connections together);
- verbal association (chaining in respect of verbal response connections);
- multiple discrimination (identifying different stimuli that resemble each other);
- concept learning (the ability to respond appropriately to a class of stimuli);
- rule learning;
- problem solving.

These types of learning are seen not just as being distinct, but also as being hierarchical, starting with 'signal learning' at the bottom and progressing to 'problem solving' at the top.

Bloom's taxonomy of educational development

Bloom (1956) and his colleagues grouped learning outcomes in three domains: the cognitive domain, the psychomotor domain and the affective domain.

Regarding the cognitive domain

Bloom proposed that it could be classified into a hierarchy going from 'knowledge', 'comprehension' and 'application', to 'synthesis' and 'evaluation'.

Regarding the affective domain

Krathwohl *et al.* (1964) proposed a five-level classification of outcomes in this affective domain.

Regarding the psychomotor domain

Harrow (1972) proposed a six-level classification of outcomes in this domain. Anderson and Krathwohl (2001), in their *Taxonomy for Learning, Teaching and Assessing*, elaborated on Bloom's original taxonomy to accommodate new ways of thinking about cognition and learning.

Bruner's cognitivist approach to learning

Bruner (1966, 1996) adopted a cognitivist approach to learning, unlike Gagne, and Skinner (1969), who adopted a behaviourist one. As he saw it, learning is not generally a matter of reflexive behaviour being reinforced by outside consequences. Rather, the activity of mind is stressed. As he sees it, learning in many cases involves:

- acquiring information;
- sorting it out;

- making sense of it;
- testing it out in a variety of ways.

He concluded that learning is about 'internal model making'. His position that there are three modes of such model making has already been considered in Chapter 12.

Surface and deep learning

A group of theories built around the concepts of surface and deep learning is also helpful. Thinking on these concepts took off in earnest in the mid-1970s in Sweden through the works of Laurillard (1979, 1993), Marton *et al.* (1984) and Marton and Saljo (1976a, 1976b). Bain summarized as follows the central argument in their works:

> if students approach their learning with the intention to reproduce facts and procedures (a 'surface' approach), then their learning will 'miss the point' of the material, it will be fragmented, its relevance to new circumstances will be missed, and misconceptions will remain intact. Alternatively, when students adopt a 'deep' approach, that is, when they seek the meaning of what they are learning and intentionally relate it to their existing knowledge, then quite different outcomes are likely to occur; the knowledge is relationally structured, it is integrated with the procedures required to put the knowledge into practice, it corrects misconceptions, and it can be applied adaptively to new circumstances.
>
> (Bain, 1994, p. 1)

This position has been developed by Bowring-Carr and West-Burnham (1997) in their model of levels of learning.

Surface learning

Bowring-Carr and West-Burnham (1997, p. 15) refer to this as 'mere memorizing', or what they term 'shallow learning'. Here, they argue, learning involves 'an increase of our knowledge about a topic, and then facts are acquired and retained so that they can be used when necessary'. Such knowledge is a necessary precursor to other learning.

Deep learning

Bowring-Carr and West-Burnham (1997) outline the following three levels of 'deep learning':

- At the first level there is the abstraction of meaning from a series of related facts.
- At the second level there is a move to an interpretative process aimed at understanding and ordering our reality.
- At the third level the learning changes the individual as a person. If what a person has 'learned' leaves him or her exactly the same as before, then the learning has been superficial, and will, sooner or later, be rejected, forgotten or ignored.

(Bowring-Carr and West-Burnham, 1997, p. 15)

Deep learning, they conclude, means there is a change, the world is seen in a different way and the perception of reality alters.

To summarize, the value to teachers in the learning theories outlined above, along with many others is not that they consist of 'true' accounts of learning (Irby *et al.*, 2013). Rather, they provide us with 'tools' for thinking intelligently about learning. It is now helpful at this point to consider the group of learning theories, namely, those that come under the general category of 'constructivism'.

Constructivist theories of learning

Constructivists are concerned with the mental models a learner utilizes when responding to new problems, or new information.

Watts and Bentley (1991, p. 4) defined constructivism as follows:

> Essentially, constructivism can be described as a theory of the limits of human knowledge, according to which all we can know is necessarily a product of our own cognition. We create our own conceptions of reality by channelling sensory data towards meditative reflections. Constructivism not only emphasises the central role of the construer but maintains that we are, at least partially, able to control constructive processes through conscious reflection.

Beyond this core position there are many views of constructivism. For example, the Russian psychologist Vygotsky (James, 2007, pp. 17–18) held that another important characteristic of learning is that 'it proceeds by interaction between the teacher (or more expert peer) and the learner, in a social context mediated by language and the social norms that value the search for understanding'.

Overall, it is reasonable to make the following generalizations about constructivism:

- Learning always involves analysing new information.
- Learning always involves transforming the new information.
- The transformation can only be achieved in light of what the learner already knows and understands.

Educationists have extrapolated from constructivist learning theories to come up with various principles to inform teaching and learning (Grennon Brooks, 2013). Snowman and Biehler (2000), for example, give us the following four:

- What a person 'knows' is not just received passively, but is actively constructed by the learner; meaningful learning is the active creation of knowledge structures from personal experience.
- Because knowledge is the result of personal interpretation of experiences, one person's knowledge can never be totally transferred to another person.
- The cultures and societies to which people belong influence their views of the world around them and, therefore, influence what they 'know'. In general, the understandings that people reach are largely consistent within a given culture.
- Construction of ideas is aided by systematic open-ended discussions and debate.

The associated metaphor of 'scaffolding' is helpful in trying to understand the teacher's role in the learning process (Groundwater Smith *et al.*, 2007). Scaffolding supports those parts of a building not yet ready to stand alone (O'Donoghue and Clarke, 2010). Once one part of the building can stand alone, however, the scaffolding is removed to be erected in another part of the building in need of support (O'Donoghue and Clarke, 2010). Similarly, the teacher can be seen as 'a facilitator of a learning process rather than the transmitter of important knowledge that needs to be learnt' (Groundwater-Smith *et al.*, 2007, p. 82). As the student learns a concept, less support is needed and 'the student becomes more independent' (Groundwater-Smith *et al.*, 2007, p. 82).

Killen (2003, p. 30) has come up with the following list of principles for practice which he has deduced from a consideration of the literature on promoting a constructivist learning approach:

- Organize learning and instruction around important ideas (such as the primary concepts, generalizations and underlying themes of the content) rather than focusing on isolated facts.
- Acknowledge the importance of prior knowledge by providing learners with a cognitive structure that they can use to make sense of new learning.
- Challenge the adequacy of the learner's prior knowledge, often by creating some conceptual conflict.
- Present students with problems that have ambiguity, complexity, uncertainty and multiple solutions.
- Teach learners how to learn, how to regulate their learning skills and how to direct their own learning efforts.
- View learning as a joint cognitive venture between learner, peers and teacher.
- Assess learners' knowledge acquisition during a lesson so that they receive immediate feedback and so that they are able to see the connection between their learning and the testing of that learning.

Issues for discussion

1   From your reading, formulate an overview of the ideas of Piaget.

2   From your reading, formulate an overview of the ideas of Vygotsky.

3   How do the two theories differ?

4   From your reading, formulate an overview of Kohlberg's theory of moral development.

5   To what extent are the theories of Piaget, Vygotsky and Kohlberg compatible?

6   Discuss the following points made by Marsh (2008, p. 32):

   a   Crain (2000, p. 16) asserts that 'Piaget portrayed pre-operational children too negatively, focusing on their logical deficiencies. We need to consider the possibility that young children's thinking has its own qualities and distinctive virtues.'

   b   According to McDevitt and Ormrod (2002, p. 148), 'challenge, readiness and social interaction are central to the theories of both Piaget and Vygotsky'.

(continued)

7   Discuss the nature and importance of the intrinsic and extrinsic motivation of students and of approaches to promoting them that can be used in the classroom and lecture hall.

8   Give examples to illustrate the position outlined of Tessmer and Richey (1997) that a certain level of adequacy must be attained in seating, acoustics, temperature and lighting for high-level learning to occur.

References

Anderson, L. and Krathwohl, D. (2001). *A Taxonomy for Learning, Teaching and Assessing: A Revision of Bloom's Taxonomy of Educational Objectives*. New York: Longman.

Bain, J. (1994). *Understanding by Learning or Learning by Understanding: How Shall We Teach?* Brisbane: Griffith University.

Barrow, R. (1984). *Giving Teaching Back to Teachers: A Critical Introduction to Curriculum Theory*. Sussex: Wheatsheaf Books.

Bloom, B. (Ed.). (1956). *Taxonomy of Educational Objectives, Handbook 1: Cognitive Domain*. New York: David McKay Co.

Bowring-Carr, C. and West-Burnham, J. (1997). *Effective Learning in Schools. How to Integrate Learning and Leadership for a Successful School*. London: Financial Times Pitman Publishing.

Bruner, J. (1966). *Towards a Theory of Instruction*. New York: Norton.

Bruner, J. (1996). *The Culture of Education*. Cambridge, MA: Harvard University Press.

Crain, W. (2000). *Theories of Development*. Upper Saddle River, NJ: Prentice Hall.

Fontana, D. (1981). *Psychology for Teachers*. London: Macmillan.

Gagne, R. M. (1970). *Conditions of Learning*. London: Holt, Rinehart and Winston.

Grennon Brooks, J. (2013). Constructivism. Transforming knowledge of how people learn into meaningful instruction (pp. 271–275). In B. J. Irby, G. Brown, R. Lara-Alecio and S. Jackson (Eds), *The Handbook of Educational Theories*. Charlotte, NC: Information Age Publishing.

Groundwater-Smith, S., Ewing, R. and Le Cornu, R. (2007). *Teaching: Challenges and Dilemmas*. Sydney: Thomson.

Harrow, A. J. (1972). *A Taxonomy of the Psychomotor Domain: A Guide for Developing Behavioral Objectives*. New York: David McKay Company

Irby, B. J., Brown, G., Lara-Alecio, R. and Jackson, S. (Eds). (2013). *The Handbook of Educational Theories*. Charlotte, NC: Information Age Publishing.

James, M. (2007). Unlocking transformative practice within and beyond the classroom: Messages for practice and policy (pp. 215–226) In M. James, R. McCormick, P. Black, P. Carmichael, M. J. Drummond, A. Fox, J. MacBeath, B. Marshall, R. Pedder, R. Procter, S. Swaffield, J. Swann and D. William (Eds), *Improving Learning How to Learn. Classroom, Schools and Networks*. Abingdon, Oxon: Routledge.

Killen, R. (2003). *Effective Teaching Strategies: Lessons from Research and Practice*. Tuggerah, NSW: Social Science Press.

Krathwohl, D. R., Bloom, B. S. and Masia, B. B. (1964). *Taxonomy of Educational Objectives: The Classification of Educational Goals*. New York: David McKay.

Laurillard, D. (1979). The process of student learning. *Higher Education*, Vol. 8, pp. 395–409.

Laurillard, D. (1993). *Rethinking University Teaching: A Framework for the Effective Use of Educational Technology*. London: Routledge.

Marsh, C. (2008). *Becoming a Teacher: Knowledge, Skills and Issues*. Frenchs Forrest, NSW: Pearson.

Marton, F. and Saljo, R. (1976a). On qualitative differences in learning: 1 – outcome and process. *British Journal of Educational Psychology*, Vol. 46, pp. 4–11.

Marton, F. and Saljo, R. (1976b). Symposium: Learning processes and strategies on qualitative differences in learning: Outcome as a function of the learner's conception of the task. *British Journal of Educational Psychology*, Vol. 46, pp. 115–127.

Marton, F., Hounsel, D. and Entwistle, N. (1984). *The Experience of Learning*. Edinburgh: Scottish University Press.

McDevitt, T. M. and Ormrod, J. E. (2002). *Child Development and Education*. Columbus, OH: Merrill Prentice Hall.

O'Donoghue, T. A. and Clarke, S. (2010). *Leading Learning: Process, Themes and Issues in International Perspective*. London: Routledge.

Skinner, B. F. (1969). *Contingencies of Reinforcement: A Theoretical Analysis*. New York: Appleton-Century-Crofts.

Snowman, J. and Biehler, R. (2000). *Psychology Applied to Teaching*. Boston, MA: Houghton Mifflin Company.

Tessmer, M. and Richey, R. C. (1997). The role of context in learning and instructional design. *Educational Technology, Research and Development*, Vol. 45, No. 2, pp. 85–116.

Watts, M. and Bentley, D. (1991). Constructivism in the curriculum. *The Curriculum Journal*, Vol. 2, No. 2, pp. 171–182.

18 Questioning some taken-for-granted assumptions about teaching and learning

In 2012, Adey and Dillon (2012) edited a book entitled *Bad Education: Debunking Myths in Education*. It demonstrates the adage that educational truths are rarely pure and never simple. Thus, it seeks to speak to policy makers, who often do not wish to consider complexity when it comes to promoting the latest education development that appeals to them. Two developments that continue to be influential at present are considered in this chapter: Howard Gardner's ideas on multiple intelligences and certain ideas on neuroscience and education.

Gardner's multiple intelligences

In a lecture given at the Institute of Education, University of London, in 2004, White (2004) addressed what he termed the possible 'myth' of Howard Gardner's (1972, 1973, 1982, 1990, 1993, 1999a, 1999b, 2003) idea that there are multiple intelligences (MI). He commenced by pointing out that MI theory identifies the following types of intelligence:

- logico-mathematical;
- linguistic;
- musical;
- spatial;
- bodily-kinaesthetic;
- intrapersonal;
- interpersonal;
- naturalist;
- existential.

At the time of White's address, as now, MI theory was very influential in school reform across the world, with many schools using it as a basis for a flexible approach to teaching and learning.

A principal assumption underlying MI theory is that children have different preferred 'learning styles'. Not everyone, it is argued, learns best through traditional methods which draw heavily on linguistic and logical skills. As a result, room should be made for children to bring to bear their other abilities, from the list of nine outlined above, in their learning. One outcome in some schools is that they give their pupils cards inscribed with their preferred intelligences.

White's main task was to question the associated idea that children are born 'hard-wired' with a whole array of abilities in varying strengths. Everything, he argued, turns on the claim that Gardner's stated intelligences actually exist. He made it clear he embraced the idea that intelligence can take many forms and is not tied to the abstract reasoning tested by IQ. Yet, he was still left asking if MI theory is a myth.

White then spelt out Gardner's procedure for identifying an intelligence. The two-stage process is as follows.

Prerequisites

A prerequisite for a theory of multiple intelligences is that it captures a reasonably complete gamut of the kinds of abilities valued by societies. They must have all been picked out for their problem solving and problem creating skills in human cultures. This raised two troubling questions for White:

- Are we talking about all human cultures, most, or only some of them? Gardner is not clear on this.
- Where is the evidence that Gardner surveyed a great number of human societies in order to reach his conclusions?

Criteria for selection

Once a candidate for intelligence has satisfied the prerequisites, it has to meet various criteria. These comprise:

- potential isolation of the area by brain damage;
- the existence in it of idiots savants, prodigies and other exceptional individuals;
- an identifiable core operation/set of operations;
- a distinctive developmental history, along with a definable set of expert 'end-state' performances;
- an evolutionary history and evolutionary plausibility;
- support from experimental psychological tasks;
- support from psychometric findings;
- susceptibility to encoding in a symbol system.

These raised the following troubling issues for White:

- Gardner's examples of high levels of development in the intelligences reflect his own value judgements. He has in mind the achievements of selected poets, composers, religious leaders, politicians, scientists, novelists and so on. It is Gardner's value judgements, not his empirical discoveries as a scientist, that are his starting point.
- Regarding Gardner's point about the potential isolation of the area by brain damage, White takes it that there are localized areas of function within the brain. If one part of the brain is damaged, one's sight is impaired; if another, one's ability to move one's left hand. All this shows, he says, is that certain physiological necessary conditions of exercising these capacities are absent; it does not help to indicate the existence of separate 'intelligences'.

- Regarding Gardner's point on the existence, in an area, of idiots savants, prodigies and other exceptional individuals, White states that what he knows of idiots savants does not lead him to think of them as intelligent. What they all have in common is a mechanical facility, one which lacks the flexibility of adapting means to ends found in intelligent behaviour. Prodigies only support Gardner's case if there is good evidence that their talents are innate. But what evidence there is seems to point to acquired abilities.
- Gardner does not justify using the particular criteria he lists to pick out intelligences.

Conclusion

Gardner holds that while nearly all children possess to some degree nearly all of the intelligences he identifies, some have particular aptitudes in one or more of them. White's concern is that if they are not part of human nature, what he calls 'wobbly constructions' on the part of their author, educators should treat them with caution. His own belief is that they do not exist. His worry is that, while children are being encouraged to see themselves, in 'Personal, Social and Health Education' lessons and elsewhere, as having innately given strengths in certain areas, if the theory is wrong they may be getting a false picture of themselves.

White also expressed concern that in many schools there is something like a simplified version of Gardner's theory being used. It divides children not into eight or nine categories, but into three. These are known by the letters VAK: 'visual', 'auditory' and 'kinaesthetic'. It comes to them 'shrink-wrapped', just like MI theory itself. But where does it come from? White says that the teachers he interviewed had no answer to this question.

Neuroscience and education

This section is directly related to the previous one. The background is the astonishing rise in recent years in the popularity of educational packages and programmes which claim to be based on the latest brain research (Purdy, 2008; Howard-Jones, 2014). Within them children are viewed in terms of having learning styles, of being either left-brained or right-brained learners. Another category that is regularly used is that they are either visual, artistic or kinaesthetic learners. This has led in some schools to children wearing badges labelled V, A or K to show their learning style for the benefit of their teachers. Teachers, in turn, are encouraged to differentiate their lesson planning to accommodate these three styles.

Some of the associated learning packages and pedagogical approaches have come in for criticism, especially from neuroscientists (Hall, 2005). This criticism led to the coining of the term 'neuromyth', which was first employed in an OECD report on brain learning (OECD, 2002) and later by Goswami (2004) and Purdy (2008). Overall, four major criticisms exist:

1   Brain-based educational packages are based on an over-literal interpretation of hemispheric specializations, 'where brain attributes are assumed to come from either one hemisphere or the other, and which has led to teachers being encouraged to identify pupils as either "left-brained" or "right-brained" learners' (Purdy, 2008, p. 197). For example, children who are artistic are seen as 'right-brained' and children who are logical are seen as being 'left-brained'. The problem according to neuroscientists is that one part of the brain rarely works

in isolation from the other parts and most cognitive tasks require both hemispheres to work in parallel.

2   The claim that certain 'critical periods' exist during which the brain 'requires a specific type of environmental stimulation in order to develop normally' (Purdy, 2008, p. 198) is highly questionable. The view is that if the biological 'window' is not exploited then the chance to learn is missed forever. Experts like Goswami (2004) argue that it would be more correct to speak in terms of 'sensitive' rather than 'critical' periods. He goes on to say that 'there seem to be almost no cognitive capacities that can be "lost" at an early age and that learning is still possible after a period of environmental deprivation' (Goswami, 2004, p. 11). The more correct view is that, while education at an early age is highly important, it does not mean that a large part of a person's education must be concentrated into the childhood years.

3   There is also criticism of the claim that the development of neural connections or synapses requires an enriched classroom environment. This is based on the notion that children require enriched classroom environments in order to facilitate normal neural development. Again, there is no scientific evidence to support this view. Purdy (2008, p. 199) concludes that, while the evidence suggests there might be a sensory threshold below which a child's brain might not develop normally, 'there is no necessity artificially to enrich a normal environment as there is no evidence to suggest that there is any benefit'.

4   Goswami (2004) has focused his criticism on the VAK classification where learners are tested to discover whether they are visual, auditory or kinaesthetic learners. He draws attention to Thompson and Maguire (2001), who outlined the supposed learning styles as follows:

- Visual learners learn better through seeing pictures, diagrams, moving images and colour, and are encouraged to use pictures, mind maps or pens of a different colour to help the brain remember better.
- Auditory learners learn by storing sounds in their brains and are encouraged to listen to music while learning, repeat their work out loud in funny voices and make up raps about their work.
- Kinaesthetic learners learn by movement or touch and should do things practically, walk around while reading, do brain gym exercises or squeeze a sponge or stress-release ball while working.

The problem, however, as Coffield *et al.* (2004) have pointed out, is that there is a great lack of independent, critical longitudinal and large-scale studies with experimental and control groups to test such claims.

Goswami (2004) has been particularly critical of the 'Brain Gym' programme, which advocates exercises to encourage whole-brain learning. This programme is based on the premise of brain laterality and promotes exercises to develop the ability to cross the brain's 'midline', from right to left, or from left to right – claiming that this is an ability fundamental to academic success. One of the sections of the programme encourages pupils to massage 'brain buttons' to the left and right of the sternum with one hand while holding the navel with the other. Such a movement, it is claimed, improves reading, coordination, the correction of letter and number reversals (central to dyslexia), consonant blending and the ability to keep one's pace while reading. Again, Goswami (2004) states that there is no reputable peer-reviewed neuroscience research to uphold these claims.

Issues for discussion

Regarding Gardner

1   Even if you accept White's argument that Gardner's theory is 'flaky', is it still possible that teachers could use it to give children self-confidence and a desire to learn?
If so, can a strong case still be made for using it?

2   Another point made by White is that MI theory reinforces the Christian belief that all human beings are born with unique God-given talents. Do you think that this may make it particularly appealing to faith schools?

3   To what extent, do you think, there may be a correspondence between the areas covered by MI theory and those that went to make up a traditional so-called 'liberal education'. If so, could it possibly provide the basis for promoting an enhanced understanding of the various worlds we inhabit?

4   Do you think that MI theory may also appeal to those who react against recent utilitarian tendencies in schooling? If so, why?

Regarding neuro-myths

1   From what has been outlined in this chapter, do you think that there is an urgent need to educate the educational community regarding the neuro-myths?
Why?
How might one go about this?

2   An alternative approach would be to promote a notion that education would be well served by acknowledging the uncertainty that exists in terms of how children learn.
Do you agree with this statement?
Do you think that neuroscientists would be quite happy to accept it?

3   Do you think that there should be more meaningful dialogue between the educational and neuroscientific communities?
How might this take place?

References

Adey, P. and Dillon, J. (Eds). (2012). *Bad Education: Debunking Myths in Education*. Berkshire: Open University Press.

Coffield, F., Mosley, D., Hall, E. and Ecclestone, K. (2004). *Should We Be Using Learning Styles? What Research Has to Say to Practice*. London: Learning and Skills Research Centre.

Gardner, H. (1972). *The Quest for Mind*. London: Coventure.

Gardner, H. (1973). *The Arts and Human Development*. New York: John Wiley.

Gardner, H. (1982). *Art, Mind and Brain*. New York: Basic Books.

Gardner, H. (1990). The theory of multiple intelligences (pp. 930–938). In N. Entwistle (Ed.), *Handbook of Educational Ideas and Practices*. London: Routledge.

Gardner, H. (1993). *Frames of Mind: The Theory of Multiple Intelligences*. London: Heinemann.

Gardner, H. (1999a). *Intelligence Reframed: Multiple Intelligences for the 21st Century*. New York: Basic Books.

Gardner, H. (1999b). *The Disciplined Mind*. New York: Simon and Shuster.

Gardner, H. (2003). *Multiple Intelligences after Twenty Years*. Paper presented at the American Educational Research Association, Chicago, IL, 21 April. http://ocw.metu.edu.tr/pluginfile.php/9274/mod_resource/content/1/Gardner_multiple_intelligent.pdf.

Goswami, U. (2004). Neuroscience and education. *British Journal of Educational Psychology*, Vol. 74, pp. 1–14.

Hall, J. (2005). *Neuroscience and Education: A Review of the Contribution of Brain Science to Teaching and Learning*. Glasgow: Scottish Council for Research in Education.

Howard-Jones, P. (2014). Neuroscience and education: Myths and messages. *Nature Reviews: Neuroscience*, Vol. 15, pp. 817–824.

OECD (2002). *Understanding the Brain: Towards a New Learning Science*. Paris: OECD.

Purdy, N. (2008). Neuroscience and education: How best to filter out the neurononsense from our classrooms. *Irish Educational Studies*, Vol. 27, No. 3, pp. 197–208.

Thompson, H. and Maguire, S. (2001). *Mind Your Head: Get to Know Your Brain and How to Learn*. Antrim: North Eastern Education and Library Board.

White, J. (2004). The myth of multiple intelligences? http://eprints.ioe.ac.uk/1263/1/WhiteJ2005Howard Gardner1.pdf.

19 Approaches to teaching

This chapter is based on a classification of approaches to teaching first made by Fenstermacher and Soltis (1986) back in the mid-1980s, and re-stated by them in 2009 (Fenstermacher and Soltis, 2009). They argued that:

- there are different ways to teach the same things very effectively;
- a teacher's approach, his or her general conception of the teacher's role, plays an important part in how one teaches.

On this, they argued that there are three basic approaches to teaching. These are:

- the executive approach;
- the therapist approach;
- the liberationist approach.

Contemporary educators have used these three different perspectives to conceive of the activities of teaching in ways they think will help teachers to teach better. Each of the three approaches can give us a way to:

- think about what one as a teacher should do;
- diagnose what one as a teacher should do;
- prescribe what one as a teacher should do.

Fenstermacher and Soltis (2009) also held that knowing about the approaches can:

- give one the power to choose ways to teach that can help one achieve the high goal of helping individuals to become fully fledged persons;
- offer ways to think about what one is doing;
- offer ways to think about what relation there is between what one intends as a teacher and what one actually does with learners.

They argue that each approach contains within it values and purposes that are useful and appropriate in certain teaching situations, as well as being morally preferable in some instances.

Features of the three approach

The executive approach

This approach views the teacher as an executor, a person charged with bringing about certain learning, using the best skills and techniques available. It can be viewed as being an instructional theory. As such, it accords with the following definition of Koch (2013, p. 237):

> An instructional theory can provide direction in helping people to learn, understand and/or apply a predetermined set of principles, concepts and/or procedures.

Contemporary research on the effects of teaching and learning is very important to advocates of the executive approach. It provides the teacher with techniques and understandings to use in the management of the classroom and the production of learning.

In the executive approach one adopts technical skills to teach pre-specified content to the learner in a way that permits him or her to acquire it to some acceptable level of competence. The knowledge and skills are highly specified so that:

- the learner's accumulated fund of knowledge and skill can be diagnosed accurately;
- an instructional prescription can be prepared;
- instruction can be given;
- an unambiguous evaluation can be administered.

A difficulty, some claim, is that knowledge and skill can be specified at so basic and detailed a level that it becomes impossible for the teacher to impart it in a manner that reflects anything but a rudimentary approach to the content.

Others, however, hold that these can be overcome by:

- learning useful techniques;
- developing effective pedagogical skills;
- holding oneself accountable for proficient instructional capabilities without forfeiting the opportunity to explore content areas in depth.

The executive approach has been given other labels by various educationists. Wink (2011), for example, has pointed out that some have considered the approach from the point of view of the students, and have termed it as seeing the 'learner as plant'. Placing the emphasis on the teacher and the notion of pouring knowledge into the student's head, she then goes on herself to term it the 'transmission' approach.

The therapist approach

This approach views the teacher as an empathetic person charged with helping individuals grow personally and reach a high level of self-actualization, understanding and acceptance. It is influenced strongly by:

- psychotherapy;
- humanistic psychology;
- existential philosophy.

The focus is on students developing their own selves as authentic persons through personally meaningful educational experiences.

In the therapist approach, the purpose of teaching is to enable the learner to become a person capable of accepting responsibility for what he or she is and to be able to make choices that define oneself as one wishes to be defined. Thus, while it is accepted that one must, and should, acquire certain bodies of knowledge that have been selected, organized and taught by others, it needs to be used to help one to understand oneself as a human being. This involves understanding one's own feelings, thoughts and ideas, and also the feelings, thoughts and ideas of others.

Just as the executive approach has been given other labels by various educationists, so also has the therapist approach. Again, Wink (2011) has pointed out that some have also considered this approach from the point of view of the students, and have termed it as seeing the 'learner as builder'. Placing the emphasis on the view that the students must engage actively in their learning, she goes on to term it the 'generative' approach.

The liberationist approach

This approach views the teacher as a liberator, a freer of the individual's mind and a developer of well-rounded human beings. The classical idea of a liberal education underpins the contemporary mainstream version of the approach. The liberationist approach places a heavy emphasis on content, with much less emphasis on specific skills or the psychological and emotional states of one's students. It requires that one consider the purpose of teaching beyond the emphasis on content. The aim should be to seek to free the student's mind from the limits of everyday experience. Thus the content of one's classes, regardless of the subject being taught, should be to select and organize it in a manner aimed at liberating the mind of the student.

Again, just as the executive and therapist approaches have been given other labels by various educationists, so also is this the case with the liberationist approach. Wink (2011), once again, has pointed out that some have also considered this approach from the point of view of the students, and have termed it as seeing the 'learner as explorer'. Placing the emphasis on the view that the students must seek to find ways to bring their learning out of the classroom and into the community, she goes on to term this the 'transformative' approach.

Some additional considerations

Fenstermacher and Soltis (2009) also made the following points regarding the approaches:

1   The content in the executive approach is highly specified. It is made up of discrete facts, ideas, topics and domains, often expressed in the form of behavioural outcomes and measurable competencies. This is necessary if objective, standardized tests are to be used to determine what the learners have gained from their teachers. The technical skills of teaching that have been proven effective for producing gains in specified knowledge are deemed most appropriate for use in the classroom or lecture hall.

2   In the liberationist approach, the manner of instruction is heavily influenced by the content itself. For example, a science teacher would desire that his or her students would become critical, sceptical inquirers in order to acquire a necessary mind-set for thinking like a scientist. The teacher should promote this mind-set amongst his or her students by being, and being seen to be, a critical inquirer in the classroom or lecture hall.

3   There is a difficult problem in the therapist approach to teaching. Each person is unique and this uniqueness is maintained by making choices on the basis of the future one constructs for oneself. But what of:

   • the future of others;
   • the future of the community;
   • the future of the state;
   • the future of the nation?

These entities, Fenstermacher and Soltis (2009) held, may exercise jurisdiction over schooling in order to ensure some common meaning and serve common purposes. This is usually achieved by governments imposing a shared programme of studies on each child in order to preserve the culture and the nation (Bradshaw, 2012; Shaw, 2014).

Issues for discussion

1   Can you relate each of the approaches to teaching to one of the orientations to curriculum considered in Chapter 12?

2   Is there a direct correspondence between each approach and each orientation?

3   Is it possible that each orientation to curriculum can accommodate a number or all of the approaches to teaching?

4   Do you think that the three approaches to teaching are compatible?

5   Would it be appropriate for a teacher to use a variety of approaches in the same lesson or lecture?

6   Given what you now know of the therapist approach, what is your reaction to it? Are you opposed to it? Are you favourably disposed to it?

7   Are you wondering whether you might, to some extent, have an executive mind, seeing the job of the teacher as one of doing an effective job of getting students to learn school subjects, while also being part therapist, recognizing the importance of encouraging them to come to grips with what they are as human beings?

8   Relating approaches to teaching to curriculum orientations is not a very difficult exercise. However, have you considered how you might relate approaches to teaching to theories of learning, including those considered in Chapter 17?

(continued)

9   The strong emphasis on subject-matter knowledge has troubled many who have looked closely at the liberationist approach. They ask:

- Is it truly possible or even desirable for all students to study the basic subjects in the way the liberationist argues, especially given the broad range of individual differences in most classrooms?
- Can all students develop the academic and scholarly minds espoused by the liberationists, or is this approach to teaching really an elitist view of education because its goals can be attained only by a select few?
- What would be wrong with a more practical approach, aimed at developing the skills and understanding needed for everyday life and work?
- How can we deal with the range of differences among teachers since many may not be able to master and teach the liberationist approach well?

Discuss each of these questions

References

Bradshaw, J. (2012). Why university students need a well-rounded education. *The Globe and Mail*, 13 October.

Fenstermacher, G. D. and Soltis, J. F. (1986). *Approaches to Teaching* (1st edn). New York: Teachers College, Columbia University.

Fenstermacher, G. D. and Soltis, J. F. (2009). *Approaches to Teaching* (5th edn). New York: Teachers College, Columbia University.

Koch, J. (2013). Instructional theory (pp. 237–238). In B. J. Irby, G. Brown, R. Lara-Alecio and S. Jackson (Eds), *The Handbook of Educational Theories*. Charlotte, NC: Information Age Publishing.

Shaw, J. S. (2014). The case for a core curriculum. *Phi Beta Cons*, October. www.nationalreview.com/phi-beta-cons/390114/case-core-curriculum-jane-s-shaw.

Wink, J. (2011). *Critical Pedagogy: Notes from the Real World*. Boston, MA: Pearson.

20 Learning through making and doing

Bruner's (1966, 1996) position, as has already been pointed out, is that learning is about 'internal model making' and that this has three modes, namely, the enactive mode, the iconic mode and the symbolic mode. Another way of putting this is that certain things are learnt through acting out, others are learnt through making things and others yet again result in learning that allows one to give some kind of an account. This type of learning can take place through the teaching of individual subjects on the curriculum. It can also take place through engagement in cross-curricular activities. Two of the best known of such activities are service learning and project work. Each of these will now be considered in turn.

Service learning

One of various productive ways of promoting student learning beyond the confines of the school is through service learning. Such learning is considered to be valuable in the contemporary era for a number of reasons. For example, Conrad and Hedin (1991, p. 743), pioneers in the field, pointed to its liberating capacity when they stated: 'the greatest power of service is that it reveals that one is not powerless, that a contribution can be given, a difference made: I can do something, I am significant'. Amongst other claims made is that service learning can:

- connect learning to life;
- give meaning to an interdisciplinary curriculum;
- promote creative skills;
- promote critical thinking skills;
- provide opportunities for introspection;
- provide opportunities for reflection.

Conrad and Hedin (1991) also concluded that service learning can have positive effects on students' social and personal responsibility, including improvement in:

- self-esteem, self-motivation, risk-taking and ability to solve real-life problems;
- taking of responsibility for one's own learning;
- one's concern for others.

Evidence of student growth in critical thinking, motivation, engagement, curiosity and citizenship has also been noted (Eyler and Giles, 1999).

Service learning appears to be one of the most important new developments in education (Mann and Patrick, 2000) as it:

- links schools and society in an increasingly technological and impersonal world;
- can be highly effective in developing a rich partnership between both the serving and the served;
- helps to move young adolescents forward on the path of civic and moral identity, and engagement can enhance teaching in school by extending student learning into the community;
- can help to foster a sense of caring for others;
- can play a part in increasing self-esteem, academic performance and social skills (Reinders and Youniss, 2006).

Strictly speaking, service learning is not community service (Mooney and Edwards, 2001) since it must be linked to the curriculum. Rather, it includes:

- a community service component in a structured learning process (Cruz and Giles, 2000);
- systematic attempts to help students to use experiences in the community to better build upon, critique and evaluate:

  a   knowledge already gained from educational experiences;
  b   messages from the mass media;
  c   influences of home and community;
  d   readings they have had.

Whatever the model (and there is quite a number of them) (Butin, 2003), service learning involves leading students to ask real and relevant questions as they take responsibility for their own learning (Eyler, 2002).

The 'Lens Model for Service Learning Educators' developed by Cone and Harris (1996) is still helpful today. It has the following characteristics:

- It stresses the importance of students being intellectually challenged through:

  o   pre-service training;
  o   exposure to concepts which they will be expected to apply and understand in the community.

- The 'lens' is the service experience itself; an experience distinct from the student's everyday experiences.
- A holistic approach to reflection involving the student's intellectual and emotional capacities as well as written and oral skills then follows the experience.

The model is adopted by:

- proceeding to introduce a vital component, namely, that reflection is most effective when guided by an educator or mentor who can facilitate the student's learning;

- inviting students to:

  - respond in writing to key questions;
  - cite observations;
  - explain their generalizations;

- ensuring the concepts become integrated into the thinking processes of the students by encouraging them to use abstract concepts frequently in:

  - observing the world;
  - thinking about the world;
  - describing the world;
  - talking about the world;

- moving students one step closer to being able to think critically and defend their point of view as the analytical methods and organizational concepts are acquired;
- returning to the learners as they integrate their experiences into new frameworks, attitudes and mind-sets.

Research in the US has indicated that when service learning is explicitly connected to the curriculum by teachers who help students process and draw meaning from their experiences, the effects on cognitive, affective and behavioural development are positive (Billig, 2000).

This linking of service with academic goals is associated in the US with progressives like John Dewey, who argued back in the 1930s that the role of education is to transform society. However, incorporating service learning into the curriculum more generally did not really take off until the early 1970s (Skinner and Chapman, 1999, p. 2). An important initiative in this regard was the establishment of the National Center for Service Learning, which provided assistance to schools introducing service learning programmes (Alt and Medrich, 1994). By the mid-2000s growth was impressive:

- The National Center for Education Statistics found that 64 per cent of all public schools had students participating in service, with almost half of all American high schools incorporating service learning within the curriculum (Skinner and Chapman, 1999).
- A 2002 report from the National Commission on Service Learning estimated that more than 13 million students participated in service, or service-learning, activities in the 2000–2001 school year.
- In 2005 it was noted that almost three-quarters of the states in the US had some form of policy addressing service learning, and one, Maryland, even made it a graduation requirement (Piscatelli, 2005, p. 59).

Also, Silcox and Leek (1997) have identified a variety of service-learning initiatives in other parts of the world aimed at helping students to develop critical thinking skills and express themselves creatively. More recent evidence in this regard has been summarized by Howard (2012).

'Project work' in Singapore

The following is a summary of an account by O'Donoghue and Clarke (2010) on another development aimed at improving student learning, namely, 'project work'. While historically this has had many meanings and approaches, a modern interpretation of what is involved is a central component of the curriculum for schools in Singapore. Students in Singapore have for a long time had a reputation for being strong in subject content knowledge and being well trained to pass examinations (Bryer, 2006). However, as in various other parts of the world, there was increasing concern towards the end of the twentieth century that this would not be sufficient to ensure economic success for the future (Ng, 2008). Particularly highlighted was the perception that students lacked the ability to generate and solve problems through application of knowledge and skills, and also that they were weak in oral communication and collaborative work (Bryer, 2006).

One of the steps taken to improve the curriculum so that students would be provided with skills to enable them to address real-life situations was the introduction of problem-based learning approaches (Ministry of Education, Singapore, 2000). 'Project work' was also introduced. This represented a move towards interdisciplinary studies and away from a view that students should be concerned almost solely with absorbing large amounts of prescribed subject content. The 'subject' was specifically timetabled in secondary schools to be conducted during regular curriculum time and curriculum content in certain other learning areas was reduced by 30 per cent to facilitate adoption. Overall, the initiative was in harmony with a more general cross-curricular initiative nationally known as the 'teach less, learn more' educational policy. Furthermore, in 1999 the Committee on University Admissions revised the admission criteria for entrance into Singapore's universities to include one's results in project work in secondary school.

The overall emphasis in the project work syllabus is on individual work and teamwork, on oral presentations and on the self-monitoring of learning (Ministry of Education, Singapore, 2000). This, it is argued, helps students to see links between and across their school subjects and to apply their knowledge. There is no body of knowledge to be reproduced in the project work syllabus (Wang *et al.*, 2011). Rather, students have to draw on their existing knowledge from across subject disciplines, seek out new knowledge and then apply it to the task they have chosen. Students cannot choose their group members. Rather, they are assigned to a group randomly. Within their group, they cooperate on tasks and are encouraged to learn from each other.

One of the main reasons for project work being conducted during regular curriculum time is to enable teachers to monitor students' progress regularly and provide feedback. The teacher's role is that of facilitator. He or she is expected to:

- raise awareness;
- generate a sense of accountability in the students;
- demonstrate leadership to ensure that students receive mentoring from lecturers in higher education institutions, including universities and polytechnics;
- let go of some of one's traditional authority to create a more conducive learning environment that facilitates the development of creativity and breaks down rigidity.

Project work has the following four domains:

- knowledge application;
- communication;
- collaboration;
- independent learning.

Within their groups, students must track their learning curve, be responsible for their own work and seek knowledge and answers for themselves.

Project work in schools in Singapore is highly regarded and a wide variety of projects are disseminated and reported publicly every year. Also, the indications are that it is contributing to a major paradigm shift in thinking about education within the nation.

Issues for discussion

1   One of the most comprehensive service learning initiatives is that which has been integral to the International Baccalaureate (IB) curriculum and which over 30 years ago was leading the field in stressing the importance of community service as part of the formal curriculum (Kulundu and Hayden, 2002, p. 30).

    a   What do you know about the IB?
    b   Why was it established initially?
    c   What is the structure of its programmes?

2   Along with the academic subjects which they are required to study, students enrolled in the IB must complete three other core elements of the programme.
   What are they?

3   One of the three core activity requirements is student participation in what is known as 'creativity, action, service' (CAS) activities. This particular requirement emphasizes compulsory involvement in service.

    a   What do you know about it?
    b   What are its requirements?
    c   What do you think its benefits might be?

4   There have been other approaches to project work in the past.

    a   Can you identify some of them?
    b   Find out what you can about the approach of William H. Kilpatrick (1871–1965).
    c   How was it, in some situations, combined with 'service work'?
    d   Was this 'service work' akin to the 'service learning' approach discussed in this chapter

---

References

Alt, M. N. and Medrich, E. A. (1994). *Student Outcomes from Participation in Community Service*. Berkley, CA: US Department of Education, Office of Research.

Billig, S. (2000). Research on K-12 school-based service learning: The evidence builds. *Phi Delta Kappan*, Vol. 81, No. 9, pp. 658–664.

Bruner, J. (1966). *Towards a Theory of Instruction*. New York: Norton.

Bruner, J. (1996). *The Culture of Education*. Cambridge, MA: Harvard University Press.

Bryer, K. (2006). Pre-university project work in Singapore: An alternative mode of assessment. www.iaea.info/documents/paper_1162a1de57.pdf.

Butin, D. (2003). Of what use is it? Multiple conceptualizations of service learning within education, *Teachers College Record*, 9 November.

Cone, D. and Harris, S. (1996). Service learning practice: Developing a theoretical framework. *Michigan Journal of Community Service Learning*, Vol. 3, pp. 31–43.

Conrad, D. and Hedin, D. (1991). School based community service: What we know from research and theory. *Phi Delta Kappan*, Vol. 7, No. 10, pp. 743–749.

Cruz, N. I. and Giles D. E. (2000). Where's the community in service learning research? *Michigan Journal of Community Service Learning*, Fall, pp. 28–34.

Eyler, J. (2002). Reflection: Linking service and learning – linking students and communities. *Journal of Social Issues*, Vol. 58, No. 3, pp. 517–534.

Eyler, J. and Giles, D. (1999). *Where's the Learning In Service Learning?* San Francisco, CA: Jossey-Bass.

Howard, J. (2012). Service learning research: Foundational issues (pp. 1–12). In S. H. Bilig and A. S. Waterman (Eds), *Studying Service Learning. Innovations in Education Research Methodology*. London: Routledge.

Kulundu, F. and Hayden, M. (2002). Creativity, action, service (CAS) activities as part of the International Baccalaureate diploma programme: A case study. *Pastoral Care*, Vol. 20, No. 1, pp. 30–36.

Mann, S. and Patrick, J. J. (Eds). (2000). *Education for Civic Engagement in Democracy. Service Learning and Other Promising Practices*. Washington, DC: Office of Educational Research and Improvement.

Ministry of Education (2000). *The Desired Outcomes of Education*. Singapore: Ministry of Education.

Mooney, L. A. and Edwards, B. (2001). Experiential learning in sociology: Service learning and other community-based learning initiatives. *Teaching Sociology*, Vol. 29, No. 2, pp. 181–194.

Ng, P. T. (2008). Educational reform in Singapore: From quantity to quality. *Educational Research for Policy and Practice*, Vol. 7, pp. 5–15.

O'Donoghue, T. A. and Clarke, S. (2010). *Leading Learning: Process, Themes and Issues in International Perspective*. London: Routledge.

Piscatelli, J. (2005). Sustaining service-learning and youth voice through policy. In National Youth Leadership Council, *Growing to Greatness*. Saint Paul, MN: National Youth Leadership Council.

Reinders, H. and Youniss, J. (2006). School-based required community service and civic development in adolescents. *Applied Developmental Science*, Vol. 10, No. 1, pp. 2–12.

Silcox, H. C. and Leek, T. E. (1997). International service learning: Its time has come. *Phi Delta Kappan*, Vol. 78, No. 8, pp. 615–618.

Skinner, R. and Chapman, C. (1999). *Service Learning and Community Service in K-12 Public Schools: Statistics in Brief*. Washington DC: National Center for Education Statistics.

Wang, J. C. K., Liu, W. C., Koh, C., Tan, O. S. and Ed, J. (2011). A motivational analysis of project work in Singapore using self-determination theory. *International Journal of Research and Review*, Vol. 7, No. 1, pp. 45–66.

21 Direct instruction

A major point made throughout this book is that there is no one correct way to teach. Rather, it is a matter of choosing what is most appropriate in a particular context. To this end, a wide array of approaches is available, including, but by no means limited to:

- discussion (Cleaver, 2015);
- small-group work (Tuttle, 2015);
- cooperative learning (Johns Hopkins School of Education, 2015);
- problem solving (Whimby *et al.*, 2013);
- student research (Cole, 2008);
- role play (Larson and Keiper, 2011);
- case study (Barnes *et al.*, 1994);
- student writing (Mingst, 1994).

Given that it has not been mentioned so far, one might at this point also think that direct instruction should be dismissed. This is not so. While the main emphasis in previous chapters has been on the importance of using approaches other than direct instruction, it is considered that for some areas of learning direct instruction still has an important part to play. The account now presented on this draws largely from O'Donoghue and Clarke (2010).

The nature of direct instruction

Direct instruction means whole-class expository teaching techniques. These include lectures and demonstrations, with the teacher delivering academic content, or 'formally' teaching some skills in a very structured manner. In other words, the emphasis is on directing the activities of learners. Its principal characteristics have been summarized by Killen (2003, p. 63) as follows:

- It is also called explicit instruction.
- It usually refers to whole-class expository teaching.
- It usually includes lectures and demonstrations.
- It usually involves the teacher delivering academic content in a highly structured format, directing the activities of learners and maintaining a focus on academic achievement.

Teachers often have to make a major effort and be very creative in order to find ways to break the dominance of this approach in their mental model of teaching. Yet it would be a mistake to argue for its total eradication. Accepting this point, Killen (2003) has put forward the 'common sense' argument that, in some circumstances, direct instruction is simply the most appropriate strategy to use. By way of illustration, he states:

- Direct instruction may be useful to develop students' basic knowledge and skills through direct instruction techniques 'before giving them a more active role in knowledge seeking through strategies such as problem solving or experimentation' (Killen, 2003, p. 63).
- Direct instruction does not have to be dull and boring: the control and structure that characterize direct instruction 'can be achieved in interesting, warm, concerned and flexible ways so that a positive classroom climate is maintained and students enjoy learning' (Killen, 2003, p. 63).

Killen (2003) has also identified the following important features of direct instruction when used effectively:

- The learning outcomes are clear to students.
- The teacher controls the time for various instructional activities.
- The teacher organizes and controls the sequencing of lesson activities.
- There is emphasis on academic achievement.
- The teacher carefully monitors students.
- Feedback to students is academically oriented.

Taking cognisance of these features, he argues that direct instruction allows one to:

- convey a personal interest in a subject (through an enthusiastic presentation) and this can stimulate the interest and enthusiasm of the student;
- provide a role model of a scholar in a particular field (showing students 'how to think like a geographer'); you can show how problems can be approached, how information can be analysed or how knowledge is generated;
- highlight important points or possible difficulties for students so that their exposure to these things is not left to chance;
- provide information for students who are poor readers or who are not skilled at locating, organizing and interpreting information.

At the same time, Killen (2003, p. 67) acknowledges that direct instruction can also have the following limitations:

- Because of the teacher's central role in direct instruction, success of this strategy depends heavily on the 'image' that the teacher projects. If the teacher does not appear to be well prepared, knowledgeable, confident, enthusiastic and well organized, the students will become bored or distracted and their learning will be hindered.
- Direct instruction depends very heavily on the teacher having a good communication style.
- Direct instruction relies very heavily on students being able to assimilate information through listening, observing and note-taking.

- It is very difficult to cater for the individual differences between students' abilities, prior knowledge, interest in the subject, rates of learning and levels of understanding during direct instruction.
- Because students have limited active involvement in direct instruction, there are few opportunities for them in this type of lesson to develop their social and interpersonal skills.
- If used too frequently, direct instruction can lead students to believe that it is the teacher's job to tell them all they need to know; they may not be encouraged to take responsibility for their own learning.

The position of Alan Luke on direct instruction termed DI

Luke (2014) has provided an exposition on his thinking on direct instruction. His fundamental position is that it is one necessary part of an effective teaching repertoire, but cannot be seen as a universal or total curriculum solution. He notes that for 40 years there has been a particular version of direct instruction entitled DI, which was developed in the USA and which has been the object of education debates, controversies and substantial research. He also notes that it has not been adopted for system-wide implementation in any state of the USA or province of Canada.

Luke goes on to differentiate as follows between direct instruction and explicit instruction.

Direct instruction

The term 'direct instruction' (DI) is affiliated with an instructional approach and curriculum materials developed in the late 1960s by American and Canadian behavioural psychologists. It relates to:

- programmes being provided for teachers and schools with packaged, programmed instructional models initially in reading and numeracy, later expanding to other curriculum areas;
- teachers following a step-by-step, lesson-by-lesson approach to teaching that has already been written for them;
- teachers saying and doing what is prescribed and scripted;
- the instruction being followed by assessment tasks and tests aligned with the behavioural goals, the results of which are fed back to modify pace, grouping and skill emphases;
- teachers having an associated pre-specified system of rewards.

Teachers receive rigorous training and a directive teachers' guidebook. The aim of these programmes is to take local variation and teacher/student idiosyncrasy out of the instructional mix.

Luke also outlines the following criticisms of the DI approach:

- It focuses on teacher control of lesson pacing and content and does not encourage engagement with student cultural resources, background knowledge and community context.
- It deskills teachers by routinizing their work and downplaying their professional capacity to vary instructional pace and curriculum content depending on the student cohort and context.
- It works through strict tracking of student progress and ability grouping, which research shows can severely disadvantage some students.

- It places the teacher and child in a rigid relationship where the teacher is always the one with the power and knowledge with limited allowance or recognition of individual and cultural difference. This relationship is not conducive to local adaptation of lessons or content to accommodate community, cultural or individual differences, creativity and innovation in teaching and learning.
- The curriculum materials, teachers' guidebooks, training and proprietary assessment instruments cost considerably more than locally developed materials.

Explicit instruction

This refers to teacher-centred instruction focused on clear behavioural goals and outcomes. Students are told:

- what they will be learning;
- how they will be learning;
- what they have to do to show that they have succeeded in learning whatever it is.

There is a strong focus on curriculum content and clarity for all about the criteria for performance expected. This is a key teaching method used commonly in schools today that has demonstrated efficacy in the teaching and learning of specific bodies of knowledge and skills. It requires that teachers possess and deploy a repertoire of strategies, approaches and methods.

Luke concludes by saying that he does not rule out 'explicit instruction' or 'direct instruction' as being valuable. Rather, he argues, these have a much better prospect of making a developmental difference for students' medium- and long-term achievement and success where they are part of a larger school-level approach and broader expansion of teacher repertoire.

Issues for discussion

1   Historically there was much emphasis in schooling on rote learning and memorization. This eventually led to a large-scale move away to a child-centred curriculum. Yet it is worth cogitating if the pendulum has swung too much. Particularly problematic is the assumption that 'critical thinking' and 'problem solving' can be seen as an alternative to factual knowledge. Experience in the real world suggests that critical thinking cannot be developed without factual knowledge of the subject to which one applies one's critical thinking. Certainly, factual knowledge does not guarantee a capacity for critical thought, yet it is difficult to imagine how one can achieve critical thought, at least about society, without factual knowledge.

   - Do you agree with this proposition?
   - Could it be that the acquisition of factual knowledge may be the most effective way of inculcating those qualities of concentration and discipline which contribute significantly towards a capacity for critical thinking and problem solving?

2   What do you think of the argument of those who hold that in a televisual world of primarily materialistic impulses, where the clamour for the 'instant fix' has become so dominant a popular impulse, it is precisely those qualities of application and concentration that are most urgently needed, not only at school, but in the wider society?

3   Killen (2003) has put forward the 'common sense' argument that in some circumstances direct instruction is simply the most appropriate strategy to use. By way of illustration, he states that it may be useful to develop students' basic knowledge and skills through direct instruction techniques 'before giving them a more active role in knowledge-seeking through strategies such as problem solving or experimentation' (2003, p. 63).
Discuss.

4   Killen (2003, p. 63) also points out that direct instruction does not have to be dull and boring. Rather, he contends, 'the control and structure that characterise direct instruction can be achieved in interesting, warm, concerned and flexible ways so that a positive classroom climate is maintained and students enjoy learning'.
Discuss.

5   What do you know about the traditional approach of the Society of Jesus (the Jesuits) to teaching, termed the 'Ratio Studiorum'. Discuss the various aspects of this pedagogical approach and its relevance (or otherwise) in the present century.

6   What do you know about Socratic Dialogue as a pedagogical approach?
Discuss how it could be used effectively in the classroom and in seminar sessions.

References

Barnes, L. B., Roland Chistensen, C. and Hansen, A. J. (1994). *Teaching and the Case Method: Text, Cases, and Readings*. Cambridge, MA: Harvard Business School Press.

Cleaver, S. (2015). 13 strategies to improve student classroom discussions. *We Are Teachers*. www.weareteachers.com/blogs/post/2015/03/18/13-strategies-to-improve-student-classroom-discussions.

Cole, R. W. (2008). *Educating Everybody's Children. Diverse Teaching Strategies For Diverse Learners*. Alexandria, VA: Association for Supervision and Curriculum Development.

Johns Hopkins School of Education (2015). *Cooperative Learning*. http://education.jhu.edu/PD/newhorizons/strategies/topics/Cooperative%20Learning/.

Killen, R. (2003). *Effective Teaching Strategies: Lessons from Research and Practice*. Tuggerah, NSW: Social Science Press.

Larson, B. E. and Keiper, T. A. (2011). *Instructional Strategies for Middle and Secondary Social Studies. Methods, Assessment, and Classroom Management*. London: Routledge.

Luke, A. (2014). Direct instruction is not a solution for Australian schools. *EduResearch Matters*, AARE, Alan Luke, 7 July. www.aare.edu.au/blog/?p=439.

Mingst, K. (1994). Cases and the interactive classroom. *International Studies Notes*, Vol. 19, No. 2, pp. 1–7.

O'Donoghue, T. A. and Clarke, S. (2010). *Leading Learning: Process, Themes and Issues in International Perspective*. London: Routledge.

Tuttle, N. (2015). Suggestions for using small groups in the classroom. *Chicago Centre for Teaching*. http://teaching.uchicago.edu/teaching-guides/small-group-work/.

Whimby, A., Lockhead, J. and Narode, R. B. (2013). *Problem Solving and Comprehension*. London: Routledge.

Part V
Leadership in education

22 Approaches to leadership

Leadership involves leaders. An early classical typology of leaders was proposed by Max Weber (1984). He identified three types:

- Traditional leaders, like monarchs, come to their role through social conventions.
- Rational leaders are appointed on the basis of their technical, professional and bureaucratic expertise.
- Charismatic leaders possess a forceful or magnetic personality, or intrinsic spiritual endowment elusively identified as charisma. The source of their power is derived from the unconscious desires of their followers, and they are provided with the sense of meaning, purpose, vocation and fulfilment that they seek.

The study of leadership grew alongside the study of leaders. Foster (1989) identified two main traditions as having influenced the social scientific definition of leadership, namely, that which comes from the political historical disciplines and that which comes from the world of business management and public administration:

- The study of leadership through the political historical model highlights the role of significant individuals in shaping the course of history. Leadership in this sense is the story of events, actions and ideas of how individuals have transformed their social milieu (Foster, 1989). Leaders are individuals who make history through the use of power and resources.
- The definition of leadership which comes from the world of business management and public administration is one which considers that:

  o leaders are persons of superior rank in an organization;
  o leadership is goal-centred;
  o goals are driven by organizational needs.

The reason for exerting leadership is achieving organizational goals. The productive function legitimizes the exercise of leadership. Leaders exercise their power within the environment bounded by tasks and responsibilities.

A typology of leadership in education

This is a summary of the typology outlined in O'Donoghue and Clarke (2010).

Managerial leadership

Bush and Glover's (2003) exposition on managerial leadership centres on functions, tasks and the behaviours of people. It takes as given that the behaviour of the organizational members is largely rational. Also, influence on people is exercised through positions of authority within the organizational hierarchy.

Instructional leadership

Bush and Glover (2003) view instructional leadership as focusing on teaching and learning, and on the behaviour of teachers when working with students in class. Student learning is the central focus of the leader's actions. The stress is on the direction and impact of influence rather than on the process. On this, Leithwood *et al.* (1999) state that instructional leaders possess the expert knowledge and the formal authority to exert influence on teachers. Furthermore, Hallinger and Murphy (1985) affirm that instructional leaders:

- define the school mission;
- manage the instructional programme;
- promote school climate.

Transactional leadership

The view in the literature on transactional leadership is that leaders and followers exchange needs and services to achieve independent objectives. Thus it is largely a bargaining process. Bartering takes place regarding the wants and needs of followers and those of the leader. These are traded and a bargain is struck. Also, positive reinforcement is given for good work and for increased performance.

Transformational leadership

The usual definition of transformational leadership is that it relates to the ability of a leader to imagine a new social condition and to communicate this to the followers. The leader inspires and transforms individual followers through adopting high levels of morality that make the promise of reward unnecessary. Bush and Glover (2003), in their interpretation of this approach to leadership, describe the influence and the increased commitment of followers to the goals of the organization. The focus is on the transformation process rather than on particular types of outcomes.

Moral leadership

The core of moral leadership lies in the values and beliefs of leaders. These beliefs and values provide the school with a clear aim (Bush and Glover, 2003). On this, Sergiovanni (1991, pp. 322–323) stated:

the school must move beyond concern for goals and roles to the task of building purposes into the structure and embodying these purposes in everything that it does with the effect of transforming school members from neutral participant to committed followers.

The embodiment of purpose and the development of followers, he concluded, are inescapably moral. The challenge for leaders is to try to marry both the managerial and the moral imperative.

Invitational leadership

Invitational leadership, according to Bennis and Nanus (1985), is based on:

- unleashing the intrinsic energy people possess;
- summoning them cordially to see themselves as capable of tackling challenges;
- overcoming obstacles;
- accomplishing great things.

It is an approach that stresses the integrity, potential and interdependence of teachers and recognizes their responsibility to work for the common good.

Interpersonal leadership

Tuohy and Coghlan (1997, p. 6) depict what they see as the 'normal' life of teachers as follows:

Much of the teachers' day is taken up in an intensity of relationships with their students; the changing context of their lives and developing appropriate and effective responses to both their personal and academic needs requires constant reflection and adjustment.

Thus, they hold, it is essential that great emphasis be placed on collaboration and interpersonal relationships. They argue for the importance of having interpersonal leaders who focus on relationships with teachers, students and other members of the school community and who embrace a morally informed collaborative leadership approach (Bush and Glover, 2003).

Distributed leadership

Leithwood *et al.* (1999) recommend that leadership should be distributed among teachers as follows:

- setting directions – vision building, goal consensus and the development of high performance expectations;
- developing teachers – providing individualized support, intellectual stimulation and the modelling of values and practices important to the mission of the school;
- organizing and building a culture in which colleagues are motivated by moral imperatives and structuring, fostering shared decision making processes and problem solving capacities;
- building relationships with the whole school community;
- promoting collaboration within and across the school through networking.

Such a view seriously challenges the traditional position of the principal within the school setting (Spillane, 2006).

On considering the wide range of approaches to leadership that exist, including those considered so far, one is prompted to ask which is the best one to adopt. It is arguable that to do so would be to fall into the trap identified by Braun *et al.* (2011, p. 585), of 'assuming best possible environments for implementation, including ideal buildings, ideal students, ideal teachers and ideal resources'. To this they add that there is often regular change taking place in staff and student profiles, including attitudes. Accordingly, it might be better to ask which leadership approach is most appropriate in what context, under what circumstances, and for whom and with whom. This is a view that context matters just as much in the realm of leadership as it does in relation to education policy, curriculum and approaches to teaching and learning.

Issues for discussion

1   Are you aware of any other approaches to leadership considered in the academic literature?

2   Do you consider that any of the approaches are in conflict with each other? Why do you say this?

3   Is it possible for a leader to adopt all of the available approaches in his or her work? Why do you say this?

4   Might some approaches be more appropriate for the achievement of certain goals and others for the achievement of other goals? Elaborate.

5   Do you think that over the duration of a regular school year priority should be given to some approaches over others?

   • Why?
   • What would your priority list be and what reasons can you give for this?

6   Consider the following quotation from Shields (2013, p. 1):

   It is no longer sufficient to manage the day-to-day operations of schools, but to ensure that every student, regardless of home situation, is able to learn to a high level. Nevertheless, world-wide, children from poverty are often less successful in schools, dropping out and failing to finish in large numbers than more affluent peers. Too often, when students fail to succeed, educators blame students and their families – an attitude known as deficit thinking and assume that without extensive changes in the social fabric of society, nothing can be done to improve the academic achievement of the most disadvantaged students. What is often missing is a willingness and ability on the part of educators to examine, and take responsibility for, their role in students' lack of success.

   What do you think the author means by 'deficit thinking' in this context?
   Do you agree with her statement in her final sentence? Why?

Her view is that transformative leadership does not tell leaders what to do or how to do it, but it does suggest some starting points and ways to think about inequity in challenging and diverse contexts. Summarize her views on this from reading her text on the matter, namely, Shields, C. M. (2013). *Transformative Leadership in Education: Equitable Change in an Uncertain and Complex World*. New York: Routledge.

7   Leadership in universities has come in for major criticism in the last two decades. Here is an example of a contention (Anonymous Academic, 2014):

> I address you as 'leaders' because, for some reason (perhaps manager comes too close to rhyming with janitor for your liking), you've increasingly taken to styling yourselves in this way. How grand. How imposing. How spurious. Leaders are followed. The capacity and willingness to drive people along with the use of the pitchfork of threatened redundancy or the flaming torch of disciplinary action does not make a leader and the mere fact that you so brazenly call yourselves leaders is evidence of the malaise that prompts me to write. For the record, if you're not Alexander, Napoleon, Monty or the modern equivalent you're not really a leader. Be neither managers nor leaders. Be provosts, masters, principals, vice-chancellors, rectors, deans, registrars, bursars. How quaint. How medieval. How refreshing.

Discuss.

References

Anonymous Academic (2014). Dear leader. *Guardian*, 2 August.

Bennis, W. and Nanus, B. (1985). *The Strategy For Taking Charge*. New York: Harper and Row.

Braun, A., Ball, S. J., Maguire, M. and Hoskins, K. (2011). Taking context seriously: Explaining policy enactments in the secondary school. *Discourse: Studies in the Cultural Politics of Education*, Vol. 32, No. 4, pp. 585–596.

Bush, T. and Glover, D. (2003). *School Leadership: Concepts of Evidence*. Nottingham, UK: National College for School Leadership.

Foster, W. (1989). Towards a critical practice of leadership (pp. 39–62). In J. Smyth (Ed.), *Critical Perspective on Educational Leadership*. London: Falmer Press.

Hallinger, P. and Murphy, J. (1985). Assessing the instructional management behaviour of principals. *The Elementary School Journal*, Vol. 86, No. 2, pp. 217–247.

Leithwood, K., Jantzi, D. and Steinbach, R. (1999). *Changing Leadership For Changing Times*. Buckingham: Open University Press.

O'Donoghue, T. A. and Clarke, S. (2010). *Leading Learning: Process, Themes and Issues in International Perspective*. London: Routledge.

Sergiovanni. T. J. (1991). *The Principalship: A Reflective Practice Perspective*. Boston, MA: Allyn and Bacon.

Shields, C. M. (2013). Leading creativity in high poverty schools: A case for transformative leadership. Paper presented at the annual conference of the European Educational Research Association, Istanbul, Turkey, September.

Spillane, J. P. (2006). *Distributed Leadership*. San Francisco, CA: Jossey-Bass.

Tuohy, D. and Coghlan, D. (1997). Development in schools: A systems approach based on organizational levels. *Education Management and Administration*, Vol. 25, No. 1, pp. 65–77.

Weber, M. (1984). Legitimate authority and bureaucracy (pp. 4–27). In D. S. Pugh (Ed.), *Organization Theories*. London: Penguin.

23 Leadership for learning

O'Donoghue and Clarke (2010), drawing from Knapp *et al.* (2003), have recognized that it is helpful to think in terms of three levels of learning within a school. These are the levels of:

- organizational learning;
- teacher learning;
- student learning.

According to MacBeath (2006, p. 20), each level is interconnected through a flow of opportunities across people, classrooms and school structures, with

- organizational learning being dependent on, and feeding into, teacher learning;
- teacher learning being enhanced by its receptiveness to students' learning needs;
- student learning being dependent on teacher learning.

Leadership for organizational learning

O'Donoghue and Clarke (2010) deem that the core concept to open up discussion on leadership of organizational learning is that of 'the intelligent school'. This then can lead one on to considering related concepts. These include:

- contextual intelligence;
- strategic intelligence;
- academic intelligence;
- reflective intelligence;
- pedagogical intelligence.

The intelligent school

A learning organization is one based on humanistic values and aspires to levels of cooperation and learning to make the organization more successful (Driver, 2002; Stoll *et al.*, 2006). The associated assumption is that since schools maintain a focus on learning, an alignment with a positive perspective on organizational learning is both understandable and justified. A school at which such an outlook can be detected can be said to be an 'intelligent school' (MacGilchrist *et al.*, 1997).

Contextual intelligence

This form of intelligence refers to:

- the capacity of a school to see itself in relationship to its wider community and the world of which it is a part;
- the ability of a school to respond to both the environment's positive and negative aspects.

Strategic intelligence

MacGilchrist (nd) explains that this form of intelligence is concerned with ensuring:

- there is clarity about goals;
- there is clarity about the standards to be achieved;
- the aims and purposes of the school are shared by everyone.

It is through the use of this type of intelligence, she argues, that:

- a school is able to plan the action needed to achieve improvement;
- a school is able to have the capacity to put vision into practice.

Academic intelligence

As MacGilchrist (nd) sees it, this form of intelligence incorporates:

- enhancing students' knowledge, skills and abilities and empowering them as critical, reflective, life-long learners;
- the characteristics of effective learning and teaching;
- the key importance of high expectations, which are collectively distinguished by an 'ethos' that encourages high achievement and performance.

Reflective intelligence

Reflective intelligence has been defined as: 'the skills and processes of monitoring, reflecting upon and evaluating the effectiveness of the school in general and, in particular, the progress and achievement of the students' (MacGilchrist, nd, p. 2).

Pedagogical intelligence

Pedagogical intelligence requires that:

- teams in schools develop their skills in reflection, inquiry and dialogue to form the basis for a shared vision of change and common commitments to action;
- a school extends its opportunities for teacher collegiality and collaboration beyond the organization by means of networks (Jackson and Temperley, 2007);
- a climate of openness and trust prevails.

Leadership for teacher learning

O'Donoghue and Clarke (2010) deem that the key concepts for gaining an understanding of leadership for teacher learning are 'collaboration', 'collaboration and inclusive education' and inter-school collaborative activities.

Collaboration

It is desirable for teachers to:

- work collaboratively;
- be reflective practitioners;
- adopt a research stance in the classroom.

Fullan and Hargreaves (1996) were amongst the early educationists to argue that collaboration must be based on mutual enquiry and sharing in order to lay the foundations of a professional learning community. Collaboration, they held, enables:

- information and insights to be shared;
- common issues to be debated;
- innovative ideas to be tested.

Engaging in these processes is likely to enhance teachers' confidence and agency, both individually and collectively, in responding critically to change.

   Little (1990) identified the following kinds of collegial relations:

- mentoring;
- action research;
- peer coaching;
- planning and mutual observation;
- feedback.

He regarded these as having the potential to promote:

- interdependence;
- collective commitment;
- shared responsibility.

Collaboration and inclusive education

Within inclusive schools, collaboration requires joint communication and decision making amongst educational professionals (Hallinger and Heck, 2010) to create an optimal learning environment for students with 'exceptionalities'.

The expectation is that teachers should not only assist in identifying students with exceptionalities, but should also collaborate in the following areas:

- the creation of individual educational plans;
- seeking out the help of special educators;
- working with parents and school administrators.

Inter-school collaborative activities

Atkinson *et al.* (2007) have identified a number of inter-school collaborative activities which have implications for the enrichment of teachers' learning. These include:

- joint planning and school development projects sometimes entailing sharing of key staff;
- sharing of curriculum facilities such as sports amenities;
- joint purchase of information technology equipment.

Atkinson *et al.* (2007) go on to contend that such endeavours can provide opportunities to:

- exchange ideas and good practice;
- expand avenues for professional learning;
- refine teaching expertise;
- provide staff with outlets to share and voice any concerns with a larger number of colleagues.

An outcome of engaging in such activities, Jackson and Temperley (2007) claim, could be gains in staff confidence, motivation and morale.

Leadership for student learning

At present, a number of education systems place great emphasis on flexible student learning (Robinson, 2007). The following propositions provide an overview of what should be involved:

- Leadership for developing flexible learners should promote student self-regulated learning.
- Leadership for developing flexible learners should promote learning in the community.
- Leadership for developing flexible learners should promote learning which is problem-based.

O'Donoghue and Clarke (2010) deem that the key concepts for gaining an understanding of leadership for student learning are:

- the promotion of self-regulated learning;
- the promotion of learning in the community;
- the promotion of learning which is problem-based.

The promotion of student self-regulated learning

Students, according to Pintrich (1995), may regulate three different dimensions of their learning:

- their observable behaviour;
- their motivation and affect;
- their cognition.

He also identifies three components of self-regulated learning that function in relation to these dimensions:

- Self-regulated learners attempt to control their behaviour, motivation and affect, and cognition.
- There is some goal the student is attempting to accomplish.
- The individual student must be in control of his or her own actions.

The sorts of activities in which teachers can engage to promote student self-regulated learning are as follows:

- Motivation: this involves goal setting, self-talk, and arranging or imagining rewards or punishments for success or failure at an academic task.
- Methods of learning: these can include rehearsal strategies, elaboration strategies and representation or mapping strategies.
- Use of time: this can include getting students to develop greater awareness of their current time usage, asking students how they want to use their time, asking students to make a short-term plan for their use of time and asking students to report on the success or failure of their new approach to time management.
- Asking students to identify different types of distractors in their study environments that interfere with attention and concentration.
- Teaching students to interrupt their habitual non-productive thought processes that will guide them through problem situations. This can involve one asking such questions of oneself as the following: What is the problem? What is my plan? Am I using my plan? How did I do? (Dembo and Eaton, 2000).

The promotion of learning in the community

In cooperative classrooms, students and teachers are continually engaged in:

- observing;
- practising;
- giving feedback about the effectiveness of their cooperative skills.

The benefits of such practices can include:

- high achievement;
- deep understanding

- learning being enjoyable;
- the development of self-esteem;
- the promotion of a sense of belonging;
- the development of skills for the future;
- the acceptance of responsibility (Barth, 1991).

Teachers need to draw upon what is known about:

- the use of discussion in class (Brookfield, 1990);
- the value of small-group work whose distinguishing feature is that students from time to time work together without direct intervention by the teacher.

The promotion of learning that is problem-based

The development of flexible learners should involve seeking to promote problem solving as a unifying curricular ideal. There is no reason why this cannot take place within a subject-based curriculum. Drake (1998) promotes this view when emphasizing the importance of students engaging in:

- multidisciplinary-based work;
- interdisciplinary-based work;
- transdisciplinary-based work.

She advocates that this be done through engagement in projects aimed at developing students' problem solving capacities.

Some concluding comments

The study of education leadership is continuously evolving. Amongst recent trends is a renewed emphasis on the moral imperative of schooling (Fullan, 2003; Resick, 2013; Shields, 2010), collaborative leadership and school improvement (Hallinger and Heck, 2010), leadership for transforming schools (Wagner *et al.*, 2006), student-centred leadership (Robinson, 2011) and system leadership (Higham and Hopkins, 2009). It is likely that these areas of study and practice will continue to be emphasized in the immediate future and soon may even become the front-running notions of leadership.

   Another interesting position is that of Clarke (2015), who argues that because of the turbulence of the contemporary education environment it is necessary to adopt more flexible approaches to leadership than has traditionally been the case. One possible approach, he contends, could be based on the paradoxical concept of 'negative capability' 'and its potential value for enhancing school leadership in circumstances of uncertainty, change and complexity' (Clarke, 2015, p. 5). What is particularly useful is his outline of the practical ways in which individuals' sense of negative capability may be enriched, especially through promoting the 'inner leader' rather than observable competencies in school leadership development.

Issues for discussion

1 Harris and Muijs (2004, p. 65) have distilled from the literature six major activities of teacher leaders which require support and development.

    a   Identify these six conditions.

    b   Discuss how each of them could be operationalized in a school, college or university setting with which you are familiar.

2 'The foundation condition for teacher learning and leadership … is closely connected with the concept of "capacity building", or releasing the human potential available in an organization' (Harris and Muijs, 2004).

    a   What do you think is meant by 'capacity building' in the above quotation?

    b   What might it mean with regard to:

- shared values;
- social cohesion;
- trust;
- staff well-being;
- moral purpose;
- staff involvement;
- care;
- valuing;
- being valued?

3 Zimmerman has identified a cyclical approach to self-regulation (Zimmerman and Risenberg, 1997). This has the following components:

- self-observation and evaluation;
- goal-setting and strategic planning;
- strategy implementation and monitoring;
- strategic-outcome monitoring.

    a   How could these four steps be used to help students solve their own academic problems?

    b   How could they be used in giving students assignments whereby they are asked to identify a learning problem and conduct their own self-management study to develop and implement a plan to solve their problems?

    c   Do you think Zimmerman and Risenberg are justified in claiming that, in time, students can, as a result of regular engagement in assignments with such a focus, learn how to take responsibility for their own learning?

4 Read Clarke's (2015) paper and summarize his interpretation of the concept of 'negative capability'.

Do you think that the practical ways he outlines by which, he claims, individuals' sense of negative capability may be enriched are achievable?

References

Atkinson, M., Springate, I., Johnson, F. and Halsey, K. (2007). *Inter-school Collaboration: A Literature Review*. Slough: NFER.

Barth, R. S. (1991). *Improving Schools from Within*. San Francisco, CA: Jossey-Bass.

Brookfield, S. (1990). *The Skilful Teacher: On Technique, Trust, and Responsiveness in the Classroom*. San Francisco, CA: Jossey-Bass.

Clarke, S. (2015). School leadership in turbulent times and the value of negative capability. *Professional Development in Education*, Vol. 42, No. 1, pp. 5–18.

Dembo, M. H. and Eaton, M. J. (2000). Self-regulation of academic learning of middle-level schools. *The Elementary School Journal*, Vol. 100, No. 5, pp. 473–489.

Drake, S. (1998). *Creating Integrated Curriculum: Proven Ways to Increase Student Learning*. Thousand Oaks, CA: Corwin Press.

Driver, M. (2002). The learning organization: Foucauldian gloom or Utopian sunshine? *Human Relations*, Vol. 55, No. 1, pp. 33–53.

Fullan, M. (2003). *The Moral Imperative of Schooling*. Thousand Oaks, CA: Corwin Press..

Fullan, M. and Hargreaves, A. (1996). *What's Worth Fighting for in Your School?* New York: Teachers College, Columbia University.

Hallinger, P. and Heck, R. H. (2010). Collaborative leadership and school improvement: Understanding the impact on school capacity and student learning. *School Leadership and Management*, Vol. 30, No. 2, pp. 95–110.

Harris, A. and Mujis, D. (2004). *Improving Schools Through Teacher Leadership*. London: Open University Press.

Higham, R. and Hopkins, D. (2009). *System Leadership in Practice*. Maidenhead, Berkshire: Open University Press.

Jackson, D. and Temperley, J. (2007). From professional learning to networked learning community (pp. 45–62). In L. Stoll and K. Seashore-Louis (Eds), *Professional Learning Communities: Divergence, Depth and Dilemma*. Maidenhead, Berkshire: Open University Press.

Knapp, M. S., Copland, M. A., and McLaughlin, M. W. (2003). *Leading for Learning Sourcebook: Concepts and Examples*. Seattle: Center for Study of Teaching and Policy, University of Washington.

Little, J. W. (1990). The persistence of privacy: Autonomy and initiative in teachers' professional relations. *Teachers College Record*, Vol. 91, No. 4, pp. 509–536.

MacBeath, J. (2006). *Self-evaluation, Background Principles and Key Learning*. Nottingham, UK: National College for School leadership. http://dera.ioe.ac.uk/5951/3/self-evaluation-background-principles-and-key-learning.pdf.

MacGilchrist, B. (nd). *Leading the Intelligent School*. Nottingham, UK: National College for School Leadership.

MacGilchrist, B., Myers, K. and Reed, J. (1997). *The Intelligent School*. London: Paul Chapman Publishing Ltd.

O'Donoghue, T. A. and Clarke, S. (2010). *Leading Learning: Process, Themes and Issues in International Perspective*. London: Routledge.

Pintrich, P. R. (1995). *Understanding Self-regulated Learning*. San Francisco, CA: Jossey-Bass.

Resick, C. J. (2013). Ethical leadership, moral equity judgments, and discretionary workplace behavior. *Human Relations*, Vol. 66, No. 7, pp. 951–972.

Robinson, S. (2007). *School Leadership and Student Outcomes: Identifying What Works and Why*. Melbourne: ACEL Monograph Series.

Robinson, S. (2011). *Student-centred Leadership*. San Francisco, CA: Jossey-Bass.

Shields, C. M. (2010). Transformative leadership: Working for equity in diverse contexts. *EAQ: The Journal of Leadership for Effective and Equitable Organizations*, Vol. 40, No. 4, pp. 558–589.

Stoll, L., Bolam, R., McMahon, A., Wallace, A. and Thomas, S. (2006). Professional learning communities: A review of the literature. *Journal of Educational Change*, Vol. 7, No. 4, pp. 221–258.

Wagner, T., Kegan, R., Lahey, L., Lemons, R. W., Garnier, J., Helsing, D., Howell, A. and Rasmussen, H. T. (2006). *Change Leadership: A Practical Guide to Transforming Our Schools*. San Francisco, CA: Jossey-Bass.

Zimmerman, B. J. and Risenberg, R. (1997). Self-regulatory dimensions of academic learning and motivation (pp. 110–125). In G. H. Phye (Ed.), *Handbook of Academic Learning: Construction of Knowledge*. San Diego, CA: Academic Press.

24 Leadership in assessment for learning

In recent years a strong argument has been put forward advocating that 'assessment of learning' should be balanced by 'assessment for learning' (Berry, 2008; Stiggins *et al.*, 2007). School leaders have a central role to play in associated practices.

Background

The discourses on assessment throughout much of the twentieth century were centred largely on the school report and the written examination (O'Donoghue and Clarke, 2010). The school report often consisted of a set of marks achieved in school-based examinations on the various subjects studied, accompanied by a few comments on behaviour (Bryce, 2003). Much more importance was attached to external examinations at both primary and secondary school levels, often being set by examination boards.

Historically, as assessment became more formalized and technical, it developed around it a particular set of concepts, including the following.

Information gathering

This relates to such matters as the following:

- what students think;
- what students feel;
- what students are able to do.

It encompasses many activities, including:

- making observations about performance;
- administering tests;
- requiring students to express their ideas in writing.

In general, it involves measurement. This can be defined as being 'concerned with making comparisons against some established scale', often using a numerical score (Smith and Lovat, 2003, p. 171).

Assessment

This involves interpreting measurement information. Historically, this has meant assigning a mark or grade to a student's performance, sometimes accompanied by qualitative comments about the work. The outcome of assessment allows one to:

- compare a student with himself or herself at some previous period in time;
- compare a student with himself or herself with other students at the present time and previously;
- compare a student against some notion of the ideal performance in what is assessed.

The two major approaches to assessment that have prevailed are norm-referenced assessment and criterion-referenced assessment.

Norm-referenced assessment

The properties of norm-referenced assessment are as follows:

- The performance of one student is compared with another.
- The same measuring 'tools' are used.
- Steps are taken to try to ensure that the contexts within which the data are collected are as similar as possible.

The most usual forms which such assessments take are external examinations and standardized tests.

Criterion-referenced assessment

The properties of criterion-referenced assessment are as follows:

- Comparison is made against a standard set of criteria.
- The criteria may relate to:
  - the content of the material measured;
  - the process of arriving at the result;
  - both of the above.

While the specification of the criteria is a subjective matter, often they are arrived at through agreement on the part of experts in the field.

Evaluation

Evaluation involves arriving at an overall composite judgement after:

- bringing together much of the information gathered;
- bringing together much of the assessment undertaken.

This can lead to a decision.

Formative evaluation

This involves the making of judgements on the basis of the results of assessment undertaken as students engage in learning activities. This is to assist the teacher to discover:

- what the students know about a topic already;
- whether students have understood the task set;
- 'whether instructions are clear and sufficient' (Smith and Lovat, 2003, p. 170).

It means that:

- it can play a diagnostic role;
- the outcomes can be provided to students as a motivational device;
- the outcomes can assist students and their parents in monitoring progress.

Summative evaluation

This takes place at the end of a unit, programme or course to:

- try to determine if students engaged in the intended activities:
- try to determine if the intended outcomes were realized;
- investigate possible reasons for the processes which actually took place;
- investigate possible reasons for the outcomes realized.

The case for 'assessment for learning'

For many years teachers, students and parents were focused primarily on summative evaluation. This was, as it still is today, because of the role that examinations play in providing entry to various occupations and to higher education. In recent times, however, formative assessment has been receiving a significant amount of attention. The key concept in this movement is that of 'assessment for learning'.

The remainder of this account is based on that by O'Donoghue and Clarke (2010). They point out that the origin of the 'assessment for learning' movement is often attributed to the influence of the research evidence made available by Black and William (1998) and the more recent summary of the evidence on studies demonstrating improvements in student achievement by Broadfoot and Black (2004). The central proposition generated from these and related works is that formative assessment, when suitably employed, can play a major role in improving student learning. Stiggins (2002, p. 8) has summarized this proposition as follows: 'Achievement gains are maximised in contexts where educators increase the accuracy of classroom assessments, provide students with frequent informative feedback (versus judgemental feedback), and involve students deeply in the classroom assessment, record keeping, and communication processes.'

- providing information to teachers to help them modify their teaching and learning activities;
- developing and supporting students' metacognition.

This is a view, as she put it, of 'students as active, engaged and critical assessors' who 'make sense of information, relate it to prior knowledge and use it for new learning' (2005, p. 10).

James *et al.* (2007, p. 6) identified the following as being likely to assist in the latter process:

- clarifying goals;
- clarifying criteria;
- reflecting on learning;
- promoting peer assessment;
- promoting self-assessment.

It may also be argued that these sorts of practices contribute to supporting pupils as flexible learners.

In similar vein, Cauley and McMillan (2005, p. 5) have summarized the evidence as follows:

> Formative assessment and, in particular, feedback and instructional correctives, can be a powerful technique to support student motivation and achievement. As teachers incorporate more formative assessment techniques into their day-to-day instruction, they will have information which they can use to modify their instruction. Teachers can also use this information about student understanding to help students self-assess and improve their own performance. When students focus on improvement and progress, they are more likely to adopt mastery goals and develop high self-efficacy and expectations for success. When students and teachers attribute student successes to effort, this attribution supports future successes. Formative assessment's emphasis on instructional modifications and student improvement supports student motivation and enables them to maintain high engagement and achievement. Using formative assessments effectively is indeed key to student motivation and achievement.

Stiggins (2002) has distinguished between 'assessment for learning' and formative assessment. In his view, while both involve teachers testing more frequently and providing students with evidence so that instruction approaches can be revised, 'assessment for learning' also involves students (Stiggins, 2002, p. 5). Successful assessors of learning, he points out:

- understand and articulate in advance of teaching the achievement targets that their students are to hit;
- inform their students about those learning goals, in terms that students understand, from the very beginning of the teaching and learning process;
- become assessment literate and thus able to transform their expectations into assessment exercises and scoring procedures that accurately reflect student achievement;
- use classroom assessments to build students' confidence in themselves as learners and help them take responsibility for their own learning, so as to lay a foundation for lifelong learning;
- translate classroom assessment results into frequent descriptive feedback (versus judgemental feedback) for students, providing them with specific insights as to how to improve;
- continuously adjust instruction based on the results of classroom assessments;

- engage students in regular self-assessment, with standards held constant so that students can watch themselves grow over time and thus feel in charge of their own success;
- involve students in communication with their teacher and their families about their achievement status and improvement.

Stiggins (2002) does not argue that in the promotion of 'assessment for learning' we should neglect 'assessment of learning'. Rather, in referring specifically to the situation in the USA, he states that what is needed is the following:

- Match every dollar invested in instruments and procedures intended for 'assessment of learning' at national, state and local levels with another dollar devoted to the development of 'assessment for learning'.
- Launch a comprehensive, long-term professional development programme at the national, state and local levels to foster literacy in classroom assessment for teachers, allocating sufficient resources to provide them with the opportunity to learn and grow professionally.
- Launch a similar professional development programme in effective large-scale and classroom assessment for state, district and building administrators, teaching them how to provide leadership in this area of professional practice.
- Change teacher and administrator licensing standards in every state and in all national certification contexts to reflect an expectation of competence in assessment both of and for learning.
- Require all teacher and administrator preparation programmes to ensure that graduates are assessment literate – in terms of promoting and of documenting student learning.

He concludes by arguing that Federal education officials, state policy makers and local school leaders need to allocate resources in equal proportions to ensure that teachers engage in 'assessment for learning' along with 'assessment of learning'.

International tests as possible constrainers of 'assessment for learning'

The foundations of the international assessments of students' performance-movement were laid down over 50 years ago with the establishment of the International Association for the Evaluation of Educational Achievement (IEA). Since then the Association has conducted assessments of the effectiveness of different education systems and identified factors related to student achievement (Owen, 2001, p. 4). A major outcome has been competition between countries.

The 1990s witnessed the following associated developments:

- two administrations of the IEA's Trends in International Mathematics and Science Study (TIMS), which by 1995 was the largest study of student achievement undertaken to date;
- the IEA Reading Literacy Study (RLS), conducted in 1990–1991 in 32 countries;
- three administrations of data collection for the International Adult Literacy Survey (IALS) in a total of 20 countries between 1994 and 1998;
- the OECD's establishment of the Programme for International Student Assessment (PISA).

There is some debate about whether the initiators of these developments had hoped to insulate the results from both extensive media coverage and those with political agendas to legitimate practices that governments already wish to implement on ideological grounds.

Certain questions relating to technical matters have also been raised, including:

- whether the tests measure what they claim to measure;
- the extent to which cultural differences may bias results;
- the extent to which performance on tests can be generalized beyond the items on the test (Rochex, 2004).

There is also very little evidence from the many countries involved in such tests that the results are put to productive use as 'assessment for learning' (O'Donoghue and Clarke, 2010). In fact, they appear to act to constrain the process by promoting a 'teaching to the test' approach, in the belief that this will help maximize the nation's results and increase its prestige in the international academic league tables.

Issues for discussion

1   Do you have schools' inspectors in your country?

- Do you think they could act as constrainers of assessment? How?
- In what ways might they add to the demands of teachers and generate anxieties?
- How might leaders act to address this in order to maintain motivation and commitment to the profession?

2   What, in your view, should be the crucial criteria for appointment as an inspector? How do these relate to the actual criteria that operate for appointment in your country?

3   In certain education systems inspectors engage teachers in 'whole school evaluation'. What, in your view, is the value of this practice in relation to:

- school ethos;
- staffing;
- accommodation;
- curriculum;
- learning and teaching;
- support for learning;
- care and welfare;
- leadership?

4   How can schools be involved in critically examining themselves in relation to:

- national priorities and targets;
- priorities of the local authority in which they are located;
- individual school development plans?

(continued)

5   When the national curriculum was introduced in England and Wales it appeared as if the requirement that teachers be involved in the assessment process as part of their normal teaching could serve both formative and summative functions. On 20 February 2009, however, the *Guardian* newspaper summarized as follows the main findings of the Cambridge Primary Review, which had conducted a wide-ranging and independent enquiry into the condition and future of primary education in England:

- Children are losing out on a broad, balanced and rich curriculum with art, music, drama, history and geography being the biggest casualties.
- The curriculum, and crucially English and maths, have been 'politicized'.
- The focus on literacy and numeracy in the run-up to national tests has 'squeezed out' other areas of learning.
- The Department for Children, Schools and Families and the Qualifications and Curriculum Authority, which sets the curriculum, have been excessively prescriptive, 'micro-managing' schools.

Do you consider that such criticisms could be levelled at the situation in your own country at this point in time?
Give reasons for your answers.

References

Berry, R. (2008). *Assessment for Learning*. Hong Kong: Hong Kong University Press.

Black, P. and William, D. (1998). Inside the black box. Raising standards through classroom assessment. *Phi Delta Kappan*, Vol. 80, No. 2, pp. 139–148.

Broadfoot, P. and Black, P. (2004). Redefining assessment? The first ten years of assessment in education. *Assessment in Education*, Vol. 11, No. 1, pp. 7–25.

Bryce, T. (2003). Could do better? Assessment in Scottish schools (pp. 709–720). In T. G. K. Bryce and W. M. Hume (Eds), *Scottish Education: Post Devolution*. Edinburgh: Edinburgh University Press.

Cauley, K. M. and McMillan, J. H. (2010). Formative assessment techniques to support student motivation and achievement, *The Clearing House: A Journal of Educational Strategies, Issues and Ideas*, Vol. 83, No. 1, pp. 1–6.

Earl, L. (2005). *Thinking About Purpose in Classroom Assessment*. Canberra: Australian Curriculum Studies Association.

James, M., McCormick, R., Black, P., Carmichael, P., Drummond, M. J., Fox, A., MacBeath, J., Marshall, B., Pedder, D., Procter, R., Swaffield, S., Swann, J. and William, D. (Eds). (2007). *Improving Learning How to Learn. Classroom, Schools and Networks*. Abingdon, Oxon: Routledge.

O'Donoghue, T. A. and Clarke, S. (2010). *Leading Learning: Process, Themes and Issues in International Perspective*. London: Routledge.

Owen, R. G. (2001). *Organizational Behavior in Education: Instructional Leadership and School Reform*. Boston, MA: Allyn and Bacon.

Rochex, J. Y. (2004). Social, methodological and theoretical issues regarding assessment: Lessons from a secondary analysis of PISA 2000 literacy tests (pp. 163–212). In G. Green and A. Luke (Eds), *Review of Research in Education, 30: Special Issue On 'Rethinking Learning: What Counts As Learning And What Learning Counts'*. Washington, DC: American Educational Research Association.

Smith, D. L. and Lovat, T. J. (2003). *Curriculum: Action on Reflection*. Tuggerah, NSW: Social Science Press.

Stiggins, R. J. (2002). Assessment crisis: The absence of assessment FOR learning. *Phi Delta Kappan*, 6 June, pp. 1–10.

Stiggins, R. J., Arter, J. A., Chappuis, J. and Chappuis, S. (2007). *Classroom Assessment for Student Learning. Doing it Right – Using it Well*. Upper Saddle River, NJ: Pearson.

25 Leadership for change

For many years educationists have argued that, in order to maximize the possibility that any proposed change in education will be successful, one needs to engage in 'situation analysis' (Endsley and Garland, 2009) and take account of what the research literature has to say about 'implementation'. This chapter provides an overview of this perspective.

Situation analysis

The reference to 'situation' in 'situation analysis' refers to 'the initial state in which the learner finds himself/herself' (Marsh, 1992). The point is that it would be folly to enact any set of education proposals without analysing what this state is. Also, while proponents recognize that many educationists are able to do this intuitively and quickly, they argue that it is worthwhile addressing it systematically by using a framework in which they distinguish between external factors to a school and internal factors to a school. The framework usually offered (Marsh, 1992, p. 79) is as follows.

Analysis of external factors to the school

- changes and trends in society which indicate tasks for schools – e.g. industrial development, political directives, cultural movements, ideological shifts;
- expectations and requirements of parents and employers;
- community assumptions and values, including patterns of adult–child relations;
- the changing nature of the subject disciplines;
- the potential contribution of teacher support systems; including teacher's centres, colleges of education and universities;
- actual and anticipated flow of resources in the school.

Analysis of the internal factors to the school

- pupils, their aptitudes, abilities, attitudes, values and defined educational needs;
- teachers, their values, attitudes, skills, knowledge, experience and special strengths and weaknesses;
- school ethos and political structure, common assumptions and expectations, including traditions, power distribution;

- material resources, including plant, equipment and learning materials;
- perceived and felt problems and shortcomings in existing curriculum.

Frameworks along this line were also devised by English and Kaufman (1975), by Soliman *et al.* (1981), by UNESCO (2004) and by The United Nations (2012). The important point on them made by Marsh and Stafford (1988, p. 107) is that they need to be used by school-based leaders to collect lots of data so that 'those involved in site-specific curriculum planning can be alerted to how their plans, cherished hopes and strategies' can not only be facilitated, but also thwarted, by the school context

While this approach has for long been advocated by curriculum theorists, it has, in more recent years, also been proposed by those who study education leadership and who realize the importance of attending to context if one is to maximize the possibility of successfully enacting educational policies and associated practices. For example:

- Gronn and Ribbins (1996) posited clearly that the approach to educational leadership in any particular circumstance needs to take that circumstance into account.
- Dimmock and Walker (1997), drawing their examples primarily from Confucian-based learning settings, highlighted the Eurocentric nature of much research, writing and practices in relation to leadership in schools. Overall, they succeeded in illustrating persuasively that different cultures have different approaches to leadership and that these have solid cultural foundations.
- Clarke and Wildy (2004) reported investigations into the ways leadership was understood and practised in the distinctive environment of the small, remote school.
- Walker (2004) provided insights from his study of the idiosyncratic characteristics of leadership in multi-ethnic schools.
- Dimmock (2005) argued that while many were writing about the appropriateness and virtues of particular approaches to leadership, very little attention was being paid to the specific contexts within which it was being exercised.
- Fitzgerald (2003a, 2003b, 2004) drew attention to how educational leadership might be practised differently by females, by indigenous leaders and by female indigenous leaders.
- Shah (2005) highlighted how the student population across much of the world is increasingly reflective of diverse cultures, religions and ethnicities. This rich diversity, she argued, could become a challenge for educational leaders, teachers and policy makers in the absence of an understanding of the diverse sources of knowledge that people draw on for directing their beliefs and daily practices.
- Clarke and O'Donoghue (2013) have illustrated the importance of educational leaders at the school level working in post-conflict societies paying attention to the contexts in which they work.

Principles of implementation for leaders

What can be learned from studies of successful and unsuccessful innovations?

A great number of studies have been carried out on successful and unsuccessful innovations. We can learn much from these for future practice. At least three ways of considering what we can learn can be considered. The following is a summary of the first of these as outlined by Marsh (2008).

Typical reasons for the failure of projects

- originated by outside experts;
- difficult to manage;
- inadequate planning;
- not understood by teachers;
- parents did not understand it.

The characteristics of an innovation that predict a high probability of success are implicit in the following questions

The following is also a summary of an outline by Marsh (2008):

Relative advantage (compared with what exists)

- Will it be more effective in promoting learning?
- Will it conserve resources more efficiently?
- Will it have a positive impact on the total programme?

Compatibility (consistent with values, experiences, needs)

- Will it fit well with other aspects of the programme?
- Will it be accepted?

Testability (can it be tried on an experimental basis?)

- Has it been tested in schools like ours?
- Can it be pilot tested?
- Can we use selected parts?

Observability (can it be seen in action?)

- Can we see a live demo with children?
- Can we see a videotaped demo?
- Can we see variations in its application?

Complexity (ease of use)

- Will teachers need special training?
- Will it add to teachers' paperwork?

Maximizing the possibility that an innovation will be accepted and will persist

The following principles have been deduced from a number of scholarly works, including Adams and Chen (1981), Adamson *et al.* (2000), Fadeeva *et al.* (2014) and Marsh (1992).

The acceptance of an innovation is a function of:

- the power that can be marshalled in its support;
- the extent to which, as a change agent, it is seen not to threaten existing power structures;
- the extent to which the expected benefits are thought to outweigh the cost involved;
- the observation of negotiation protocols;
- the extent to which the rhetoric used conveys similarity to the status quo.

The persistence of an innovation is a function of:

- the extent to which the innovation is perceived as credible by those expected to implement it;
- the outcome of both formative and summative evaluations;
- the availability of a critical mass of resources – personnel, plant and equipment;
- the stability of personnel.

More recently, Goodson (2001) proposed a model that stressed the importance of taking external, internal and personal influences in an institution into consideration. On this, he identified the following four issues that need to be addressed in this regard:

1   *Mission: institutionalize new purposes*: even though the mission of a particular curriculum change may arise external to the institution, to succeed it must become part of the mission of those within it.
2   *Micro-politics: re-negotiate school practices*: there must be an internal re-negotiation of professional practices of those who work most closely with a curriculum change and this must be handled delicately in each situation.
3   *Memory work: engage the community*: it is necessary to take cognizance of local opinion and to develop community awareness of new reforms.
4   *Movement: generalize to other schools*: often, for a curriculum change to be successful a school needs to form coalitions with other similarly minded schools so that chains of support will become available.

Issues for discussion

1   Do you consider that it is important to engage in situation analysis regarding curriculum at the school, college and university level?
Give reasons for your answer.
Address how the answer to this question might be different if you work in an environment where the curriculum is centrally prescribed as opposed to an environment where it is developed locally.

2   Do you consider that it is important to engage in situation analysis regarding teaching and learning at the school, college and university level?
Give reasons for your answer.
Again, address how the answer to this question might be different for one who works in an environment where the curriculum is centrally prescribed as opposed to that for one who works in an environment where it can be developed locally.

3   If you have answered 'yes' to each of the above questions ask yourself if there are any possible problems associated with this point of view.

4   Consider the curriculum in a situation with which you are familiar.
Would you like to see any aspect of it changed?
If so, how would you like to see it changed?
How would you go about bringing about the change?

5   Consider any approach to teaching and learning in a situation with which you are familiar.
Would you like to see any aspect of it changed?
If so, how would you like to see it changed?
How would you go about bringing about the change?

6   Consider any approach to management and administration in a situation with which you are familiar.
Would you like to see any aspect of it changed?
If so, how would you like to see it changed?
How would you go about bringing about the change?

7   McNeil (1985, p. 203) has challenged us to describe a situation in which one or more of the following conditions exist:

   * a social climate conducive to change;
   * an imbalance in the power structure;
   * a crisis;
   * an element of self-interest.

What kind of a policy change could be successfully implemented in view of the condition(s) described?

(continued)

> What kind of a curriculum change could be successfully implemented in view of the condition(s) described?
>
> What kind of a pedagogical change could be successfully implemented in view of the condition(s) described?
>
> What kind of leadership change could be successfully implemented in view of the condition(s) described?

References

Adams, R. S. and Chen, D. (1981). *The Process of Educational Innovation: An International Perspective.* London: Kogan Page.

Adamson, B., Kwan, T. and Chan, K. K. (2000). *Changing the Curriculum: The Impact of Reform on Primary Schooling in Hong Kong.* Hong Kong: Hong Kong University Press.

Clarke, S. and O'Donoghue, T. A. (Eds). (2013). *School-level Leadership in Post-conflict Societies: The Importance of Context.* London: Routledge.

Clarke, S. and Wildy, H. (2004). Context counts: Viewing small school leadership from the inside out. *Journal of Educational Administration*, Vol. 42, No. 5, pp. 555–572.

Dimmock, C. (2005). The leadership of multi-ethnic schools: What we know and don't know about values-driven leadership. *Educational Research and Perspectives*, Vol. 32, No. 2, pp. 80–96.

Dimmock, C. and Walker, A. (1997). Comparative educational administration: Developing a cross-cultural conceptual framework. *Educational Administration Quarterly*, Vol. 34, No. 4, pp. 558–595.

Endsley, M. R. and Garland, D. J. (Eds). (2009). *Situation Awareness Analysis and Measurement.* New York: Routledge.

English, F. W. and Kaufman, R. A. (1975). *Needs Assessment: A Focus for Curriculum Development.* Alexandria, VA: Association for Curriculum Development.

Fadeeva, Z., Galkute, L., Mader, C. and Scott, G. (2014). *Sustainable Development and Quality Assurance in Higher Education.* New York: Palgrave Macmillan.

Fitzgerald, T. (2003a). Interrogating orthodox voices: Gender, ethnicity and educational leadership. *School Leadership and Management*, Vol. 23, No. 4, pp. 431–444.

Fitzgerald, T. (2003b). Changing the deafening silence of indigenous women's voices in educational leadership. *Journal of Educational Administration*, Vol. 41, No. 1, pp. 9–23.

Fitzgerald, T. (2004). Powerful voices and powerful stories: Reflections on the challenges and dynamics of intercultural research. *Journal of Intercultural Studies*, Vol. 25, No. 3, pp. 233–245.

Goodson, I. (2001). Educational change and professional biography. Paper presented at the Annual Conference of the American Educational Research Association, Chicago.

Gronn, P. and Ribbins, P. (1996). Leaders in context: Postpositivist approaches to understanding school leadership. *Educational Administration Quarterly*, Vol. 32, No. 3, pp. 452–473.

Marsh, C. (1992). *Key Concepts for Understanding Curriculum.* London: The Falmer Press.

Marsh, C. (2008). *Becoming a Teacher: Knowledge, Skills and Issues.* French Forest, NSW: Pearson.

Marsh, C. and Stafford, K. (1988). *Curriculum: Practices and Issues.* Sydney: McGraw-Hill.

McNeil, J. D. (1985). *Curriculum: A Comprehensive Introduction.* Boston, MA: Little, Brown and Company.

Shah, S. (2005). Educational leadership: An Islamic perspective. *British Educational Research Journal*, Vol. 32, No. 3, pp. 363–385.

Soliman, I., Dawes, L., Gough, J. and Maxwell, T. (1981). *A Model for School-based Curriculum Development.* Canberra: Curriculum Development Centre.

UNESCO (2004). *FRESH Tools for Effective School Health.* Paris: UNESCO.

United Nations (2012). Situation analysis (np). In United Nations, Virtual Knowledge Centre to End Violence Against Women and Girls. New York: United Nations Entity for the Gender Equality and the Empowerment of Women.

Walker, A. (2004). *Priorities, Strategies and Challenges. Proactive Leadership in Multi-ethnic Schools.* Nottingham, UK: National College for School Leadership.

26 Some challenging positions for leaders in education

The position underpinning this chapter is that education leaders should not see their role as simply perpetuating the status quo. Rather, they should constantly reflect on it. One valuable way of doing this is for them to consider their situation in relation to challenging positions from a wide variety of perspectives. A separate text could be produced to assist education leaders in this process. A much more modest approach is adopted here, namely, presenting some challenging sociological, pedagogical and management positions in education.

Education and social reproduction

In their book on education in capitalist America, Bowles and Gintis (1976) argued that education cannot be understood independently of the society of which it is a part. On this, they held that it serves to perpetuate or 'reproduce' the capitalist system. The following account is based on the summary by Blackledge and Hunt (1985) on how this is supposed to take place in schools.

Legitimation

Bowles and Gintis (1976) argued that the education system transmits the ideology of equal educational opportunity and meritocracy. They promoted the view that schools justify inequalities of income, wealth and status to students on the grounds that the most valued positions in society need to be filled by the most talented. Because these people need to undergo a lengthy period of preparation, often at significant cost, they need to be rewarded with high incomes and prestige. Bowles and Gintis' view, however, is that, in general, it is one's position in society in the first instance, rather than one's ability, that is the most significant factor in determining if one is able to embark on such a course of preparation.

Socialization

On this, Bowles and Gintis (1976, p. 127) stated: 'It is clear that the consciousness of workers – beliefs, values, self-concepts, types of solidarity and fragmentation, as well as modes of personal behaviour and development – are integral to the perpetuation, validation and smooth operation of economic institutions.' All of these, they hold, develop in a person's social relationships, including in the education system. Schools, so their argument goes, reward:

- docility;
- passivity;
- obedience.

Schools also, in their view, penalize:

- creativity;
- spontaneity.

They do this, it is argued, because industry requires a compliant and obedient workforce in order to maximize profits.

The correspondence principle

Blackledge and Hunt (1985) summarize this principle of Bowles and Gintis as follows:

- Students, like workers, have little power: their control over the curriculum is minimal and is similar, therefore, to that of the workers over the content of their jobs.
- Education, like work, is seen as a means to an end rather than an end in itself. Neither are intrinsically satisfying but are undertaken:

  o   for the sake of 'external' rewards – qualifications and wages;
  o   to avoid unpleasant consequences – educational failure and unemployment.

- The division of labour at work, which confers on each person a narrow range of tasks and engenders a disunity among the workforce, is repeated in the specialization and compartmentalization of knowledge, and in the unnecessary competition between students.
- The different 'levels' of education correspond to, and prepare people for, the different 'levels' of the occupational structure. In secondary schools the stress is on 'doing as you are told'. In higher education, such 'external' controls become inappropriate; students are now expected to get on with their work unsupervised and be self-directing.

Education, social class and language

Blackledge and Hunt (1985, pp. 134–148) summarized Bernstein's (1977) position on education, social class and language. Put simply, they stated, he argued that:

- Members of one group in society adopt a 'positional approach' to their children in which:

  o   the demands they make on the child are related to his or her age, sex and status;
  o   the child learns that what is expected of him or her depends on factors outside of his or her control;
  o   the child also learns that parts of life are divorced from each other – the life of the baby, child and youth are separated and unrelated;
  o   family socialization is characterized by 'strong classification' of language;

  ○ they use a 'restricted' code of language. This code works on the assumption that the lis-tener has the same experience as the speaker and has an implicit understanding of the speaker's meanings.

- Members of another group adopt a 'personal' approach to the raising of their children in which:

  ○ they are sensitive to the changes and development of the child;
  ○ they modify their demands and expectations as the child develops;
  ○ the child learns that the different parts of his life are related and flow into each other, because of the way he or she has been treated by his or her parents;
  ○ family socialization is characterized by 'weak classification' of language;
  ○ they use an 'elaborated' code of language that allows its user to see relationships between aspects of experience that are hidden to users of the 'restricted' code and it enables people to make explicit their meanings. This is the code of education. Thus, middle-class students who arrive in school with the elaborated code are better placed for educational success than working-class children.

The importance of encouraging solitude

Deresiewicz (2009) holds that while the current emphasis on the use of social media in education is valuable, it needs to be accompanied by a reinstatement of an emphasis on solitude. His argument is that the contemporary self wants to be recognized, to be connected, to be visible. The great contemporary terror is anonymity.

 In developing his argument, Deresiewicz holds that ICT is taking away our privacy, our concentration and our ability to be alone. He draws particular attention to the fact that solitude has traditionally been a societal value which was democratized by the Reformation and secularized by Romanticism. It accommodated reading which, for many, became an act of great inwardness and subjectivity, facilitating self-discovery. By the latter half of the twentieth century, however, our great fear, he holds, was isolation from the herd. As he put it:

> The child who grew up between the world wars as part of an extended family within a tight-knit urban community became the grandparent of a kid who sat alone in front of a big television, in a big house, on a big lot. We were lost in space.
>
> (Deresiewicz, 2009, np)

The advent of the internet was promoted as an antidote to the latter position on the grounds that it would allow isolated people to communicate with one another and allow marginalized people to find one another, which it did for a while, and still does in many cases.

 Deresiewicz goes on to say, however, that as the internet's dimensionality has grown, it has quickly become too much of a good thing. On this, he elaborates as follows:

> Ten years ago we were writing e-mail messages on desktop computers and transmitting them over dial-up connections. Now we are sending text messages on our cell phones, posting pictures on our Facebook pages, and following complete strangers on Twitter.
>
> (Deresiewicz, 2009, np)

The goal of the individual now, as he sees it, is simply to become known, to turn oneself into a sort of miniature celebrity, where one is regularly asking oneself the following sorts of questions:

- How many friends do I have on Facebook?
- How many people are reading my blog?
- How many Google hits does my name generate?

Visibility, Deresiewicz holds, secures our self-esteem, becoming a substitute, twice removed, for genuine connection. Not long ago, it was easy to feel lonely. Now, it is impossible to be alone. Regarding the latter, Deresiewicz makes the following points:

- Young people today seem to have no desire for solitude, have never heard of it, can't imagine why it would be worth having. In fact, their use of technology seems to involve a constant effort to stave off the possibility of solitude. Yet, the more we keep aloneness at bay, the less are we able to deal with it and the more terrifying it gets.
- The inability to sit still; 100 text messages a day creates the aptitude for loneliness, the inability to be by yourself. They have lost the ability to be alone, their capacity for solitude.

And in losing solitude, he holds, people have lost:

- the propensity for introspection, that examination of the self;
- the related propensity for sustained reading. The internet has remapped our attention spans: 'reading now means skipping and skimming; five minutes on the same web page is considered an eternity' (Deresiewicz, 2009, np).

Steiner schools

Rudolf Steiner (1861–1925) established Steiner or Waldorf schools. The first Waldorf school was opened in 1919 in Stuttgart, Germany. Currently, there are thousands of independent Waldorf schools around the world. Steiner adopted a humanistic approach to pedagogy, emphasizing the role of imagination in learning and striving to integrate holistically the students' intellectual, practical and artistic development. He also placed a major emphasis on hands-on activity.

When conducted in a manner that shows total fidelity to the principles of their founder, Steiner schools do not have school principals, directors or superintendents (Oberman, 1997). Rather, the sorts of responsibilities usually performed by these individuals are dispersed amongst:

- a college of teachers;
- a board of trustees, or a board of directors;
- paid-administrators and/or an administrative committee.

Where teachers do perform administrative duties they are not entitled to greater decision making power than others involved in the school, nor are they expected to be the sole providers of school leadership. Sometimes they are referred to as 'powerful powerless people'; powerful because they administer the budget, but powerless because they do not determine its distribution. Even choosing students for particular classrooms is conducted by a committee with the classroom teacher; administrators do not assign students to classrooms.

The real power in Waldorf schools is held by teachers and staff members who have made a special commitment to the care and growth of the school. These individuals belong to the College of Teachers, which provides spiritual and pedagogical guidance to the school. During college meetings, usually held weekly, teachers make decisions regarding any issue that has pedagogical implications. These include development of academic standards, teacher evaluation, dress code, expulsion and the hiring and firing of teachers.

Most college work is conducted in committees. Some committees such as 'prospective teachers committee' or 'the high school committee' are often open only to college members. Other committees might be open to both college and board members, and others yet again are open to everyone. Each major committee has at least one college member on it. By diffusing power into smaller committees and then ensuring that college teachers serve on them, the college retains control of the school.

Waldorf schools are usually formed by parents. Those who are most active form a board of directors to govern the school (Stehlik, 2003). They are responsible for legal and financial affairs and attempt to promote effective development efforts. The board usually meets once a month. The board's ultimate liability requires a close working relationship between the board and college in order for the school to run smoothly. The functions of the board include legal incorporation, financial overview, budget review and approval, fund raising, the planning of building developments and advising to the faculty of 'general issues'.

Issues for discussion

Regarding education and social reproduction

1 One might argue that Bowles and Gintis are wrong in their analysis. To do so, however, would be to presuppose that they claimed they were right. This would not be correct if in fact their claim is that what they gave us is not fact, but a theory.
   Discuss.

2 Bowles and Gintis assert that creativity is not rewarded in education. However, many would argue that education does foster and reward creativity.
   Discuss.

3 Bowles and Gintis make little reference to the content of education. This suggests it is unimportant in the process of reproduction.
   Do you think that this may be an odd omission? Why?

Regarding education, social class and language

4 Do you think that the distinctions made by Bernstein are as clear-cut as he suggests they are?
   Even if they are so, does it mean that one is condemned to remain in one group or another?

(continued)

5   In an age of mass communication is it not possible for everyone to develop an elabo-rated code of language?

6   What do you know about the effects on the literacy levels of those from deprived back-grounds where there is lack of reading material in the home, and parents who do not engage in reading to any significant extent?

7   How might this group suffer educationally during vacation breaks from not engaging in reading?
What might this tell us about the folly of relying on schools alone to develop students' literacy levels?

8   Cultural capital is a process of powerful practices: ways of behaving, talking, acting, thinking, moving and so on. These practices are determined unconsciously by the dominant culture and are used to promote success for specific groups in our society? (Wink, 2011, p. 63).
Discuss.

9   Consider the following quotation:

> I argue that deficit-based teacher talk about students and families of color reflects and may reinforce teachers' low expectations and negative assumptions about stu-dents of color. Low expectations for students may diminish teachers' sense of self-efficacy and professional responsibility, while justifying differential teaching practices, policies, and teacher behaviors – all of which are associated with inferior educational experiences and opportunities for students of color.
>
> (Pollack, 2012, p. 888)

What do you think, within this context, is meant by 'deficit-based teacher talk'?
Is it possible that a particular reading of Bernstein's position might encourage us to engage in such deficit thinking?
If so, how might this manifest itself?
How could we learn from Bernstein's work and not become involved in deficit thinking?

10 MacRuairc (2011) has highlighted research that has pointed to the benefits for chil-dren's learning when schools take account of, rather than negate, children's home lan-guage in the teaching and learning process.
What do you think these benefits are?
What practices might a school engage in that could negate children's home language in the teaching and learning process?
What practices might a school engage in that would take account of children's home language in the teaching and learning process?

Regarding the importance of encouraging solitude

11 Discuss the following claims made by Deresiewicz (2009, np):

- Solitude enables us to secure the integrity of the self as well as to explore it. We are not merely social beings. We are each also separate, each solitary, each alone in our own room, each miraculously our unique selves and mysteriously enclosed in that selfhood.
- To hold oneself apart from society is to begin to think one's way beyond it. Historically the university facilitated this. Today it does everything possible to keep students from being alone, 'lest they perpetrate unfashionable thoughts'.
- No real excellence, personal or social, artistic, philosophical, scientific or moral, can arise without solitude.

Regarding Steiner schools

12 Read and discuss the views on Steiner education in the following sources:

Lee, A. (2012). What every parent should know about Steiner-Waldorf schools. *The Quackometer*. www.quackometer.net/blog/2012/11/what-every-parent-should-know-about-steiner-waldorf-schools.html

Sklan, S. (2014). Extremist: Steiner schools are no such thing. *Guardian (Australian edition)*, 22 July.

References

Bernstein, B. (1977). *Class, Codes and Control*. London: Routledge and Kegan Paul.

Blackledge, D. and Hunt, B. (1985). *Sociological Interpretations of Education*. London: Routledge.

Bowles, S. and Gintis, H. (1976). *Schooling in Capitalist America*. London: Routledge and Kegan Paul.

Deresiewicz, W. (2009). The end of solitude. *The Chronicle of Higher Education*, 30 January.

MacRuairc, G. (2011). They're my words – I'll talk how I like! Examining social class and linguistic practice among primary school children. *Language and Education*, Vol. 25, No. 6, pp. 535–559.

Oberman, I. (1997). Waldorf history. Case study of institutional memory. Paper presented to Annual Meeting of the American Education Research Association, 24–28 March.

Pollack, T. M. (2012). Unpacking everyday 'teacher talk' about students and families of color. Implications for teacher and school leader development. *Urban Education*, Vol. 48, No. 6, pp. 863–894.

Stehlik T. (2003). Parenting as a vocation. *International Journal of Lifelong Education*, Vol. 22, No. 4, pp. 367–379.

Wink, J. (2011). *Critical Pedagogy: Notes from the Real World*. Boston, MA: Pearson.

Part VI
Teacher preparation

27 The evolution of teacher preparation

The evolution of approaches to teacher preparation has varied from country to country (Fraser, 2006; Gardiner *et al.*, 2011). Nevertheless, it is helpful to put forward as an 'ideal type' a basic model of that evolution. One can then use it to consider the extent to which the situation in one's own country has been in harmony with, or deviated from, that 'ideal type'. The basic position is that teacher preparation progressed through a series of stages. These can be termed 'the teacher apprenticeship stage', 'the college-based teacher training stage' and 'the college or university-based teacher education stage'. Each of these is now considered and a brief overview of developments across the stages, based on an exposition by O'Donoghue and Whitehead (2008), is then presented.

A basic historical model of teacher preparation

The teacher apprenticeship stage

In the first of these stages, teachers in schools for the better-off were deemed sufficiently prepared if they held a university degree, but the teachers of the great majority were prepared through apprenticeship. They learnt on the job from practising teachers the basic skills required to instruct and control very large classes taught according to a factory model. Also, the system of training was the same for all; there was one way to teach, just as there was a uniform schooling for all. Within such a system, it was taken for granted that the role of the teacher was largely to tame and civilize the masses, and provide them with basic skills in numeracy and literacy.

The college-based teacher training stage

The second stage was the college-based teacher training stage. In some cases the model pursued in this stage was promoted by various Christian churches, in others by the state, and in others yet again by both of these societal institutions. What was established were residential teacher-training colleges. The length of time spent in them varied from country to country and was brief, although it lengthened somewhat over time.

At least three general variations of the teacher training curriculum offered in this stage existed in different countries (and even within countries) and at different times.

- There was teacher training in school subject-specific teaching methods, along with some general training in generic teaching methods and classroom management. However, apart from ensuring that students lived within a regimen dictated by the strict morals of the day, little attention was given to the possibility that their personal development might also be important. Also, the assumption was that there was no need for an extension of the basic knowledge-base which the students had acquired at school. Rather, it was sufficient that in their work they be 'one page ahead of the students'.

- A second model was very similar to the first one, except that attention was also given to upgrading the students' subject content knowledge over what they had learnt in school.

- A third model was built on the second in that some attention was given to the students' personal and 'cultural' development, while additional studies were undertaken aimed at giving them some theoretical foundation to their work. In particular, student teachers began to be exposed in their courses to the history of education and the basic elements of educational psychology. Both subjects were designed to place teaching on a more professional footing, with history being aimed at locating teaching within 'a great tradition' and psychology being aimed at giving it a scientific basis.

The college or university-based teacher education stage

The third historical phase in teacher preparation which seems to have evolved in many countries can be termed the college or university-based teacher education stage. This stage is characterized by teacher training colleges having developed very strong affiliations with university education departments, or being absorbed totally within universities, although the nature of what this relationship should be can itself sometimes be contested. Associated with this development was a lengthening of the preparation period. The foundation disciplines of history and psychology were also enriched by the addition of various other theoretical strands, including the study of the progressive education movement and the study of child development. Later came an introduction to the philosophy and sociology of education. Increased emphasis was also placed on students acquiring a strong foundation in one or more of the academic subjects they would teach, while all of the time continuing to maintain a practical focus through the simulation of classroom practice and through spending a period of time on practice teaching in schools. In certain situations, attention was also paid to developing a sense of social justice among the student teachers and even a commitment to social reconstruction.

To reiterate what was said at the outset, the three historical stages of teacher preparation proposed here are very general. As such they approximate to the notion of 'an ideal type'. This basic device, which can be used for comparative study, is formed by the synthesis of a great many diffuse, discrete, more or less present and occasionally absent concrete individual phenomena which are arranged into a unified analytical construct.

In promoting the notion of the historical stages through which teacher preparation moved, no case is being made that all countries, or even any one country, conform exactly to the pattern presented. It also has to be recognized that there was variation from country to country in progression through the stages, while within each stage there was variation in:

- the length of teacher preparation;
- the nature of the components of the curriculum;
- the emphasis placed on some aspects of these components over time.

Also, in some countries, institutions stretched their provision to include such specialist areas as the preparation of early childhood teachers and special education teachers, alongside the more generalist primary and secondary school teachers. At the same time, the pattern suggested by the three stages proposed does allow one to consider how any particular country relates to and deviates from it, thus allowing one to consider the situation relating to that country in a systematic way and to talk about it in a structured manner.

Overview of developments across the stages of teacher preparation

Bruno-Jofre and Johnston (2014) have offered the following overview of shifts in recurrent themes across the stages of teacher preparation:

- There has been a shift in the geographic and ideological context in which teacher preparation has been taking place over the period. While the central point of emphasis during the nineteenth century was the nation state and the education of citizens, this focus has been replaced by an ideal increasingly oriented to an international context since the beginning of the twentieth century.
- There has been a shift from moral and religious narratives towards scientific and rationalist ones. In the nineteenth century, the education of young students was conducted with an almost missionary zeal. In the twentieth century, however, teaching methods became coupled with an ideal that the teacher should not appear as a religious moralizer. Instead, he or she should act according to strictly rational and scientific criteria.
- In the nineteenth century, the teaching of the history of education was central in courses of teacher preparation. In the twentieth century, however, experts with international influence held that it should be replaced with references to the future, a time when 'a world unified by standardization in education and science could promise to solve the increasingly interdependent problems of a globalized world' (Bruno-Jofre and Johnston, 2014, p. 28).
- There has been a significant turning away from a fixed education canon towards an increasingly constructivist concept of knowledge. As a consequence, 'cognitive structures and abstract, mathematical, and logical problem-solving abilities became privileged over historically and culturally bound knowledge concerning the world' (Bruno-Jofre and Johnston, 2014, p. 28).

Issues for discussion

1   Consider any course of teacher preparation with which you are familiar, or through which you progressed or are currently progressing.
    How does it relate to the general pattern outlined for the college or university-based teacher education stage outlined above?

2   What do you know about the evolution of approaches to teacher preparation in the institution which you attended, or are currently attending?

(continued)

3　What do you know about the evolution of approaches to teacher preparation in your own country?

4　Which approach to teacher preparation do you favour, the concurrent approach or the consecutive approach? Give reasons for your answer.

5　What are your views on the movement in some countries to remove teacher preparation as much as possible from universities and colleges and locate it within schools?

References

Bruno-Jofre, R. and Johnston, J. S. (Eds). (2014). *Teacher Education in a Transnational World*. Toronto: University of Toronto Press.

Fraser, J. (2006). *Preparing America's Teachers: A History*. New York: Teachers' College Press.

Gardiner, D., O'Donoghue, T. A. and O'Neill, M. (2011). *Constructing Education as a Liberal Art and as Teacher Preparation at Five Western Australian Universities: An Historical Analysis*. New York: Edwin Mellen Press.

O'Donoghue, T. A. and Whitehead, C. (Eds). (2008). *Teacher Education in the English-speaking World: Past, Present and Future*. Charlotte, NC: Information Age Publishing.

28 A model to inform planning for teacher preparation

In this chapter, as in the last one, an 'ideal type' is put forward. This time it is of a model to inform planning for teacher preparation, based on an exposition by O'Donoghue and Whitehead (2008). It is not being suggested that the proposed approach is the one that should be adopted in every teacher preparation institution in every country. Rather, it constitutes a model to which one can relate when considering what might be the most appropriate way to proceed in particular circumstances. This is followed by a related informing account, namely, an overview of recurrent themes regarding teacher preparation across a variety of countries.

The model

Teacher demand and supply

Ideally, a perfect match should exist between teacher demand and teacher supply. In other words, a system should prevail whereby institutions responsible for teacher preparation are all the time able to ensure that sufficient graduates are available to match any expansion in demand for new teachers, while they should also be equally able to ensure there is no oversupply in times of contraction. This, of course, is easier said than done. Indeed, failure to work out an effective system has long been a major headache in many countries. Nevertheless, this is no reason why efforts should not continue to be made to find a system which works in this regard.

Who should be selected?

Related to the supply and demand of teachers is the question of who should be selected for teacher preparation. Again, the ideal scenario would envisage both primary and secondary school applicants for teacher preparation programmes having at least five years of secondary school education. Furthermore, those selected from the pool of graduates should be high academic achievers and display a strong aptitude for teaching.

The location of teacher preparation programmes

Another feature of the ideal scenario is that both primary and secondary school teacher preparation should take place in institutions which are an integral part of the university system. Here they should be exposed to a programme with three main properties:

- They should be involved in studies which will bring them to an undergraduate degree-level of achievement in a number of academic subjects related to the school curriculum. This can take place either consecutively (enrolling in an undergraduate degree only, in the first instance) or concurrently (undertaking a programme with degree-level academic studies alongside their professional studies). What is important regardless of the model adopted, however, is that the students are exposed to, rub shoulders with and benefit from engaging with undergraduate peers intent on other career paths.

- The students' professional studies should involve exposure to such bodies of educational theory as would provide them with a solid background to understanding both generic and subject-specific pedagogical theory. There is no one or best way to teach. The relationship between particular teaching and classroom management approaches and such theory should also be made clear. Concurrently, there should likewise be an exposure to the social foundations of education, including developing a sense of the role of the teacher in the promotion of equity and social justice.

- The third property of the ideal programme of teacher preparation is that it should have a significant degree of teaching practice. The traditional practices of observational visits to schools, simulation of teaching activities at the university and actual practice teaching periods in schools should all be maintained. Added to this is a desire for partnerships with allied schools so that teaching internships can be facilitated and experienced practising teachers can play a major role as mentor teachers for the neophytes. Tying much of this together is the notion that teacher education programmes should produce reflective teachers.

Here it is helpful to recall Van Manen's (1977) three levels of reflectivity outlined in Chapter 1. These levels may well encompass the variety of perspectives involved in integrating the various components of the ideal scenario that has been depicted. Level one is reflection at the level of 'technical rationality'. The primary emphasis in 'technical rationality' within the teaching context, it will be recalled, is on the efficient and effective application of educational knowledge for the purpose of attaining given ends. Reflection at this level is concerned with questioning the appropriateness of various courses of action in the classroom, but does not enquire about purposes.

Reflection at level two for Van Manen is that of 'practical reflection'. At this level, it will be recalled, what is involved is the clarification of the assumptions that are the basis of practical action. The focus is on the moral, ethical and value considerations of the educational enterprise. In engaging in reflection at this level the concern is with deciding the worth of competing educational goals and experiences, not just harnessing energies for their attainment.

Level three is the level of 'critical reflection'. Reflection at this level, it will be recalled, focuses on the ways in which the goals and practices become systematically and ideologically distorted by structural forces and work constraints in various social settings, including schools.

The teacher educators

The quality of the teacher educators is also paramount. They should:

- be highly qualified academically (preferably to doctorate level);
- be outstanding academics who maintain for education studies a reputation of being equals in the university academic community;

- have wide teaching experience at the schools' level;
- be able to demonstrate to their students the intellectual and cultural as well as practical relevance of their areas of expertise to teaching, to the professional status of teachers and to the wider education community, including policy makers.

Societal attitudes

The graduate teachers should, on taking up their first appointment, find themselves operating in a society which values their work highly. This should be reflected in societal practices indicating that teachers command deep respect. These practices should be accompanied by salaries deemed to be commensurate with such respect and by the existence of a professional self-regulating association. The outcome should be teachers who experience high esteem.

It is difficult to point to any country where the situation approximates the scenario outlined so far (O'Donoghue and Whitehead, 2008). In many countries, however, the state plays a major role in shaping the preparation of teachers. The ever-present power of the public purse, the widespread influence of neo-liberalism in shaping government attitudes towards education and the overriding belief in the need for public accountability by providers of social services, including education, have generated deep-seated philosophical and practical tensions in both schools and universities that are involved in teacher education. So-called market forces currently drive government economic management in many countries. As a consequence, there is now a real fear among many educators that predominantly economic and short-term motives rather than more deep-seated moral and liberal education objectives will dictate future ways of staffing schools and educating future generations.

Some recurring themes regarding teacher preparation across various countries

The degree of professional regulation of teaching and the level of influence of this regulation on programmes of teacher preparation

At one end of the spectrum are countries that do not have any professional regulating body. Rather, control typically lies with government, with policy makers and with educational bureaucrats. Two of the major countries which stand out as located at this end, namely, the USA and Singapore, are established on very different political assumptions. Reasonably close to the other end of the spectrum are the two Canadian provinces of British Columbia and Ontario. The initiatives taken there would seem to indicate a greater level of influence, power and control by teachers over teacher preparation than in England and Wales, and Scotland. This observation suggests that the latter jurisdictions lie somewhere along the middle of the spectrum. And then there are those not easily located at this moment in time as they work towards putting structures in place to facilitate the emergence of self-regulating bodies.

The influence across many countries of the movement which favours highly prescriptive centralized sets of professional standards for teacher preparation

This has led to a whole industry in North America centred on teacher portfolio writing and to the involvement of personnel in various other jurisdictions in much 'busy work', extensively documenting how standards are assessed and covered in their respective institutions. It has also led to much stress for teacher educators where performance reports in teacher preparation programmes are published for perusal by the general population without any attempt to contextualize what is going on. Associated with the latter is the anxiety generated by a market-driven approach to the provision of teacher preparation programmes. This could possibly promote a purely technocratic approach at the expense of the provision of opportunities for students aimed at promoting their personal development and nurturing their commitment to the caring role of teachers.

At the same time one cannot overlook arguments, like those emanating from South Africa in particular, that having norms and standards for teacher preparation, as for the schools' curriculum nationally, are important in trying to ensure equity within the educational system. Also, it is true that there are exceptions when it comes to the movement which favours highly prescriptive centralized sets of professional standards for teacher preparation.

In New Zealand, the movement which favours highly prescriptive centralized sets of professional standards for teacher preparation has facilitated the emergence of great diversity in the teacher education environment; the argument seems to be that it does not matter who provides so long as what is provided facilitates the attainment of the standards. On the other hand, concern has been expressed in some quarters that provision for teacher preparation outside of the long-established parameters may make the funding of the activity an increasingly complex task in future. Also, there are those who argue that it may also lead to a major dilution in the view that central to teacher preparation programmes is a notion of teaching as a moral enterprise.

Developments in Scotland are seen in certain quarters as safeguarding against some of the drawbacks noted above. While on the surface they display many of the features of government-driven notions of effectiveness and efficiency aimed at ensuring an approach to teacher preparation in the interest of producing an economically productive workforce, the approach adopted is not a market-driven one. Rather, it has led to a situation whereby institutions tend to attract students collaboratively. This has been attributed partly to the Scottish tradition of egalitarianism and of education being seen as a public good rather than being for private advantage.

Issues for discussion

1   Are you familiar with alternative approaches to teacher preparation to that outlined above, such as 'Teach For America' and 'Teach For Australia'?

- How are these approaches different?
- Can you outline their characteristics?
- Can you see any advantages in these approaches?
- Can you see any disadvantages?

2   How would you characterize the attitudes of your society to teachers?

3   How would you characterize the attitudes of your society to teacher preparation?

4   Are you familiar with the academic entry requirements for teacher preparation in your country?

     Do you think these are of an appropriate standard?

5   Are there any additional requirements for teacher preparation in your country apart from having an academic teaching qualification?

     •   If so, are they appropriate?
     •   If there are none, do you think there should be?

References

O'Donoghue, T. A. and Whitehead, C. (Eds). (2008). *Teacher Education in the English-speaking World: Past, Present and Future*. Charlotte, NC: Information Age Publishing.

Van Manen, M. (1977). Linking ways of knowing with ways of being practical. *Curriculum Inquiry*, Vol. 6, No. 3, pp. 205–228.

29 Globalization, internationalization and teacher preparation

Dale (2014) contends that neo-liberal education has had a notable direct effect on teacher preparation across the world. In particular, he states: 'It has reinforced at transnational levels the mantra that in a global knowledge economy all countries need effective systems that will ensure the production of appropriately skilled and "knowledged" (*sic*) students' (Dale, 2014, p. 38). Dale (2014) also highlights the prevalence of 'the notion that the effectiveness of those forms of education is due in considerable degree to the effectiveness of teachers'. Building on the latter points, he draws attention to:

- the notion that the effectiveness of teachers is closely associated with the effectiveness of teacher education;
- the involvement of 'countries and systems being in competition with each other, which places teacher education at the forefront of the global battle' (Dale, 2014, p. 38);
- the view that competition, in turn, 'necessarily produc[es] more losers than winners, which partly accounts for the denunciation of national teacher education systems for their contribution to lack of national economic success' (Dale, 2014, p. 38);
- changes that have taken place in the expectations of the teaching profession and its organization, which themselves have direct repercussions for teacher education and which have led to considerable restructuring of the teacher workforce in many countries.

Dale also points to suppression of the 'bureaucratic-professional' model of teaching by the 'evaluative state' or 'quasi-market' model. This 'is clearly closely linked', he argues, 'to the striking increases in the accountability demands placed on teachers' (Dale, 2014, p. 38). He concludes by drawing attention to the 'pervasive shift in how "quality" is defined and appraised in teacher education' (Dale, 2014, p. 38), from its meaning of cultural competence, ethical practice and responsiveness to learners within a broad definition of curriculum 'to definitions that seem set to feature test scores and value-added measures of literacy and numeracy'.

The European Movement in teacher preparation

Dale (2014, p. 41) qualifies his position in pointing out that if we consider the particular case of teacher preparation in Europe, and in particular the reforms introduced under the Bologna Process, we find that it is one of the areas least affected in university activity. Here the structure of teacher education is strongly bound and shaped by national context and history. The state, as the main employer of graduates, tends to have a strong influence on the structure and content of teacher preparation, and the related requirements generally to lower the flexibility of provision in this field. The programmes cater largely for national labour markets.

The situation described above does not mean, Dale (2014) says, that the European Union has not had ambitions to be involved in teacher education, or has been inactive in the field. He offers the following two reasons why efforts to bring more coherence to teacher education in Europe have not been very successful:

1   There is no consensus on what school education is about, on the priorities for curriculum, on the skills and qualities required to be a teacher or the responsibilities to be taken.
2   The constitutional position, which limits the EU to assisting member states to improve quality in the area of education has essentially precluded it from direct involvement. Thus its activities have been limited to exhortation, pointing out to member states the importance of good teaching and of teacher education as a means to bring this about, with actual activities essentially confined to the sharing of good practice and peer learning activities.

Yet, there are linkages discernible between various forms of European cooperation in higher education, through the Bologna Process, as well as the EU's 'Lisbon agenda'; essentially its framing of what is required to make Europe into the most competitive dynamic, knowledge-based economy in the world. This common agenda influences the institutional contexts within which the rather different forms of teacher education find themselves operating.

Some implications for teacher preparation

Arising out of the nature and extent of globalization, Bottery (2006) has argued that educators, including teachers, are likely to experience the following tensions in their work:

*   Their attempts to satisfy the greater demands of both clients and governments for an improved service will be hindered by the need to reduce expenditure and increase efficiencies.
*   The need to respond to nation-state attempts to strengthen its legitimacy as the sole provider of citizenship will be in conflict with the increased claims of sub-national groups, and supranational organizations, which may produce demands for more 'nested' forms of citizenship.
*   The pressure to use private sector concepts and practices, primarily based around questions of efficiency, economy and profit, will likely conflict with public sector values and practices, based more around care and equity.
*   Governments will continue to want to control their thought and activity, yet will also wish them to be flexible and creative in developing students for a competitive knowledge economy.
*   Teachers are likely to experience a similar tension in terms of trust, as governments see the need to allow an enhanced autonomy and creativity, yet feel unwilling or unable to abandon policies which result in low-trust cultures of targets, performativity and compliance.

A consequence of these tensions, Bottery (2006) concludes, is that teachers need to be prepared not only in terms of knowing their subject and knowing how to teach it, but they also need to:

- have a greater ecological and political awareness – they need to have the mental apparatus to reflect on education beyond the classroom, and not just locally and internationally, but globally, in order to understand the factors that constrain, steer or facilitate their practice;
- express supporting notions of public good – educators must be much clearer and vociferous in espousing notions of a public good; they should strive to make a difference to the quality of society;
- embrace a sophisticated accountability – this would manifest itself in the recognition that forms of accountability are not simply 'done' to them, but are a product of, and contribute to, the ecology within which they practise; they would then work towards forms which would display how aspects of professional practice, neglected in current forms of accountability, are essential to a rich conception of education;
- build trust and build accountability – this in part can be done by involving and educating other stakeholders in the nature, purpose and constraints of their job and a greater commitment to explain current practice; this involves more communication and more inter-professional research between public sector workers;
- embrace an epistemological provisionality – they need to be suitably humble about their own capacity to 'know' any final answers, and to recognize that others have significant input here, not least those normally described as 'clients';
- engage in a greater degree of professional self-reflection – this must manifest itself in a greater appreciation of the contexts within which professionals find themselves, of their need to debate the purposes of their profession and to continue to ponder on the balance between their purposes, and then interrogate them; this calls for a degree of professional self-knowledge and self-reflection.

Issues for discussion

1   During the second half of the twentieth century, teacher education was seen primarily as the responsibility of the nation state because it was an integral part of preparing national citizens. The role of teacher education was to prepare pre-service teachers to pass on to the next generation national culture and traditions, as well as the skills and knowledge necessary for fulfilling different roles in the national society. However, with the increased influences of economic and cultural globalization, the notion of the nation state and its functions has been reframed.

(Aydarova, 2012, np).

On the matter raised above, Aydarova (2012) has posed the following questions which you should consider:

- If the nation state is rescaled due to the increased influence of transnational organizations and its functions are curbed to ensure the existence of free and unfettered markets, what role can and should it play in shaping education and teacher education?

- If globalization has contributed to the creation of a 'borderless' world, then what kind of preparation should teachers receive?
- What cultures and what traditions should be passed on in a world dominated by discourses of competitiveness and global markets?
- With the increasing role of international comparisons and the growing rate of transferred educational reforms and models, what cultures and what traditions end up being taught in the teacher education programmes?

2   The research community can help policy makers make informed decisions related to globalization, teaching and teacher education. First, it is important to describe the realities of globalization and its impacts on schools, teachers and teacher education to help policy makers and practitioners develop a deep understanding about them. Second, it is critical to conceptualize the issues and problems emerging from these realities and to develop theoretical assumptions that are useful to policy makers and to practitioners for developing and implementing effective teaching practices. Third, it is necessary to verify empirically these concepts and assumptions so that potentially detrimental consequences of policy decisions and practices may be mitigated.

(Wang *et al.*, 2011, p. 115)

a   What is involved in describing the realities of globalization and its impact on schools, teachers and teacher education to help policy makers and practitioners develop a deep understanding about them?

b   Why is it critical to conceptualize the issues and problems emerging from these realities and to develop theoretical assumptions that are useful to policy makers and to practitioners for developing and implementing effective teaching practices?

c   Why is it necessary to verify empirically these concepts and assumptions so that potentially detrimental consequences of policy decisions and practices may be mitigated?

3   A strategy for internationalizing the curriculum and developing greater intercultural competence in students is to take advantage of the human capital that already exists on university campuses in the form of international students. Most universities tend to view international students as people who need to learn about how to be successful at an overseas university. While this is of course true, at the same time international students speak other languages and have knowledge of other cultures that is rarely tapped ... these 'funds of knowledge' need to be a resource to internationalizing the curriculum.

(Cordeiro *et al.*, 2003, p. 15)

a   What is your view on adopting this type of strategy?
b   Are you aware of any institution that adopts this type of strategy?
c   Can you think of any way in which you might adopt it, or encourage it to be adopted?

(continued)

4   Education is a future-oriented business because it aims to prepare today's children for the future. In this sense, teacher education is an even more future-oriented business for it aims to prepare teachers for future educational institutions. Thus, discussing teacher education cannot afford to ignore the forces that will shape education in the future, which will prepare our children to live in an even more distant future world.

(Zhao, 2010, p. 422)

Discuss.

5   What implications does globalization have for teacher preparation in your country?
What knowledge, skills and dispositions will best serve teachers in responding to globalization?
What opportunities does globalization present for programmes of teacher preparation?
What pitfalls does globalization present for programmes of teacher preparation?

References

Aydarova, O. (2012). Globalization and teacher education. http://e12.cgpublisher.com/proposals/129/index_html.

Bottery, M. (2006). Education and globalization: Redefining the role of the educational professional. *Educational Review*, Vol. 58, No. 1, pp. 95–113.

Cordeiro, P. A., Bloom, D. A., Englebrecht, G., Gonzalez, B., Kissock, C. and Wan, Y. (2003). A call for the internationalization of teacher education in an era of globalization. Paper presented by the Global and International Teacher Education Committee of the American Association of the College of Teacher Educators. Melbourne: International Council on Education for Teaching.

Dale, R. (2014). Globalization, higher education and teacher education: A sociological approach (pp. 33–53). In R. Bruno-Jofre and J. Scott Johnston (Eds), *Teacher Education in a Transnational World*. Toronto: University of Toronto Press.

Wang, J., Lin, E., Spalding, E., Odell, S. J. and Klecka, C. L. (2011). Understanding teacher education in an era of globalization. *Journal of Teacher Education*, Vol. 62, No. 2, pp. 115–120.

Zhao, Y. (2010). Preparing globally competent teachers: A new imperative for teacher education. *Journal of Teacher Education*, Vol. 61, No. 5, pp. 422–431.

30 Teacher induction

Huberman (1989, 1993) generated a very helpful model for considering career stages in teachers' professional work. While this model was developed later by others, including Steffy and Wolfe (2001) and White (2008), their work was largely an elaboration on the three main phases that Huberman proposed. They are as follows:

1   the novice stage;
2   the mid-career stage;
3   the late-career stage.

The principal characteristics of each stage, as summarized by White (2008), are outlined below.

Huberman's model of teacher development

The novice stage

The student-teaching/early-novice sub-stage

Here the primary concern is with surviving. One finds oneself saying to oneself and others: 'I'm not sure that I can teach'.

The middle-novice sub-stage

Here the primary concern is with the task of teaching. One finds oneself saying to oneself and others: 'Just let me teach! I'm working as hard as I can, but how am I supposed to teach all of these kids with so few materials and so many extra duties?'

The late-novice sub-stage

Here the primary concern is with one's impact on students. One finds oneself saying to oneself and others: 'I think I've almost mastered this teaching thing! Now how do I make sure every student learns in my class?'

The mid-career stage

The stabilization sub-stage

Here experienced teachers usually feel confident about their professional skills and knowledge, and settle into a comfortable and predictable pattern of teaching.

The sub-stage of experimentation

Here seasoned teachers often look for ways to make their teaching more interesting, experimenting with new approaches and activities in their classrooms.

The sub-stage of taking stock

Here teachers with a decade or more of experience may reflect on their careers, contemplating both the worth of their past work and their plans for continued work in coming years. Some, in the midst of a mid-career crisis, look back over their careers with distaste and find nothing to look forward to but 'more of the same'.

The late-career stage

The sub-stage of serenity

Here teachers with many years of experience are usually comfortable with classroom life and their role in it.

The sub-stage of disengagement

Here, as they approach retirement, some older teachers start focusing on their lives beyond the classroom and they begin to distance themselves emotionally from their students.

Huberman does not promote his phases as being linear. He also holds that the lines are blurred between the stages and the sub-stages. Furthermore, it would be wrong to see his model as representing exactly how each teacher develops as that would be to ignore such factors as:

- personal experiences;
- social environment;
- organizational influences.

Teachers can also move in and out of the various phases. For example, late-career teachers can return to being novices if faced with totally new requirements. What the model does do, however, is give us a framework by which we can talk about teacher development.

Teacher induction

For many years the attitude towards beginning teachers was one of 'sink or swim'. This was inappropriate since not only did they encounter particular difficulties, excessive burdens were also often placed on them. In the 1990s, for example, it was noted in the US that novice teachers were typically given the most difficult classes, had more courses to teach than their older peers and also had more extracurricular duties (Andrews and Andrews, 1998; Darling-Hammond, 1997; Darling-Hammond and Sclan, 1996). By this stage, however, some countries, most notably Japan and Germany, were inducting new teachers into the profession through clinical, real-world training processes.

Soon it became recognized internationally that at the beginning of one's teaching career, the provision of support is vital and complex. It was recognized that for induction and mentor programmes to be effective, they need to be structured, comprehensive and well monitored (Wong, 2001). The most prevalent arguments were that:

- a mentor should be assigned to the beginning teacher;
- observation of, and by, experienced colleagues should be arranged;
- opportunities to help one develop critical self-reflection should be provided.

Plans to help one to create safe classroom environments and to work effectively with parents should be put in place (Conway *et al.*, 2009).

It was also argued that the beginning teacher needs protected time for:

- review meetings;
- structured discussion with colleagues;
- systematic collection of evidence for a crucial summative assessment.

Exemplars of intelligent practices

The BTSA programme

In the US, California's BTSA programme is recognized as an exemplar programme. It is state-mandated and provides a focused and intensive support framework for beginning teachers for the first two years of teaching. This is based on research carried out by the California New Teacher Project (CNTP) (Shields *et al.*, 2002), which highlighted the need for focused induction support with sufficient intensity to make a difference to beginning teachers in terms of:

- performance;
- retention;
- satisfaction.

Careful attention is paid to building explicit structural and conceptual links between the different partners in teacher education, namely:

- the university;
- school contexts;
- policy makers.

Its principal characteristics are as follows:

- Trained mentors support beginning teachers as they develop quality teaching practices, habits and skills.
- A series of collaborative reflective processes keeps a consistent focus on student learning and teacher learning.
- Beginning teachers are supported by mentors to collect and interpret evidence of their teaching performance, to reflect on their practice and to identify meaningful professional development that is specifically targeted to individual needs.
- Mentors work with individual teachers to examine practice decisions in order to align them more closely with Californian curricular frameworks and standards for student learning.
- There is a consistent focus on planning for improving student learning.
- Specialists and partner teachers model lessons for new teachers.
- Partner teachers work with beginning teachers on lesson plans, grading issues, preparing for parent conferences and other aspects of classroom practice.
- Partner teachers work at identifying targeted professional development sessions to meet individual needs.
- Scheduling for release time and budgeting for materials are allowed for.

The beginning teacher's portfolio in the BEST programme

Connecticut's BEST programme for beginning teachers is along similar lines. In this model, the mentor teacher also helps the beginning teacher to become a member of a community of learners and to construct a professional portfolio in relation to state standards, which is used in one's assessment for one's licence to teach. The portfolio has the following characteristics:

- It is used as a situated assessment tool.
- A beginning teacher must present a portfolio during his or her second year of teaching and assessment criteria are linked explicitly to context, grade and subject area.
- A beginning teacher must provide a written commentary to explain and evaluate instructional decisions and relate this to his or her plans for student and teacher learning.
- Specially trained state assessors provide written feedback on the competence of the beginning teacher.
- It is used as a deliberate collection of school-site evidence in response to a set of questions for purposes of licensure and professional development. Moreover, the portfolio is designed to evoke the knowledge, skills and dispositions necessary to determine that professional standards are being met over time (Arends and Regazio-DeGilio, 2000, p. 11).

Intelligent practices and the beginning teacher in New Zealand

From 1989, New Zealand moved to decentralized education decision making and implemented a series of major educational reforms. There has been a shift in responsibility for teacher induction from government bureaucrats to local administrators and teachers. Local programmes support new teachers' transition to the culture of teaching through school-designed and implemented 'advice and guidance programmes' for the first two to five years of teaching.

Characteristics of New Zealand's beginning teacher induction programmes are as follows:

- 20 per cent release time for new teachers and their mentors to participate in support activities;
- mentoring, observations and in-service;
- a focus on assistance rather than assessment;
- a high degree of camaraderie and collegiality;
- experienced teachers considering it their duty to pass on to the next generation of teachers their knowledge, skills, and experience (Kleinhenz and Ingvarson, 2007).

Intelligent practices in other countries

Poland

Here, beginning teachers have the benefit of an experienced teacher employed in the school at 'appointed' or 'chartered teacher level' who supports them throughout the first three-and-a-half years of teaching (Conway *et al.*, 2009).

Singapore

Here, beginning teachers have a reduced workload of 80 per cent. They are mentored by experienced teachers within the school. Co-teaching is also a feature of induction. An emphasis is placed on beginning teachers learning through observing one another teaching, through mutual feedback and through sharing lesson plans and pedagogical techniques (Conway *et al.*, 2009).

Scotland

Here beginning teachers have reduced teaching hours, time for professional development and an experienced teacher as a probationer supporter. The scheme has attracted extensive interest internationally (Conway *et al.*, 2009).

Issues for discussion

1   If you are a teacher:

- Were there any special programmes or services available for first-year teachers when you began teaching?
- If there was a lack of special programmes and services available for first-year teachers, do you think it had a negative influence on your teaching experience during the early years of your career?

(continued)

2   Regarding the mentoring of beginning teachers:

- Why should today's beginning teachers be mentored?
- Might we be justified in saying that 'the way we've always done it' no longer works?
- What might be the benefits to the mentee of mentoring beginning teachers?
- What might be the benefits to the school of mentoring beginning teachers?
- What might be the benefits to the principal of mentoring beginning teachers?

3   Can any teacher be a mentor?

4   What does a mentor do?

5   What training do you think a mentor needs?

6   New teachers have varied backgrounds, educational experiences, skills and learning styles; consequently their rate of development and needs are different. These differences must be acknowledged throughout the teacher induction programme. The content and delivery of the teacher induction programme must be tailored to meet these unique needs.

(Brock and Grady, 2006, p. 7)

Consider how the needs of the following individuals may vary:

- those of a traditional graduate of a teacher education programme;
- those of a non-traditional graduate of a teacher education programme;
- those of an individual entering the teaching field after leaving a different career;
- those of an experienced teacher returning to teaching;
- those of an individual who completed an alternative certification programme;
- those of an experienced teacher moving to a new school;
- those of an experienced teacher changing grade levels or subject areas.

References

Andrews, T. E. and Andrews, L. (Eds). (1998). *The NASDTEC Manual 1998–1999. Manual on the Preparation and Certification of Educational Personnel*. Dubuque, IA: Kendall/Hunt.

Arends, R. and Regazio-DeGilio, G. (2000). Beginning teacher induction: Research and examples of contemporary practice. Paper presented at the annual meeting of the Japan–United States TeacherEducation Consortium (JUSTEC).

Brock, B. L. and Grady, M. L. (2006). *Developing a Teacher Induction Plan: A Guide for School Leaders*. Thousand Oaks, CA: Corwin Press.

Conway, P. F., Murphy, R., Rath, A. and Hall, K. (2009). *Learning to Teach and Its Implications for the Continuum of Teacher Education: A Nine Country Cross-national Study*. Dublin: The Teaching Council.

Darling-Hammond, L. (1997) *Doing What Matters Most: Investing in Quality Teaching*. New York: National Commission on Teaching and America's Future.

Darling-Hammond, L. and Sclan, E. M. (1996) Who teaches and why. Dilemmas of building a profession for twenty-first century schools (pp. 67–101). In S. E. J. Sikula, T. Buttery and E. Guyton (Eds), *Handbook of Research on Teacher Education*. New York: Association of Teacher Educators.

Huberman, M. A. (1989). The professional life cycle of teachers. *Teachers College Record*, Vol. 91, No. 1, pp. 31–57.

Huberman, M. A. (1993) *The Lives of Teachers*. New York: Teachers College Press.

Kleinhenz, E. and Ingvarson, L. (2007). *Standards for Teaching. Theoretical Underpinnings and Applications.* Wellington: New Zealand Teachers Council. http://research.acer.edu.au/cgi/viewcontent.cgi?article=1000&context=teaching_standards.

Shields, P. M., Esch, C. E., Humphrey, D. C., Young, V. M., Gaston, M. and Hunt, H. (2002). *Teaching and California's Future. The Status of the Teaching Profession: Research Findings and Policy Recommendations*. Santa Cruz, CA: Center for the Future of Teaching and Learning.

Steffy, B. E. and Wolfe, M. P. (2001). A life-cycle model for career teachers. *Kappa Delta Pi Record*, Vol. 38, No. 1, pp. 16–19.

White, R. (2008). Teachers' professional life cycles. *International House Journal of Education and Development*, Vol. 24. http://ihjournal.com/teachers-professional-life-cycles.

Wong, H. (2001). Mentoring can't do it all. *Education Week*, Vol. 20, No. 43, pp. 46–50.

31 Alternative models of teacher preparation

Zeichner (2008) has documented some alternative models of teacher preparation that have emerged in the US since the 1980s. This move has been a result of a number of private foundations, state governments and the Federal Department of Education encouraging the development of programmes that have less emphasis on professional education content apart from that which is acquired while teaching, and which still can lead to certification to teach in public schools. Overall, the move can be seen as an expansion of the initiatives undertaken throughout the 1950s and 1960s when the Ford Foundation spent over US$70 million on initiatives that encouraged the development of post-baccalaureate programmes on top of an undergraduate degree with a full academic major (Stone, 1968).

In recent years, a number of school districts and private providers have also initiated pre-service teacher preparation programmes and projects like the 'New Teacher Project' and 'Troops to Teachers' (Feistritzer, 2005). The focus has been on recruiting specific populations such as recent graduates from elite universities and retired military personnel into teaching. Following through on this became possible because, while the Federal education law known as 'No Child Left Behind' requires that all teachers meet certification requirements in the particular states in which they are teaching, there is great variation across the US in what prospective teachers need to do to meet these requirements.

The American Board for the Certification of Teaching Excellence (ABCTE) (Zeichner, 2008) programme became recognized in five states as providing certification to teach. Certification was gained by individuals who could pass two paper tests, one on academic content and the other on professional education content. It required no formal college-based teacher preparation. Such developments encouraged various critics of college and university-based teacher education programmes to call for the elimination of state licensing of teachers and to give the public schools the right to hire anyone they wish. The argument they put forward is a simple one, namely, that if teachers are not successful they will not be rehired.

Distance education for teacher preparation

Back in 1995, Jegede et al. (1995) argued that while the technologies used to support distance learning are important for a well-functioning distance education programme, more critical for teacher learning are the type and quality of instruction offered with and through these technologies. The following is a summary of what Burns (2007), with this in mind, considered to be some of the basic principles to keep in mind when deciding on some of the 'best' or optimal teaching and learning methods across all modes and models of distance education:

- Good teachers matter in all nations. Creating an effective distance education system for teacher preparation and teacher on-going professional development means immersing the students in high-quality learning experiences with instructors who themselves embody the characteristics of good teaching.
- Many distance education programmes have been characterized as 'one step ahead for technology and two steps back for pedagogy' (Mioduser *et al.*, 2000), with a great emphasis on didactic approaches. If distance education is to help develop good teaching, appropriate technologies must be matched with appropriate instructional methods. This is because distance education raises instructional issues that depend on:

  o whether the course is taught synchronously (in real time) or asynchronously;
  o what technology is used – videoconferencing is very different from online instruction;
  o what the educational outcomes of the distance learning programme are.

- Student teachers and practising teachers must be taught using the same instructional methods with which they are expected to teach students and, as much as possible, participate in a variety of appropriate instructional models. These include:

  o direct instructional models (transmission of concepts, skills and procedures);
  o cognitive models (inductive reasoning, teaching via analogy);
  o social models (learner-centred instruction) (Boethel and Dimock, 1999; Maor and Zariski, 2003; Gaible and Burns, 2007; Dede *et al.*, 2005).

- Distance programmes that combine face-to-face instruction, supervision, tutoring and modelling have a greater chance of success than those that use a single approach (Perraton, 2002).
- All effective distance learning content materials – both digital and text-based – must be developed by people with successful school experience. These developers must not only understand how people learn and how the design of content contributes to learning, but must also be aware of the skills, abilities and culture of the pre-service and in-service teachers for whom they are producing the content.
- Materials must be of high quality and must be sufficiently engaging to advance the diverse aims of various courses by supporting instructional efforts to model good teaching and learning. These efforts require:

  o focusing on classroom and school;
  o integrating theory and practice;
  o linking to specific teacher assessment outcomes;
  o explaining and modelling subject-specific pedagogy;
  o inculcating declarative, procedural and conceptual knowledge about a particular subject area (Commonwealth of Learning, 2008).

- Teachers must be helped to develop the characteristics of good teaching. To this end, distance learning programmes need to provide teachers with on-going opportunities to improve their:

  o content knowledge;
  o instructional skills;
  o knowledge about how students learn;
  o understanding of learning from a student's point of view.

- Quality distance education needs to provide on-going professional development that:

    o   is based on proven best practices;
    o   builds in continual support;
    o   helps teachers become not just a community of learners, but a community of practitioners.

- Distance learning programmes must prepare their instructors and learners to succeed in a distance environment through:

    o   orientation;
    o   preparation;
    o   support;
    o   leadership.

- All components of distance learning programmes must be designed according to quality standards so that:

    o   courses and learning experiences may be developed;
    o   teachers are assessed;
    o   programmes are evaluated;
    o   quality is assured by measurement against these standards.

- Distance learning designers must integrate rigorous evaluation into programme design so that programmatic and contextual factors can be addressed and remedied if needed. These components should be incorporated into a coherent distance education system.

Burns (2007) concluded that the designers of many distance education programmes have approached the task of improving teacher quality with too much complacency and too little ambition, and have little to show for it as a result. Other programmes have focused too much on careful attention to technology inputs and infrastructure and not enough on human inputs and human infrastructure. The outcome, she argues, is little measurable improvement in quality.

The 'Teach For' movement

Dale (2014, p. 39) has drawn attention to the contemporary idea 'that competition will lead to the improvement of teacher education, and the encouragement of alternatives to the traditional university-based form, from both public and private suppliers'. One of the most interesting and pervasive of the groups of associated initiatives, he points out, has been the 'Teach For' movement. These consist of:

> social-enterprise-based organizations, claiming to recruit outstanding graduates to teach in schools where the majority of pupils come from the poorest families. They typically receive abbreviated forms of training and are expected to teach in disadvantaged schools for two years, before moving into leadership positions in education or in the wider business world.
>
> (Dale, 2014, p. 39)

Back in 1989, an American student, Wendy Kopp, came up with an idea of 'Teach For America'. The following is a summary by Exley (2014, np) of subsequent developments:

> The idea Kopp had was that high-flying graduates should be recruited to teach in low-performing schools in the most impoverished communities. They should be sent on short, intensive courses to learn the basics, before being placed into schools with a teacher shortage. Kopp's proposal was taken up by Mobil (now ExxonMobil), who approved funding of $26,000 to get the programme underway. By 2012, 22 years on, the programme had received more than 48,000 applications, resulting in 5,800 teachers being posted to schools across 46 regions in the US, from Alabama to Washington.

In 2002, social entrepreneur Brett Wigdortz founded 'Teach First', a similar UK scheme, which has grown from an initial cohort of 180 to become the biggest graduate recruiter in the country. From 2015, it was expected to be taking on more than 2,000 graduates each year. Then, in 2007, Wigdortz and Kopp joined forces to create 'Teach For All', a network to promote and support the spread of their shared views to countries around the world. Today, Teach For All has more than 30 international partner organizations spanning five continents.

Concerns expressed

- Some have questioned the ethics of 'experimenting' on children from the poorest communities with inexperienced teachers.
- Others hold that the zeal with which the Teach For All movement promotes its achievements, and cultivates support – both financial and political – from politicians and businesses, has led some critics to portray it as an educational 'cult' wielding enormous power over policy makers.
- Others yet again claim that the programme is used to staff struggling schools on the cheap, with eager graduates more interested in boosting their CVs than improving the lives of vulnerable children.
- Some argue that the schemes bring little tangible benefit when the significant amounts of public and private funding being thrown into them are considered.
- At the 'Free Minds, Free People' education conference in Chicago in 2013, a meeting entitled 'Organizing resistance to Teach For America and its role in privatization' was held. It was set up by several former Teach For America participants whose experiences had turned them against the movement.
- Some question much of the academic evidence produced to demonstrate Teach For America's effectiveness on the grounds that there is very little peer-reviewed academic research.
- Dale (2014, p. 39) claims that the movement implies that:

> teaching is not a job that requires careful training and induction, and is not a career that the 'best' candidates would want to stay in for more than two years, though it may provide good training for a more lucrative leadership role in business.

Declared benefits

- The Teach For All movement points to numerous pieces of research demonstrating that it delivers both value for money and good results for students.
- Those who promote the movement argue that some of the recruits even outperform more experienced colleagues who have come through the traditional teacher training route.
- England's schools inspectorate, Ofsted, judged Teach First's training provision to be outstanding in every category.
- A key piece of 2004 research on Teach For America found that average test scores in mathematics classes taught by participants were higher than those of other teachers.
- Research by Rebecca Allen of the University of London's Institute of Education found that Teach First increases GCSE grades across participating schools.
- Whereas most of the Teach For All programmes are targeted at working-class students in deprived urban areas, Teach For China focuses on driving up attainment in rural schools.

Issues for discussion

1   A competencies-based approach to teacher preparation is favoured by many. Discuss the following problem with such an approach as posed by O'Donoghue and Chapman, 2010, p. 85):

> The competencies-based approach 'asserts that knowledge is constituted in what people need to know in order to perform or demonstrate a particular skill' (Soucek, 1993, p. 51). While this might be fine in relation to the needs of the economic system, education surely requires preparation also for the social, cultural, and ethical aspects of life. Such preparation, while benefiting from the acquisition of pre-ordained competencies, equally requires the development of the individual's critical thinking skills, and the outcomes of the exercise of these skills is, by definition, not capable of being stated in pre-ordained form. To put it another way, a problem with a competencies-based approach is that it conceptualizes knowledge as static, or as something which the learner only needs to acquire, rather than to produce as an autonomous thinker.

2   Do you think that Soucek (1993, pp. 50–52) is justified in raising the following associated issues?

   - Competency cannot be defined in advance because 'it is always situationally specific. As a consequence, predetermined knowledge might not guarantee a competent performance in altered circumstances' (Soucek, 1993, p. 50).
   - Because the assessment of a competent performance is at least partially dependent on the assessor's subjectivity, it 'assumes that the personal values and knowledge of the assessor and the tested person are identical or at least similar. This might not be the case. A question might arise as to who is the most competent performer, the assessor or the person being assessed' (Soucek, 1993, p. 51).

- The competency-testing approach cannot anticipate all possible permutations of occupational situations. Its 'focus on performance rather than on the knowledge, therefore, might fail to equip the future practitioner with the capacity to deal effectively with unforeseen situationally specific problems' (Soucek, 1993, p. 52).

3 Another problem proposed for advocates of both a competencies-based approach and a distance-education approach to teacher preparation is that they provide little room for those who consider that the curriculum should pay attention to the dynamics of interpersonal relationships. The importance of the interpersonal in education was put as follows by Buber (1965, p. 89), the existential philosopher:

> There was a master, a philosopher and a coppersmith, whose journeymen and apprentices lived with him and learned by being allowed to share in it, what he had to teach them of his handwork or brainwork. But they also learned without their or his being aware of it; they learned without noting that they did, the mystery of the personal life.

This personal encounter, according to Buber, is the other half of education. Teachers and lecturers are moral agents who initiate students into the human conversation, into a way of life and a culture (Burke, 1992, p. 212; Kerr, 1987). Similarly, Goodlad (1988, p. 108) stated his belief that 'the craft of teaching must be honed within the context of moral intention. Otherwise, it is little more than mechanics and might be performed better by a machine'.

- Do you consider these positions to be valid?
- Do you consider them to be important?
- Do you think that they are accommodated within all approaches to teacher preparation? If, not, which approaches do not accommodate them?

4 Most teacher preparation programmes, even those that adopt alternative approaches to those traditionally operating, prepare teachers for 'regular' schooling. However, a great variety of alternative approaches to schooling exist.

- Find out what you can about the following six alternative approaches:

  o Maria Montessori
  o A. S. Neill
  o Edward Harkness
  o Reggio Emilia
  o Sudbury Schools
  o Rudolf Steiner

- Consider what teacher preparation programmes might be appropriate for schooling based on each of these types.

References

Boethel, M. and Dimock, K. V. (1999). *Constructing Knowledge with Technology: An Overview of the Literature*. Austin, TX: Southwest Educational Development Laboratory.

Buber, M. (1965). Education (pp. 80–93). In M. Buber (Ed.), *Between Man and Man*. New York: Macmillan.

Burke, A. (1992). *Training of Trainers*. Dublin: Department of Education.

Burns, M. (2007). *Distance Education For Teacher Training: Modes, Models and Methods*. Washington: Education Development Center, Inc.

Commonwealth of Learning. (2008). *Education for a Digital World: Advice, Guidelines and Elective Practice from Around the Globe*. Burnaby, BC: Commonwealth of Learning. www.col.org/resources/education-digital-world-advice-guidelines-and-effective-practice-around-globe.

Dale, R. (2014). Globalization, higher education and teacher education: A sociological approach (pp. 33–53). In R. Bruno-Jofre and J. Scott Johnston (Eds), *Teacher Education in a Transnational World*. Toronto: University of Toronto Press.

Dede, C., Clarke, J., Ketelhut, D., Nelson, B. and Bowman, C. (2005). *Fostering Motivation, Learning, and Transfer in Multi-User Virtual Environments*. Paper presented at the American Educational Research Association Conference, Montréal, Canada.

Exley, S. (2014). The unstoppable rise of Teach For America. *Times Higher Education Supplement*, 3 January.

Feistritzer, E. (2005). *Alternative Certification: A State by State Analysis*. Washington, DC: National Center for Education Information.

Gaible, E. and Burns, M. (2007). *Using Technology to Train Teachers: Appropriate Uses of ICTs for Professional Development*. Washington, DC: World Bank.

Goodlad, J. J. (1988). Studying the education of educators: Values driven enquiry. *Phi Delta Kappan*, Vol. 70, No. 2, pp. 105–111.

Jegede, J. O., Fraser, B. and Fisher, D. (1995). The development and validation of a distance and open learning environment scale. *Educational Technology Research and Development*, Vol. 43, No. 1, pp. 89–94.

Kerr, D. H. (1987). Authority and responsibility in public schooling (pp. 20–40). In J. J. Goodlad (Ed.), *The Ecology of School Renewal*. Chicago: University of Chicago Press.

Maor, D. and Zariski, A. (2003). Is there a fit between pedagogy and technology in online learning? In *Proceedings of the 12th Annual Teaching Learning Forum, 11–12 February 2003: Partners in Learning*. Perth, Australia: Edith Cowan University. https://ctl.curtin.edu.au/events/conferences/tlf/tlf2003/abstracts/maor-abs.html

Mioduser, D., Nachmias, R., Lahav, O. and Oren, A. (2000). Web-based learning environments: Current pedagogical and technological state. *Journal of Research on Computing in Education*, Vol. 33, No. 1, pp. 55–76.

O'Donoghue, T. and Chapman, E. (2010). Problems and prospects in competencies-based education: A curriculum studies perspective. *Educational Research and Perspectives*, Vol. 37, No. 1, pp. 85–104.

Perraton, H. (Ed.). (2002). *Distance Education for Teacher Training*. London: Routledge Press.

Soucek, V. (1993). Flexible education and new standards of communication competence (pp. 33–72). In P. Watkins, V. Soucek, S. Robertson and P. Brown (Eds), *Economising Education: The Post-Fordist Directions*. Victoria: Deakin University.

Stone, J. C. (1968). *Breakthrough in Teacher Education*. San Francisco, CA: Jossey-Bass.

Zeichner, K. (2008). America (pp. 7–22). In T. O'Donoghue and C. Whitehead (Eds), *Teacher Education in the English-speaking World: Past, Present and Future*. Charlotte, NC: Information Age Publishing.

Part VII
International developments in education

32 Standardized testing

Critical to educational developments in many countries in recent years has been the measuring and auditing of educational practices and relationships, with a major focus on human capital agendas that link education to international economic competitiveness. This top-down approach to educational accountability is in response to a perceived 'crisis' in schools (Shine and O'Donoghue, 2013). It has involved the introduction of national curricula and a drive for higher professional standards and accountability for teachers. Regarding the latter, the introduction of standardized testing as a tool for educational reform and a measure of student, teacher and school success is a great source of contention among students, parents, educators, politicians and policy makers alike (Thompson and Price, 2012). Results of tests such as those of the Programme for International Student Achievement (PISA) that compare the academic achievement of students around the world have been used to justify and intensify national reform agendas (Smith, 2016). In the early 2000s, Finland emerged as a leader in such student achievement tests.

What are standardized tests?

Standardized tests refer to tests that are designed externally and aim to create:

- conditions;
- questions;
- scoring procedures;
- interpretations

that are consistent across schools (Wang *et al.*, 2006).

   Primarily, the function of such tests is to monitor and evaluate a country's educational system and answer the following questions:

- Are students achieving national standards?
- How well is the education system functioning?

Evaluation of student performance and analysis of data are used to check performance against stated goals and identify corrective actions. Thus, national test results are used not only as indicators of the quality of teaching and the performance of teachers, but also to measure the overall effectiveness of education policies and practices. Underlying this purpose is the assumption that test results will be used to determine how students compare to standards and that information gained will be used to improve student outcomes.

In many countries the tests are used to assess students, teachers and schools. However, substantial differences exist in the purpose, design, implementation and use of such tests. Also, recent educational reforms around the world indicate a greater reliance on the use standardized tests than previously.

Standardized tests can be classified as 'high-stakes testing' or 'low-stakes testing'. The term 'stakes' refers to the judgements passed based on test results and the severity of the consequences attached to the test.

High-stakes testing

This type of testing has high-level consequences not only for the student but for the teacher and the school. In the USA, results in high-stakes testing directly determine whether a child passes a grade, graduates from high school or qualifies for entry into higher education. Furthermore, test scores in high-stakes testing are linked with conclusions about the quality of teaching, teacher remuneration and even the decision to close 'under-performing' schools (Morris, 2011).

Low-stakes testing

These are tests like those used for monitoring purposes that have little or no consequences on the student's career.

Some reasons why standardized tests have been adopted in many countries

1   Tests used for the purpose of national monitoring, accountability or evaluation purposes are commonly a reflection of government efforts to incorporate business practices into public service management (Figlio and Kenny, 2009; Thompson and Price, 2012). A growing emphasis on quantitative measures of output, improving efficiency and effectiveness, and accountability, are all distinct features of the 'corporate model'. In relation to education, efficiency and effectiveness are measured by such outputs as test scores and graduation rates rather than by inputs such as funding or resources.

2   At the core of the corporate model and related business management techniques is the establishment of indicators or benchmarks as a tool to measure efficiency and achievement. These are called Key Performance Indicators (KPIs). In the educational sector they have been called 'benchmarks' or 'standards' and play a significant role in determining the extent to which the education system is meeting national standards and goals (Morris, 2011). They provide a relatively easy and convenient quantitative measure of output by which judgements about students, teachers and schools can be made (Shine and O'Donoghue, 2013).

3   Poor results in international comparative tests of student achievement are often cited as a motive for educational reform and a push towards testing and accountability. Government-directed investigations on perceived underperforming education systems often result in a

reliance on standardized tests as the primary source of information gathering regarding student achievement and teacher effectiveness.

4   Standardized testing has readily been accepted into education systems around the world because of the belief by both business and government that the future economy depends on a highly educated workforce. Popular opinion dictates that we need to drive our children further and harder with a more rigorous curriculum focusing on 'twenty-first century skills', ensuring continued economic success.

5   In many countries, through powerful lobbying, the test industry has applied great pressure on governments to rely on their tests for national monitoring and evaluation purposes. In the USA alone, testing required by the No Child Left Behind Act requires that approximately 45 million tests be conducted annually (Toch, 2006).

6   Attaching accountability measures to test results is closely related to the growing trend of 'Results Based Management' (RBM) or 'New Public Management' (NPM), which aims to analyse public sector operations by improving cost effectiveness and quantifying output.

7   In Australia, England, Wales and the USA, results are published through various outlets and reported in the media. Parents can use this information to make decisions on their child's schooling and compare and rank schools. The publication of results can also serve to increase awareness of educational issues and place education on the public agenda. Conversely, it is argued that by publishing such information, governments can divert the focus of poor student performance away from themselves and shift the blame onto teachers and schools (Shine and O'Donoghue, 2013).

8   In some systems, teachers are held accountable for student performance and find their professional performance being evaluated on the basis of test results. These judgements about teacher performance can then be linked to rewards or sanctions.

Summary of regularly stated advantages of standardized testing

Phelps (2005) proposed four main benefits of standardized testing:

1   improved diagnosis of students' strengths and weaknesses;
2   improved prediction and selection for college, scholarships and employment;
3   improved achievement;
4   popularity in the community as parents want comparative test data about their children and the schools they attend.

Summary of regularly stated disadvantages of standardized testing

Cizek (2005) has identified the following common criticisms of standardized testing:

•   increased teacher frustration;
•   stress and pressure on students resulting in tears and even vomiting;
•   increased student dropout;
•   reduced classroom instructional time;
•   measuring only lower order content;

- diminishing academic excellence;
- narrowing of curriculum;
- widening of the achievement gap;
- reproduction of social inequalities;
- promoting cheating;
- bias.

Finland

The Programme for International Student Achievement (PISA) is an Organization for Economic Co-operation and Development (OECD)-led project investigating the educational attainments of 15-year-old students in all member countries. Since the first PISA tests in 2000, Finland has demonstrated an exceptionally high level of attainment in all three domains (reading, mathematics and science). Also, variations in performance among students and schools in Finland were amongst the lowest in the PISA countries, demonstrating that the Finnish education system was not only among the best in the world but also the most consistent and egalitarian. This has aroused continuous international interest in the Finnish educational system and made it a 'model' for education systems around the world.

Decentralization and the absence of standardized testing

School principals, teachers and support staff work cooperatively to develop a school curriculum that interprets and reflects national and municipal guidelines, incorporating the national goals, study content and cross-curricular themes but translated into the individual school's action plan. Within this plan, strategies are outlined for the support of students with special learning needs, multicultural education, student guidance and counselling, and student physical and mental well-being (Kupiainen *et al.*, 2009).

According to Välijärvi and Malin (2002), non-differentiation is the secret in the success of the Finnish comprehensive school. Instead of tracking and streaming students, Finnish teachers are in a position to cater for the needs of individual students. This is thanks to the Finnish teacher who is a highly educated, pedagogical expert. In addition, due to the absence of any national tests or examinations upon completion of compulsory schooling, teachers' assessment of their pupils is all the more important. Finland does have national grading guidelines for performance but, according to the Finnish PISA team, these are flexible and allow for a broad definition of student achievement (Välijärvi and Malin, 2002).

Due to the underlying philosophy of educational equality, streaming of students and competitive high-stakes testing are not a feature of the Finnish education system. In the Finnish model, the role of evaluation is formative, with the aim of developing and supporting schools, not controlling them. Under new legislation, schools are obliged to evaluate their own operations and effects. Once again, this indicates the great trust of society and government in teachers as pedagogical and content-specific professionals. It is believed that academically educated teachers are the best experts to design their teaching, albeit within the fairly loose framework of national curricula. Rigorous standards have often been viewed in Finland as restricting the innovative thinking and pedagogical freedom of teachers and as counter-productive to achieving educational aims.

Reasons for Finland's educational success

The relative success of an educational system is a product of many and varied interrelated and inter-dependent factors. The outstanding PISA results of 2000 came as quite a shock to those responsible for, and making decisions about, education in Finland. The country had moved from seeing itself as following the examples of others to now serving as a model for them (Välijärvi and Malin, 2002).

Following the Finnish success in the 2000 PISA, a vast body of research has sought to identify and explain the elements of the Finnish educational system responsible for such success. While many factors are proposed as contributors, the following emerge as being the most predominant:

1   an inherent cultural importance of education, where teaching and learning, which have roots in its Lutheran tradition, hold a high priority and value in Finnish society:
2   a national philosophy of a free and egalitarian education for all students regardless of gender, ethnicity, disability and socio-economic status, with a particular focus on providing special education and the absence of differentiation through streaming and selection;
3   a high quality of teacher preparation, resulting in the elevated status of teachers that engenders trust in educational policy, teachers and schools to deliver relevant curriculum and pedagogy;
4   a purposeful and progressive education policy that empowers decentralized control, leading to the freedom of schools to develop differentiated curricula based on local needs and require-ments and a broad societal acceptance and agreement on education policy;
5   evaluation and assessment of learning outcomes in the absence of standardized testing and based on a philosophy where competition is not the driving force for raising the quality and developing the system;
6   cultural homogeneity of the Finnish population.

Issues for discussion

1   The Finnish system relies heavily on the professional abilities of teachers and hence invests heavily in teacher education. Highly trained teachers are considered to be subject-specific and pedagogical experts and are trusted to lead educational reform.
   What can your country possibly learn about what, if anything, can be adopted and adapted from the Finnish system?

2   Equality and an egalitarian approach to education are central to Finland's model and its comparative success.
   Are there inequality issues that exist and that need to be addressed in your country?

3   Central to the argument promoting the use of standardized tests is the assertion that raising accountability measures will motivate students to improve their performance. The underlying assumption, therefore, is that students and teachers are indolent and need to be made accountable.
   Do you accept this?
   If so, why?
   If not, why not?

   (continued)

4   The assumption mentioned above fits neatly into an economic rationalist/business model of measuring input and output. However, such a perspective fails to consider the many other individual, economic and social factors that contribute to student achievement.

What might these factors be?

5   What do you think might be the unintended consequences of standardized testing?

References

Cizek, G. J. (2005). High-stakes testing: Contexts, characteristics, critiques, and consequences (pp. 23–54). In R. Phelps (Ed.), *Defending Standardized Testing*. Mahwah, NJ: Lawrence Erlbaum Associates.

Figlio, D. N. and Kenny, L. W. (2009). Public sector performance measurement and stakeholder support. *Journal of Public Economics*, Vol. 93, No. 9, pp. 1069–1077.

Kupiainen, S., Hautamäki, J. and Karjalainen, T. (2009). *The Finnish Education System and PISA*. Helsinki: Ministry of Education.

Morris, A. (2011). *Student Standardised Testing: Current Practices in OECD Countries and a Literature Review*. Paris: OECD Publishing.

Phelps, R. (Ed.). (2005). *Defending Standardized Testing*. New York: Psychology Press.

Shine, K. and O'Donoghue, T. (2013). *Schoolteachers in the News: A Historical Analysis of Coverage in The West Australian Newspaper*. New York: Cambria Press.

Smith, W. C. (Ed.). (2016). *The Global Testing Culture: Shaping Education Policy, Perceptions, and Practice*. Oxford: Symposium Books.

Thompson, G. and Price, A. (2012). Performance pay for Australian teachers: A critical policy historiography. *The Social Educator*, Vol. 30, No. 2, pp. 3–12.

Toch, T. (2006). Turmoil in the testing industry. *Educational Leadership*, Vol. 64, No. 3, p. 53.

Välijärvi, J. and Malin, A. (2002). The effects of socio-economic background on the school-level performances (pp. 123–165). In S. Lie, P. Linnakylä and A. Roe (Eds) *Nordic Lights: PISA in Nordic Countries*. Oslo: Department of Teacher Education and School Development, University of Oslo.

Wang, L., Beckett, G. H. and Brown, L. (2006). Controversies of standardized assessment in school accountability reform: A critical synthesis of multidisciplinary research evidence. *Applied Measurement in Education*, Vol. 19, No. 4, pp. 305–328.

33 National curriculum

Economic globalization has increased competition within and between countries and the world's regions. Economic competitiveness is commonly seen as a valid index for judging a country's level of economic prosperity. There is also the argument that both primary and secondary school education significantly contribute to economic development and growth. This position recognizes people as human capital and demonstrates how increased investment in knowledge, skills and health provides future returns to the economy through increases in labour productivity (Cohen and Soto, 2007).

Many recent large-scale education reforms have been justified by the urgent need to increase labour productivity and promote economic development and growth through expanded and improved education. It is generally assumed that to increase economic competitiveness, citizens must acquire knowledge, skills and attitudes necessary for civic success and the knowledge-based economy. In the last two decades, expectations of education, and especially the qualities desired of educated and trained people in these knowledge-based economies, have changed dramatically (Sahlberg, 2006).

Any new policy for official curricula represents a set of decisions and enshrines particular values and purposes, thus making them contentious. Curriculum is never simply a neutral assemblage of knowledge somehow just appearing in texts and classrooms. Rather, it is always a part of a selective tradition, some group's vision of legitimate knowledge. Teachers, politicians, parents, students and school authorities are likely to fall into different camps based on these decisions. Some may feel side-lined, others may view the official curriculum as largely irrelevant to what occurs in the classroom, and others yet again might sanction such reforms as a much-needed redirection (Brennan, 2011).

Some precedents

A national curriculum can be defined as a common programme of study in schools that is designed to ensure nationwide uniformity of content and standards in education (Prideaux, 2003). In the USSR, uniform curriculum prescription became official state policy in 1918. Following World War II, a common curriculum was introduced in France. The notion of a broadly based, general, non-specialized curriculum had also become common in other European countries, promoted largely on the grounds of its necessity to ensure equality of opportunity in education for all members of society.

At the same time, federated systems, including that in Canada, the USA, Germany, Mexico and Switzerland, still manage to participate in cross-national arrangements, including the international comparative testing programmes, without having a national curriculum (Brennan, 2011). Also, some non-federalized countries which previously had a national curriculum have moved away from them or are in the process of doing so. Furthermore, as the last chapter has indicated, Finland, whose education system is amongst the highest achieving and most egalitarian in the world, has continued to move from a system of centrally controlled and highly prescribed national curriculum to a decentralized system operating within a national framework that accommodates flexibility and school-based curriculum planning based on the particular needs of the student population.

In the late 1980s, highly prescribed national curricula were introduced in the UK. The justification for this was that it was needed to address issues relating to the provision of equal access to quality education. Extensive reviews have led to further reform and the development of a more flexible model that allows schools to determine the best ways to engage students.

Regularly proposed advantages and disadvantages of a national curriculum

The key arguments presented in support of a national curriculum are usually that it leads to:

- public accountability;
- improved standards in education;
- greater national consistency in learning outcomes;
- the possibility of comparing student and school results;
- improved education standards;
- enhanced national competitiveness;
- improved workforce productivity.

In the 2004 global competitiveness ratings, countries like the USA (second) and Norway (sixth) ranked highly in competitiveness, but only modestly or poorly in assessment of their students' learning achievement in international comparative tests like PISA. Conversely, Korea, Canada and the Netherlands ranked highly on student achievement levels, but not in economic competitiveness rankings (twenty-ninth, fifteenth and twelfth, respectively). Indeed, some countries seem to exhibit results at opposite ends of the measurement spectrum for these two ratings. At the same time, there are examples of countries that do achieve well in both rankings (Sahlberg, 2006).

The potential to address and resolve long existing problems of educational inequality have also been cited as a reason for the implementation of a national curriculum. In the UK, for example, the national curriculum was introduced to eradicate the acute variations in curriculum content which were contributing to variation in the quality of educational provision (Tymms and Merrell, 2007). A regular position also put forward is that a single national curriculum is fair as each child will be exposed to the same curriculum. At the same time, there is the argument that uniformity is not synonymous with fairness and equality. Furthermore, if students are to have fair and equal access to education there is also a need to ensure that there are appropriate capital resources and highly prepared and skilled teachers. Also, teacher preparation and effective pedagogy must play a part in equal provision of education to all.

There is a strong argument that issues of inequality in education are best tackled at the school and classroom level by teachers being actively engaged in diagnosing learning difficulties and adapting the curriculum to suit the specific needs of students. Brennan (2011) also contends that a national curriculum cannot adequately cater for the diversity of students in order to reduce some of the educational inequalities that exist: 'A document does not provide for diversity of resources, student body, family educational background and experiences or community location' (Brennan, 2011, p. 276).

On the latter matter, some point to a reported decline in standards following the introduction of the national curriculum in the UK; students' ability levels declined in biology, English literature, French, geography, history and mathematics in the first decade of implementation. There is also the potential for interest groups to exert control over a national curriculum in selecting the 'best' one. In the UK, such a situation led to difficulties in deciding what was to be included in the curriculum and what was to be left out. Various groups clamoured to ensure that subject content which reflected their interests was included in the core content of the national curriculum, leading to a lack of clarity of what should be taught (Rawling, 2001). This resulted in the curriculum being overcrowded and unwieldy, forcing teachers to adopt a 'tick the box' mentality in order to get through the content (Dearing, 1994). Accompanying this was an overbearing assessment programme which had an adverse impact on teaching and learning (Oates, 2010).

Another argument for a national curriculum is that it will assist those families who need to regularly relocate with school-aged children to different locations in a country from time to time (Farrelly, 2007). Again, in the UK, effective student transfer between different regions in the country was reported as a benefit of the national curriculum. On this, however, one has to ask if this is a justification for having a national curriculum or just a positive side effect?

Issues for discussion

1 Do you think one can distinguish between a national curriculum and a national curriculum framework?
   Spell out what might be involved in such a distinction.

2 Can a national curriculum address issues of inequality in education?
   How might it do so?

3 To what extent might the introduction of a national curriculum be motivated by economic and/or political agendas rather than education goals?

4 What lessons can other nations learn from the British experience with its national curriculum?

5 Who serves to benefit most from a national curriculum?

6 A notion regularly associated with that of a national curriculum is that education should be in some way balanced between the humanities and the sciences.

   •   Do you agree with this notion?
   •   Discuss the practicalities of what would be involved in producing such a balance.

(continued)

7   Another notion regularly associated with the concept of a national curriculum is that of a core curriculum.

  •   How would you define a core curriculum?
  •   What learning experiences should be selected?

      o   Who should select them?
      o   What might be the best core curriculum design?

8   Recall what you found out already about Kohlberg's (1975) theory of moral development and discuss it in relation to its possible implications for a national curriculum.
    How does it relate to Piaget's stages of cognitive development?

9   How would you define moral education?

  •   Should it have a place in a national curriculum?
  •   If so, should it be a separate subject?
  •   How might moral education be conceived as a set of processes of valuing to be used across the curriculum?

10 Is there a place for career education in a national curriculum?

11 Politicians in many countries are advocating for a far greater emphasis than previously on science, technology, engineering and mathematics, while at the same time most of them have humanities degrees. Their qualifications have given them the ability to engage in critical thinking, problem solving, communication, and not to approach problems with linear one-solution models.
    How might we be able to account for this paradox?

References

Brennan, M. (2011). National curriculum: A political-educational tangle. *Australian Journal of Education*, Vol. 55, No. 3, pp. 259–280.

Cohen, D. and Soto, M. (2007). Growth and human capital: Good data, good results. *Journal of Economic Growth*, Vol. 12, No. 1, pp. 51–76.

Dearing, R. (1994). *The National Curriculum and its Assessment: Final Report*. London: School Curriculum and Assessment Authority.

Farrelly, R. (2007). National curriculum: A bipartisan bad idea. *Policy*, Vol. 23. No. 2, pp. 38–41.

Kohlberg, L. (1975). The cognitive development approach to moral education. *Phi Delta Kappan*, Vol. 56, No. 10, pp. 670–677.

Oates, T. (2010). Could do better: Using international comparisons to refine the National Curriculum in England. *Curriculum Journal*, Vol. 22, No. 2, pp. 121–150.

Prideaux, D. (2003). ABC of learning and teaching in medicine: Curriculum design. *British Medical Journal*, Vol. 326, No. 7383, p. 268.

Rawling, E. (2001). *Changing the Subject: The Impact of National Policy on School Geography 1980–2000*. Sheffield: Geographical Association.

Sahlberg, P. (2006). Education reform for raising economic competitiveness. *Journal of Educational Change*, Vol. 7, No. 4, pp. 259–287.

Tymms, P. and Merrell, C. (2007). *Standards and Quality in English Primary Schools over Time: The National Evidence*. Cambridge, UK: Primary Review, University of Cambridge Faculty of Education.

34 Education in countries in transition

Transitional societies are those that have undergone political, economic and social change in the previous two decades. There are many such societies in the modern turbulent era in which we live. Regarding these, Mebrahtu et al. (2000) state that we can learn a lot from their efforts to transform education policy and practice.

In order to understand the changes that have taken place, it is important to understand the concept of transition. Birzea (1994) defines it as a historical stage which leads to substantial transformations in every domain of society, but whose duration cannot be determined while it is lasting. To illustrate his position, he detailed differences between two models of education that have operated in the countries of Eastern Europe. He pointed out that the Soviet model of education was based on teaching one universal truth equally to everyone from the same curriculum and textbooks across the country, while the liberal model of education in the post-Soviet area states that it aims to provide equality of opportunity and nurture pluralism through the provision of tailor-made curricula.

Birzea explains that in the various Eastern European countries that moved to democratic forms of government, there was a short time period during which a whole set of interdependent economic, political and social reforms were brought about to bridge the two mutually incompatible models of education. For a period, the change taking place was too rapid and led to individual and social disorientation (Birzea, 1994).

Amongst the groups of countries at the present time that are in transition are those moving from socialism to democracy. This implies a linear transition from one social order to the next. Such a process is determined by the starting point (totalitarianism), the destination (liberal democracy) and the content of transition (the passage to political pluralism and a market economy). The situation can be illustrated by briefly examining the situation in Mongolia.

Mongolia

Wedged between two political giants yet defiantly distinct is Mongolia. Once the centre of the largest empire on the planet, Mongols are deeply proud of their rich history. They have an intrinsic respect and love of their land and many still embrace living a way of life not too dissimilar from that of Chinghis (Genghis) Khan and his warriors of the Steppe. With a population of less than three million occupying a territory of 1.56 million square kilometres, Mongolia is often perceived as isolated, rural, nomadic and unique. A deep spiritual influence of both Buddhism and traditional

Mongolian Shamanism gives Mongols a spiritual connection with their land and traditional lifestyle. With the last century being a turbulent story of political influence and occupation of the land by both the Russians to the north and the Chinese to the south, Mongolia now finds itself in the twenty-first century as a country with the modern political world suddenly thrust upon it.

Soviet influence on Mongolian education

Never officially a Soviet satellite, Mongolia's relationship with the Soviet Union throughout the twentieth century was akin to that of a younger brother. It was Soviet Communism that was responsible for 'modernizing' the country (Batbayar, 1999). One outcome was that cities were established, trading of resources was integrated and a network for the provision of quality education was established throughout the country (Steiner-Khamsi and Stolpe, 2006). At the end of the period of Soviet occupation, the country had a literacy rate of 96.5 per cent (Badrach *et al.*, 1997).

The Soviet Union invested heavily in education and introduced its own influence in Mongolia's schools and in higher education. The Mongolian State University was established in 1942 in Ulaanbaatar and modelled after Russian institutions (Badrach *et al.*, 1997). As with most satellite Soviet states, education was approached as a resource to further progress the socialist ideology (Steiner-Khamsi and Stolpe, 2006). Educated Mongolians developed a somewhat socialist perspective on academia without having great regard for the more humanitarian aspects of education (Urtnasan, 1991). Generations of Mongolian school children also had lessons devoted to chanting such slogans by rote as 'Down with the British Empire' and 'Down with American Imperialism' (Becker, 1992). Concurrently, reactionaries were sought out and removed through political purges.

With the disintegration of the Soviet Union Mongolia had to re-evaluate its education policies. It was faced with a series of major questions:

- How would adequate education be sustained without the economic support of a gigantic elder brother?
- Would Mongolian independence bring about opportunities for new education ideals and freedom?
- How would transition to a market-based economy influence education in Mongolia?

Concerns in a post-Socialist vacuum

Soviet influence led to an urbanization of the country to the extent that, by 2004, 52.4 per cent of the population was urban, with most living in the capital, Ulaanbaatar (United National Development Program, 2004). The traditional nomadic lifestyle has become significantly surpassed with urbanized and globalized life. This has meant that education in Mongolia has had to be geared towards the strikingly polarized rural and urban communities within the country.

Economic concerns

When its influence was at its peak, the USSR contributed 30 per cent of Mongolia's gross domestic product (Robinson, 1995). The country was also integrated within a localized Soviet satellite trade network which worked to support the country financially. With the Soviet system abandoned, the capacity for government support for education declined. It was considered that for Mongolia to become financially self-sufficient as a country the government would have to embrace aspects of a market economy orientated towards a larger international community. It was also recognized that in order to do so it would be necessary to borrow money internationally and that this would have a significant impact on education reform within the country (Badrach *et al.*, 1997).

The economic concerns of Mongolian education are also those of the local population. One third of Mongolians can be classified as being poor or very poor. Also, a third of the people are nomadic pastoralists. These are people who cannot easily afford such basic resources as textbooks, uniforms and school fees (United National Development Program, 2004).

Political concerns

The education system of Mongolia quickly became largely privatized. New educational institutions were established in Ulaanbaatar and a wider range of educational opportunities became available for those who could afford them. By 2004, 30 per cent of primary and secondary schools and 78 per cent of tertiary institutions were privately owned (United National Development Program, 2004).

Quality teachers began to be lured away from government institutions by the private sector (United National Development Program, 2004). With less government financial assistance being available to schools, teachers could earn more money teaching at the new private institutions. Privatization also led to greater corruption throughout all levels of the Mongolian education system (Tsend, 2000), with local officials holding on to money allocated for educational materials and teachers' salaries (Rossabi, 2005).

Privatization brought about particular difficulties for education in rural areas. Private institutions were not available in the Mongolian countryside and with the neglect of the Socialist network of rural education centres many traditional herders no longer had education options available to them (Robinson, 1995). Quality education could generally be obtained only in Ulaanbaatar, a world away from the rural population's nomadic life.

Social concerns

Since the disintegration of Soviet influence Mongols have embraced the opportunity to explore and embrace their own culture and religion. Statues of Lenin in town centres have been replaced with those of Chinghis Khan. New religious freedoms brought about an embracing of traditional Mongolian beliefs to be practised without fear of persecution (Becker, 1992).

With an increase in rates of school dropout amongst students, many ended up being less educated than their parents (Steiner-Khamsi and Stolpe, 2006). Also, throughout all levels of education, including tertiary education, there were more female than male students enrolled. A shift towards employment of males in the labour market is one likely explanation for this trend, while rural pastoralist families are also very dependent on skilled workers to sustain themselves in their nomadic or semi-nomadic lifestyle.

The perceived necessity for educational borrowing

Mongolia saw a value in seeking views from abroad on educational reform. Some were keen to embrace an education system similar to that of the USA (Rossabi, 2005). Instead, the country turned towards New Zealand. Throughout the 1990s, every member of the Mongolian parliament and all senior-level staff at ministries went to New Zealand to study government and administrative policy (Steiner-Khamsi and Stolpe, 2006, p. 136). These study tours were funded in part by the Asian Development Bank.

It was decided that the academic subjects on the school curriculum would remain largely untouched. The New Zealand emphasis, however, was felt in the adoption of an outcomes-based education (OBE) approach to curriculum planning (Steiner-Khamsi and Stolpe, 2006). Yet, to say that Mongolia embraced an OBE system would be a gross exaggeration. Mongolian students were not assessed by specific measureable 'outcomes', they were not working towards 'standards-based assessments' and there was a freedom for them to be assessed in a variety of forms (Takala, 2012). Where Mongolia has embraced aspects of OBE is in relation to the less student-oriented principles of teacher management.

Mongolian teachers associated OBE with the daily completing of pro forma notebooks designed for educational self-assessment. Teachers were required to complete notes of lesson and course planning as well as notes on students in a specific journal that had to be submitted monthly to the directors of schools (Steiner-Khamsi and Stolpe, 2006). The journals were seen as being overly bureaucratic by many Mongolian teachers and resulted in the adoption of a sceptical perspective on OBE, some stop-work strikes and legal action (Steiner-Khamsi and Stolpe, 2006, p. 139). Many believed that the journals and the embracing of OBE were tactics designed to lead to a reduction in teachers' salaries.

Mongolia needed financial assistance throughout the nineties, as it does today. The sources of the funds have been varied. Launched in 1991, the European Union's TACIS programme aimed to aid in the transition of old Soviet bloc countries. While Mongolia was not included within TACIS' primary network of assistance, the EU did offer financial assistance for some specific projects in education. These included the introduction of new history texts and of the English language as a school subject (Rossabi, 2005). The Japanese government provided funds for the construction of six new schools and the Nordic Development Fund donated US$140,000 for dormitory repairs (Rossabi, 2005, p. 163). UNESCO made a contribution to non-formal distance education and UNICEF assisted with primary school teacher training and non-formal education for school drop-outs. Denmark, Germany, Korea, Australia, Canada and the USA also made small contributions to Mongolia's education 'reforms' (Weidman, 2002).

The largest influence on education 'reform' in Mongolia was a US$15.5 million loan from the Asian Development Bank (ADB) (Weidman, 2002). Mongolian schools were to be guided towards the ideals of a 'Western classroom'. The money was channelled towards the training of administrators, school principals and assistant principals (Weidman, 2002). Non-essential teachers were removed and classroom student numbers subsequently increased.

Privatization of Mongolian education was also promoted. This was undertaken against a background of government liberalizing prices, devaluing the country's currency and reducing public expenditure. There was little incentive for a private education institution to establish itself anywhere other than in the financial capital, Ulaanbaatar. Independent rural village schools were, as a result, neglected and many were abolished.

Other policies had a positive influence. New freedoms were introduced in education. A comprehensive policy framework for technical and vocational training was drawn up (Weidman, 2002). Also, the culturally relevant subjects of Mongolian history and traditional Mongolian script, which had been excluded from the curriculum under the Soviet system, were introduced (Becker, 1992, p. 106)

Some present concerns with education in Mongolia

* The infrastructure of schools is a major concern. Most buildings are getting old and in need of renovation.
* Throughout the Mongolian winter, with the temperature dropping to 40°C, many students cannot attend schools when the heating systems are broken and money is not being spent on trying to fix them.
* While teachers are still highly regarded professionals in Mongolian society, this is not reflected in their meagre pay. As a result, it is difficult to encourage them not to move to better-paying positions.
* The neglect of rural schools only serves to compound the urbanization of Mongolia and the reduction of education in rural Mongolia. Also, for a traditionally pastoralist and nomadic society, urbanization can be seen as representing a change to their very way of life such that it affects their interest in participating in education (Dyer, 2001). It is not that nomads don't value education. Rather, in its urbanized form, it has little relevance for them.

Some positive developments

* In an effort to reintegrate education centres throughout the regional breadth of the country, a 'National Program for Non-formal Education' has been established. Supported by UNESCO, UNICEF, World Vision, Peace Wind Japan and Danish International Development Assistance (DANIDA), the programme hopes to increase literacy, education levels and professional labour training outside the conventional school system.
* Also supported by DANIDA, UNESCO and the Mongolian government is the 'Gobi Women's Project'. This incentive seeks to provide non-formal education for up to 15,000 nomadic women throughout the Gobi Desert region. The project is providing access to information and knowledge, changing attitudes and developing skills for self-reliance for traditional Mongolian women.
* The use and importance of ICT has been identified as a particular area of focus for improvement of education in Mongolia. The 'E-Mongolia National Programme' is working to establish the foundation of a knowledge-based society (Uyanga, 2005). Moves have been taken to implement computer-based online distance schooling throughout all provinces of the country. Efforts to increase literacy in ICT throughout the country have also been undertaken to assist in the integration of education within the country and a realization of Mongolia's role in a global community.
* The Asian Development Bank made US$17 million available to be directed towards access to preschool feeding programmes, secondary school textbooks, and operation and maintenance of schools, safeguarding the incentives of the previous grant of the 1990s and further 'budget monitoring and evaluation' (Takala, 2012).

Issues for discussion

1   Select a country in transition and do some research on a key education policy document that has been produced there. Regarding this policy document, ask yourself the following:

- What is the format of the policy document?
- What is the language of the policy document?
- How understandable is the policy document?
- Who can have access to the policy?
- Is the policy open to interpretation?
- What were the forces or pressures leading to the policy formulation process?
- What was the context or environment in which the policy formulation process commenced?
- What were the stages in the development of the policy?
- Who was involved in the policy making process?
- Whose interests are served by the policy?
- Are there likely to be winners and losers?
- How was the policy received?
- Why was the policy adopted?
- How has the policy been implemented?
- Have there been any unintended consequences of the policy being implemented?
- Has the policy been reviewed or evaluated?

2   A particular type of country in transition is that of a post new-war country.

- Define what is meant by a post new-war country.
- Distinguish a new war from an old war.
- Identify the ways in which a clear-cut distinction cannot be made between these two kinds of wars.
- Identify the particular challenges faced by a post new-war country.
- Identify the particular education problems faced by a post new-war country.
- Identify the various ways in which these problems are being tackled in any post new-war country.

3   Some countries are new countries.

- Identify some countries that have emerged as independent states in the last 25 years.
- Identify some of the problems they have faced.
- Identify some of the specific education problems they continue to face.
- Identify how these problems are being addressed.

4   Many countries receive what is known as 'development aid'.
Define what is meant by development aid.
Study some of the literature on development aid and discuss the advantages which it is claimed it brings to recipients.

There is also a large literature on the problems that development aid creates for recipients. Identify them and discuss them.

What role do non-government agencies, popularly known as NGOs, play in the process?

Do they have any advantages over government aid agencies?

Do NGOs have any advantages over non-government aid agencies?

References

Badrach, D. B., Gerel, O. and Weidman, J. (1997). Mongolia (pp. 199–216). In G. M. Postiglione (Ed.), *Asian Higher Education: An International Handbook and Reference Guide*. Westport, CT: Greenwood Press.

Batbayar, B. (1999). *Mongol Relations with Russia. History of Mongolia, From World Power to Soviet Satellite*. Cambridge: University of Cambridge.

Becker, J. (1992). *The Lost Country: Mongolia Revealed*. London: Sceptre.

Birzea, C. (1994). *Educational Policies in the Countries in Transition*. Paris: Council of Europe Press.

Dyer, C. (2001) Nomads and Education for All: Education for development or domestication? *Comparative Education*, Vol. 37, pp. 315–327.

Mebrahtu, T., Crossley, M. and Johnson, D. (2000). *Globalisation, Educational Transformation and Societies in Transition*. Oxford: Symposium Books.

Robinson, B. (1995). Mongolia in transition: A role for distance education? *Open Learning: The Journal of Open and Distance Learning*, Vol. 10, No. 3, pp. 3–15.

Rossabi, M. (2005). *Modern Mongolia: From Khans to Commissars to Capitalists*. Los Angeles, CA: University of California Press.

Steiner-Khamsi, G. and Stolpe, I. (2006). *Educational Import: Local Encounters with Global Forces in Mongolia*. New York: Palgrave Macmillan.

Takala, T. (2012). Changing conceptions of development assistance to education in the international discourse on post-Soviet countries. *The International Journal for Academic Development*, Vol. 32, No. 1, pp. 2–4.

Tsend, A. (2000). *Leadership Practices in Higher Education in Mongolia*. Blacksburg, VA: University Libraries, Virginia Polytechnic Institute and State University.

United Nations Development Program (2004). *Development of the Education System in Uzbekistan*. Tashkent, Uzbekistan: United Nations Development Program.

Urtnasan, N. (1991). Bolovsrolyn asuudal [Educational issues]. *Ardyn Erkh*, November, np.

Uyanga, S. (2005). The usage of ICT for secondary education in Mongolia. *International Journal of Education and Development Using Information and Communication Technology*, Vol. 1, No. 4, pp. 101–118.

Weidman, J. (2002). Developing the Mongolia Education Sector Strategy 2000–2005: Reflections of a consultant for the Asian Development Bank. *Current Issues in Comparative Education*, Vol. 3, pp. 99–108.

35 Shadow education

In recognizing the importance of education for economic and social development, policy makers have long focused their interest and effort on such mainstream institutions as kindergartens, schools and universities. In doing so, they neglected the role of private supplementary tutoring. This tutoring is widely known as shadow education as it attempts to replicate the mainstream experience. Furthermore, as Bray and Lykins (2012) have pointed out, as the content of mainstream education changes so does the content of the shadow, and as the mainstream grows, so also does the shadow.

While shadow education is to be found in many parts of the world, it has grown at a great rate in Asia in recent decades. Bray and Lykins (2012) provide the following statistics on this:

- In the Republic of Korea nearly 90 per cent of elementary students receive some sort of shadow education.
- In Hong Kong, China, about 85 per cent of senior secondary students do so.
- In West Bengal, India, nearly 60 per cent of primary school students receive private supplementary tutoring.
- In Kazakhstan a similar proportion of students do so at the senior secondary level.

They list the following beneficial dimensions of private tutoring:

- It can help slow learners to keep up with their peers.
- It can help high achievers reach new levels.
- The extra learning may contribute human capital for economic development.
- Many families consider extra lessons to be a constructive way to use the spare time of adolescents.

The following negative dimensions of private tutoring have also been noted:

- Private tutoring may reduce the time available for sports and other activities, which are important for well-rounded development (Bray and Lykins, 2012; Rowley, 2012).
- It can maintain and exacerbate social inequalities, with rich families being able to pay for better quality and greater quantities of tutoring than middle-income and poor families.

- It can create inefficiencies in education systems, especially if teachers deliberately reduce the effort that they devote to their regular classes to reserve energy for private tutoring.
- In many countries, individuals can become tutors without training, and the effectiveness of some forms of tutoring is questionable.

The findings of research on whether shadow education delivers higher academic grades is mixed, with much depending on both the motivations and abilities of the students and the motivations and abilities of the tutors.

Bray and Lykins (2012, p. 2) also offer the following advice to policy makers:

- Shadow education should be brought much more actively into the research arena and policy makers should take cognisance of results to consider various ways to encourage desirable forms of shadow education and discourage undesirable forms.
- Systems of assessment and selection, which are among the most immediate drivers of demand for shadow education, might need to be reformed.
- It might be wise to devise and implement regulations on the tutoring industry since, in general, it tends to be poorly supervised and inadequately regulated, especially in comparison with mainstream schooling.
- For reasons of social equity and for the efficiency of education systems there is a need to investigate what can be done in the mainstream to make supplementary tutoring less desirable and necessary.

Shadow education in South Korea

The Republic of Korea (South Korea), as has already been pointed out, is one country where shadow education is extremely common; a very large number of students proceed from their schools at the end of the day to some form of private tutoring to continue their learning. This can be a range of formal after-school academic activities, such as individual or group tutoring, self-study or practice exam questions (Lee and Shouse, 2011). A study conducted in 2010 found that 86.8 per cent of elementary and 72.2 per cent of middle school students undertook shadow education (Bray, 1999).

A major problem with the shadow education system in South Korea is that it is extremely expensive and not every family can afford it. Nevertheless, it was reported as far back as 1999 that 'typical' households spent approximately US$1,500 a year on tutoring each child in primary school and US$1,950 a year on tutoring each child in secondary school (Bray, 2014).

The supplementary private tutoring institutions that make up the shadow education system in South Korea are called 'hagwons', which means 'study place' in Korean (Rowley, 2012). There are many different kinds of hagwons:

- For the younger students, they are where they get additional help to excel in school, with the most popular subjects being mathematics and English (Zhou and Kim, 2006).
- For high school students, the main aim of the hagwons is to exclusively:
  - prepare students for the highly competitive college entrance examination;

o   help test-takers who do not score high enough to get into their college of choice to retake the exam with a better score the following year (Zhou and Kim, 2006).

Reasons offered as to why the shadow education system has expanded so greatly in South Korea

1   The country has experienced dramatic economic and social development over the past few decades, which has strained its ability to distribute education resources fairly and equitably (Lee and Shouse, 2011). Students and parents face tremendous competition in obtaining higher levels and quality of schooling. This has triggered the expansion of the shadow education system (Lee and Shouse, 2011).
2   There is a perceived lower quality of formal schooling. This has been seen to significantly increase the demand for shadow education in many areas in South Korea (Kim, 2004). South Koreans regard education very highly and demand better education in order to pursue places in the highest ranked universities, propelling the shadow education phenomenon further (Lee, 2014). The government has attempted with numerous efforts to decrease parent expenditure on shadow education. However, none of these efforts have appeared to be effective (Lee and Shouse, 2011).
3   Shadow education ensures there are vast amounts of employment opportunities. Some tutors are mainstream teachers who gain extra income from supplementary lessons and others are employees of companies that provide tutoring (Bray, 2006).

Lee (2014) argues that shadow education has now become complicated by being so integrated into the education system and social expectations in South Korea that it is no longer possible to compare the success of children who take advantage of it with those who do not. In other words, shadow education has become the norm. According to Bray (2014), the main questions that now need to be asked are as follows:

- What are the types, qualities and quantities of shadow education?
- What durations and intensities in shadow education work in what types of learning domains?
- What works for what sorts of students and in what sorts of circumstances?

Disadvantages of shadow education in South Korea

Along with the disadvantages associated with shadow education in general, as outlined in the first part of this chapter, the following have also been noted in relation to South Korea in particular:

- The 13-hour day that many students spend in formal education activities because of shadow education is longer than an average adult works at his or her job. As a result, shadow education contributes to fatigue of both the students and the teachers and can create dissonance with lessons in mainstream classes (Bray, 2006).
- Those who are unable to afford shadow education may well have lower performance and are at risk of having a lower sense of self-worth and a higher risk of developing depression (Heyneman, 2011).

- The heavy financial burden placed on families with low income is cited as a key factor explaining Korea's extremely low birth rate (Jones, 2013).
- Halak and Poisson (2007) state that the high fees of private tutoring services and the mono-poly of certain education centres lead to particular corrupt practices plaguing shadow educa-tion: 'shadow education has become a source of distortion that adversely affects mainstream education' (Halak and Poisson, 2007, p. 258).
- While students from wealthy families and children of parents with higher education levels are more likely to receive shadow education, it is still considered to be a social norm (Lee, 2005, 2014). This renders psychological and financial burdens for parents, especially those unable to afford shadow education.

Due to the social inequalities and economic burden that shadow education imposes on families in South Korea, the government has attempted to decrease the role of these education institutions. To accomplish this, the government has been trying to:

- improve the quality of public education;
- expand the diversity of the types of secondary schools;
- de-emphasize the role of the examinations in the university admission process (Jones, 2013).

It is argued that the government needs to pursue such reforms, while improving vocational educa-tion, to provide high-quality alternatives to university (Jones, 2013). At the same time, it is believed the shadow education system will continue to play an important role. Therefore, improv-ing access for low-income families is suggested as an alternative.

Issues for discussion

1   Discuss the following extract from a report prepared for the European Commission by the Network of Experts in Social Sciences of Education and Training (2011, p. 1):

> A first key message from this report is that private tutoring is widespread. It has reached such a scale, and has such strong implications for equity, for the work of schools, and for the lives of children and families, that it must be addressed. We need to recognise and evaluate it. We also need to heed the signals it sends about the nature of mainstream schooling. A second key message is that private tutoring has not taken hold to the same extent in all EU Member States. Southern Europe has particularly high rates of tutoring. Tutoring is also widespread in Central and Eastern EU Member States. While in Western Europe the scale of tutoring greatly increased during the last decade, the Nordic Member States appear to be the least affected by the phenomenon so far. A third key message from this report is that private tutoring is much less about pupils who are in real need of help that they cannot find at school, and much more about maintaining the competitive advant-ages of the already successful and privileged.

(continued)

2   Parents now feel tutoring has become a necessity rather than a top-up in order to stand a chance. Sir Peter Lampl, chairman of the Sutton Trust, said:

> Parents naturally want to do the best for their children and the pressure to succeed in exams is stronger than ever, and not just for a child who is falling behind. Parents who find that independent school fees are too expensive want to ensure their child gets the grades they need to get good GCSEs and A-levels while at state school, and get to a good university. Spending a bit of extra money to give them that extra edge is a lot cheaper than private school. But of course this is an option only open to those who can afford it: £25 an hour is quite a lot for someone on low or average incomes.
>
> (Ensor, 2013, np)

The observation outlined above has been made in relation to the situation in England.

- Does it apply to the situation in your own country?
- Does it apply to the situation in your own region?
- Is this state of affairs justified?
- Does it call for government intervention? Why? How?

3   There is also a form of shadow education operating at university level. Discuss the following comment on this this:

> Unless universities find ways to confront the impact of search technologies on students' ability to cut corners, their own reputations will suffer while students rob themselves of a rigorous education and 'shadow scholars' make out like bandits. We might witness, perhaps, a return to oral examinations to demonstrate competence, or collaborative group projects that require each student to contribute in real-time to a collective project that cannot be so easily faked – or bought. Either way, the 'shadow scholars' salvo in the academic establishment's premier journal is a wake-up call to all who argue that American higher education produces the best and the brightest.
>
> (Khanna and Khanna, 2014, np).

References

Bray, M. (1999). *The Shadow Education System: Private Tutoring and Its Implications for Planners*. Fundamentals of Educational Planning Series, Number 61.

Bray, M. (2006). Private supplementary tutoring: Comparative perspectives on patterns and implications. *Compare*, Vol. 36. No. 4, pp. 515–530.

Bray, M. (2014). The impact of shadow education on student academic achievement: Why the research is inconclusive and what can be done about it. *Asia Pacific Education Review*, Vol. 15, No. 3, pp. 381–389.

Bray, M. and Lykins, C. (2012). *Shadow Education*. Manila: Asian Development Bank.

Ensor, J. (2013). One in four children privately tutored in 'shadow education system'. *The Telegraph*, 6 September.

Halak, J. and Poisson, M. (2007). *Corrupt Schools, Corrupt Universities: What Can Be Done?* Paris: International Institute for Educational Planning, UNESCO.

Heyneman, S. P. (2011). Private tutoring and social cohesion. *Peabody Journal of Education*, Vol. 86, No. 2, pp. 183–188.

Jones, R. S. (2013). *Education Reform in Korea*. Paris: OECD.

Khanna, P. and Khanna, A. (2014). The shadow education economy. *Big Think*. http://bigthink.com/hybrid-reality/the-shadow-education-economy.

Kim, T. (2004). *Shadow Education: School Quality and Demand for Private Tutoring in Korea*. Seoul: KDI School of Public Policy and Management.

Lee, C. (2005). Korean education fever and private tutoring. *Korean Educational Development Institute Journal of Educational Policy*, Vol. 2, No. 1, pp. 98–108.

Lee, S. K. (2014). Local perspectives of Korean shadow education. *Reconsidering Development*, Vol. 2, No. 1, pp. 1–22.

Lee, S. and Shouse, R. C. (2011). The impact of prestige orientation on shadow education in South Korea. *Sociology of Education*, Vol. 84, No. 3, pp. 212–224.

Network of Experts in Social Sciences of Education and Training (2011). *The Challenge of Shadow Education: Private Tutoring and Its Implications for Policy Makers in the European Union*. Brussels: European Commission.

Rowley, A. (2012). The dark side of Asian shadow education. *The Business Times*. http://web.edu.hku.hk/f/news/1680/07052012_BT.pdf.

Zhou, M. and Kim, S. S. (2006). Community forces, social capital, and educational achievement: The case of supplementary education in the Chinese and Korean immigrant communities. *Harvard Educational Review*, Vol. 76, No. 1, pp. 1–29.

36 The challenge of ICT in the classroom

The term information and communications technology (ICT) refers to any communication device or application. It encompasses radio, television, cellular phones, computer and network hardware and software, and satellite systems, as well as the various services and applications associated with them, such as videoconferencing and distance learning. In recent years, the proliferation of the use of ICT in an educational context has raised questions as to the extent to which it should be used in the classroom. Specifically in relation to computers, for example, some argue that students must be skilled with computer competency to enter a twenty-first century workforce. Conversely, others suggest that technology can have a detrimental impact on students' interpersonal skills and limit their ability to learn.

The argument for ICT, and especially computers, in the classroom

- National professional standards for teaching in various countries describe the necessity for teachers to use ICT to facilitate students' learning and broaden their opportunities to engage with an extensive variety of resources.
- By using ICT one can create multi-sensory classrooms in which 'students can experience highly sophisticated visual images, text, animation, sound – all sorts of sensory experiences' (Marsh, 2010, p. 244).
- The internet is deemed to be the 'ultimate learning tool', as it can enhance interactivity and connections with peers (Marsh, 2010, p. 93). It allows children to reimagine themselves and their relations to the world. As they connect with other parts of the world, they can become tied to other cultures (Jenkins, 2008, p. 19).
- Teachers can use ICT to tailor learning programmes to suit various levels of learning (Woolfolk and Margetts, 2012).

Some possible disadvantages

- Jenkins (2008, p. 17) holds that 'even the most media-literate kids are often not asking hard questions about the ways media reshape our perceptions of the world'. Students should be engaged in critical thinking about how technology has an impact on their lives.
- Turkle (2012) argues that students can begin to slip into virtual worlds and distance themselves from each other through technology. He suggests that as we use technology to mediate our

relationships we become less and less connected to each other as a result of a fear of intimacy. Young people who have grown up with technology as 'always on' become accustomed to not switching off and also to a whole host of new insecurities; 'when media are always there, waiting to be wanted, people lose a sense of choosing to communicate' (Turkle, 2012, p. 163).

- There is a related argument that if one is too well 'connected' through ICT one stops thinking. The constant absorption of other people's thoughts interfere with the deep abstraction required to find one's own way.
- In a world where students are constantly attached to computers and digital technology, at times the school environment provides an escape through which they can disconnect from virtual worlds and reconnect with the real world.
- To help students to live in an environment filled with human-made products we need to first help them know and respect what cannot be manufactured (Monke, 2005), namely, the living and inanimate things in nature.
- 'The child has effectively merged with the computer – albeit in a rather benign version of the science-fiction cyborg' (Buckingham, 2007, p. 34). Monke (2005, p. 1) supports this claim by stating that 'the computer is a purely symbolic environment; users are always working with abstract representations of things, never with the things themselves'. A common approach is to use computers as a method of conveying information. Teachers, however, should also use computer programmes to facilitate interactive learning.
- In a classroom environment students can begin to debate ideas, test theories and develop their sense of self. Adolescence is a stage of growth in which 'the years of identity formation can be a time of learning what you think by hearing what you say to others' (Turkle, 2012, p. 175). Turkle (2012) expresses concern that this period of emotional and social growth can be hindered by technology and that the benefits of collaborative learning can be lost.
- There is also the argument that it could be beneficial to limit the use of technology in schools because much classroom work with technology is bound to appear unexciting when compared with the complex and extensive multimedia experiences some students have outside school.

The particular case of the iPad

Apple launched the mobile touchscreen tablet computer, the iPad, in 2010. By 2011 it was reported that some 250,000 applications (apps) had been written for the device (Murray and Olcese, 2011). In 2012, the iPad was rated as the most desired consumer electronic device for children aged 6 to 12 years of age in the USA (Brown-Martin, 2012). Whilst not designed specifically for the education market (Molnar, 2013), the iPad has been introduced into Kindergarten to Year 12 (K-12) classrooms at a rate that surpasses any previous computing device, including laptops and desktops (Vu *et al.*, 2014). The iPad dominates the tablet computer market (94 per cent of tablet computers in K-12 schools are iPads) (Molnar, 2013). In 2010, 60 per cent of the largest deployment of iPads were to the education sector (Gentile, 2012). iPads have begun to replace textbooks and pencil cases in student backpacks (Timmerman, 2010), students of all ages find them easy to use (Heinrich, 2012) and they have been considered an affordable alternative to educational technologies. As a result, they are being heralded by some as 'game changers' in education (Culen and Gasparini, 2013).

Concerns that have been raised

- Schools are rushing to invest in iPads before their educational value has been demonstrated (Vu *et al.*, 2014).
- They are sometimes deployed as a quick fix solution for underlying educational problems (Kucirkova, 2014).
- Their effectiveness in education may be unrealistic sales hype (Falloon, 2015).
- It is simply a cleverly marketed commodity.
- Traxler (2011) expresses concern that the education sector has taken devices such as the iPad that were not intended for educational purposes and attempted to use them to foster educational gains. Murray and Olcese (2011) report that lower acquisition costs of the iPad compared to other technologies, their increased capability and a lack of compelling arguments against their purchase are encouraging politicians and educational administrators to support schools in purchasing them.

Some current evidence

- Melhuish and Falloon (2010) recommend that technological developments in schools can only be successful when the benefits and challenges of the innovation have been carefully weighed up against effective teaching and learning outcomes.
- Culen and Gasparini (2012) advise that if schools are to go ahead with implementing iPads in the classroom, all stakeholders, from students to policy makers, need to be included when designing educational initiatives supported by the iPad.
- Some urge schools to be cautious in their decisions and suggest that no single technology can influence learning on its own; the iPad is just one tool that, if used effectively, can have a positive impact on teaching and learning. They suggests that schools should not treat the decision to implement iPad programmes lightly and must consider carefully the initial and on-going costs associated with them, the ownership models, the life cycle of the technology and the need for on-going evaluation and monitoring.
- Dhir *et al.* (2013) believe that for iPad adoption in a school to be successful the hurdles that need to be overcome are the inflexible curriculum, constraints of pedagogy and administration, technicalities of the iPad, as well as time constraints of the school schedule, lack of sufficient skills for manipulating the iPad (especially by teachers), demands of the traditional education system and insufficiency of the iPad as an all-purpose device.
- Others do not believe schools should assume that iPads can replace fully featured computers. Rather, they should complement them. They argue that they should be used for different functions: iPads for consuming media and providing simple responses and fully featured computers for content creation and editing.
- Jahnke *et al.* (2013) observed iPad use in 15 classrooms and found that use was only high when teaching objectives, learning activities, social relations and use of ICT in the classroom were well aligned.
- Lynch and Redpath (2014) advise schools considering iPad purchases that it is those technologies that fit with existing classroom practices that are more likely to be implemented in programmes, as opposed to technologies that require large-scale changes to teaching and learning methods.

- Johnson *et al.* (2013) advise schools that, while the introduction of new ICT may pose challenges to students, teachers and administrators, the key to successful integration is to provide teachers with effective training; if teachers are left without the tools and skills to effectively integrate the new technology into their teaching methods the investment will be underutilized or used in a way that does not have a positive effect on teaching and learning.

Issues for discussion

1   Bell *et al.* (2015) have summarized Greenfield's position as follows:

> Through appearances, interviews, and a recent book, Susan Greenfield, a senior research fellow at Lincoln College, Oxford, has promoted the idea that internet use and computer games can have harmful effects on the brain, emotions, and behaviour, and she draws a parallel between the effects of digital technology and climate change.
>
> (Bell *et al.*, 2015)

They go on to offer a critique of the position. Read it and ask yourself with whom do you agree.

2   Discuss the following propositions:

- Digital media can give students the information they need in an instant, but this could be to the detriment of their interpersonal skills and ability to think critically.
- Information is widely available on the internet, but we need to educate students about how to use it effectively. As teachers, we need to set clear goals of our expectations of what technology can achieve.
- As a society, we should constantly address the role technology plays in our lives and examine its impact on our perspectives as human beings.
- The role of technology is important in the classroom, but teachers need to constantly assess its relevance to the specific task and subject.

3   Read and discuss the following works:

Baurerlein, M. (2009). *The Dumbest Generation. How the Digital Age Stupefies Young Americans and Jeopardizes Our Future (Or, Don 't Trust Anyone Under 30)*. Los Angeles, CA: Tarcher.

OECD (2015). *New Approach Needed to Deliver on Technology's Potential in Schools*. Paris: OECD. www.oecd.org/education/new-approach-needed-to-deliver-on-technologys-potential-in-schools.htm.

Parr, R. (2013). Students opposed to online learning. *Times Higher Education Supplement*, 30 March.

Rogers, J., Usher, A. and Kaznowska, E. (2011). *The State of E-learning in Canadian Universities 2011: If Students are Digital Natives, Why Don't They Like E-learning?* Toronto: Higher Education Strategy Associates. http://higheredstrategy.com/wp-content/uploads/2011/09/InsightBrief42.pdf.

(continued)

4   Armand Marie Leroi, professor of evolutionary developmental biology at Imperial College London, published an article entitled 'Mind-expanding and free: Are Moocs the perfect drug?' (Leroi, 2015, p. 22). In it he makes the following points:

a   'David Bromwich, Sterling Professor of English at Yale, effectively admits he's a Luddite.... Bromwich's article, "Trappe in the virtual classroom", is a jeremiad against "Moocs – Massive Open Online Courses", which many universities now produce and stream to the world. Bromwich's complaint is that they keep students and teachers physically apart. That's bad, since teaching is not just about the transmission of facts, but also about the craft of intellectual inquiry, which requires face-to-face talk. It's a good, if modest, point, but there's more. Moocs are emblems of humanity's "robotification". We are, Bromwich asserts, becoming information-processing machines, and any knowledge that cannot be codified into machine-readable form is doomed to disappear.'

b   'Before we consider whether any of this makes sense, a word in the defence of Moocs. At their best they're like the perfect drug: mind-expanding, abundant and free ... [lectures can be] beautiful: clear, concise, precise and self-effacing. They're highly engineered knowledge-transmission machines.'

c   'The purpose of Moocs is efficient learning. As such they leave little room for witty apercus, erudite allusions, sweeping generalisations or inspiring slogans – tools of the humanities professor as star.'

d   '[Humanities professors] will still be needed to teach the intangible craft of criticism ... this requires that teacher and student jointly contemplate the world. I know this because I too teach craft: science. And let me further allay his (Bromwich's) fears: his craft won't be crushed by the march of the Moocs, for modern civilisation rests on it.'

Discuss each of the points above.

References

Bell, V., Bishop, D. V. M. and Przybylski, A. K. (2015). The debate over digital technology and young people needs less shock and more substance. *British Medical Journal*, Vol. 351, No. 3064, pp. 1–2.

Brown-Martin, G. (2012). Technophobia has no place in education. *TES Magazine*. www.tes.co.uk/article.aspx?storycode=6162155.

Buckingham, D. (2007). *Beyond Technology: Children's Learning in the Age of Digital Culture*. Brisbane: Wiley.

Culen, A. and Gasparini, A. (2012). Acceptance factors: An iPad in classroom ecology. Paper presented at International Conference on E-Learning and E-technologies in Education, Lodz, Poland, 24–26 September, pp. 140–145.

Culen, A. and Gasparini, A. (2013). The iPad in a classroom: A cool personal item or simply an educational tool? Paper presented at the Sixth International Conference on Advances in Computer-Human Interactions. www.thinkmind.org/index.php?view=article&articleid=achi_2013_8_40_20302.

Dhir, A., Gahwaji, N. M. and Nyman, G. (2013). The role of the iPad in the hands of the learner. *Journal of Universal Computer Science*, Vol. 19, No. 5, pp. 706–727.

Falloon, G. (2015). What's the difference? Learning collaboratively using iPads in conventional classrooms. *Computers and Education*, Vol. 84, pp. 62–77.

Gentile, M. (2012). The importance of managing iPads in the classroom. *The Education Digest*. http://eric.ed.gov/?id=EJ1002980.

Heinrich, P. (2012). *The iPad as a Tool for Education: A Study of the Introduction of iPads at Longfield Academy, Kent*. Nottingham, UK: NAACE. www.e-learningfoundation.com/Websites/elearningfoundation/images/PDF%20Documents/Longfield-The_iPad_as_a_Tool_for_Education.pdf.

Jahnke, I., Norquist, L. and Olsson, A. (2013). Digital didactical designs in iPad-classrooms, Proceedings of the European Conference of Technology-Enhanced Learning, Cyprus.

Jenkins, H. (2008). Media literacy – Who needs it? (pp. 15–39). In T. Willoughby and E. Wood (Eds), *Children's Learning in a Digital World*. London: Blackwell Publishing.

Johnson, L., Adams Becker, S., Cummins, M., Estrada, V., Freeman, A. and Ludgate, H. (2013). *NMC Horizon Report: 2013 K-12 Edition*. Austin, Texas: The New Media Consortium. www.nmc.org/pdf/2013-horizon-report-k12.pdf.

Kucirkova, N. (2014). iPads in early education: Separating assumptions and evidence. *Frontiers in Psychology*, 8 July. http://dx.doi.org/10.3389/fpsyg.2014.00715.

Leroi, A. M. (2015). Mind-expanding and free: Are Moocs the perfect drug? *The Financial Times*, 20 September, p. 22.

Lynch, J. and Redpath, T. (2014). Smart technologies in early years education: A meta-narrative of paradigmatic tensions in iPad use in an Australian preparatory classroom. *Journal of Early Childhood Literacy*, Vol. 14, No. 2, pp. 147–174.

Marsh, C. (2010). *Becoming a Teacher*. Frenchs Forest, NSW: Pearson Australia.

Melhuish, K. and Falloon, G. (2010). Looking to the future: M-learning with the iPad. *Computers in New Zealand Schools: Learning, Leading, Technology*, Vol. 22, No. 3. www.otago.ac.nz/cdelt/otago064509.pdf.

Molnar, M. (2013). Educators weigh iPad's dominance of the tablet market. *Education Week*, 22 November. www.edweek.org/ew/articles/2013/11/22/13ipad_ep.h33.html.

Monke, L. (2005). The overdominance of computers. *Educational Leadership*, Vol. 63, No. 4, pp. 20–23.

Murray, O. T. and Olcese, N. R. (2011). Teaching and learning with iPads, ready or not? *Tech Trends*, Vol. 55, No. 6, np.

Timmerman, P. (2010). 'Is my iPad in my backpack?' *Journal of Digital Research and Publishing*, University of Sydney.

Traxler, J. (2011). Mobile learning: Starting in the right place, going in the right direction? *International Journal of Mobile and Blended Learning*, Vol. 3, No. 2, pp. 57–67.

Turkle, S. (2012). *Alone Together*. New York: Basic Books.

Vu, P., McIntyre, J. and Cepero, J. (2014). Teachers' use of the iPad in classrooms and their attitudes toward using it. *Journal of Global Literacies. Technologies and Emerging Pedagogies*, Vol. 2, No. 2, pp. 58–76.

Woolfolk, A. and Margetts, K. (2012). *Educational Psychology*, third edition. Frenchs Forest, NSW, Australia: Pearson Australia.

INDEX